YOUR 15-MONTH CANDID,
COMPLETE AND INDIVIDUAL FORECAST

SAGITTARIUS
November 23 - December 20

1991
SUPER HOROSCOPE

ARROW BOOKS LIMITED
20 Vauxhall Bridge Road
London SW1V 2SA

CONTENTS

THE PUBLISHERS REGRET THAT THEY CANNOT ANSWER INDIVIDUAL LETTERS REQUESTING PERSONAL HOROSCOPE INFORMATION.

FIRST PUBLISHED IN GREAT BRITAIN BY ARROW BOOKS 1990
© GROSSET & DUNLAP, INC., 1974, 1978, 1979, 1980, 1981, 1982
© CHARTER COMMUNICATIONS, INC., 1983, 1984, 1985
COPYRIGHT © 1986, 1987, 1988, 1989, 1990 THE BERKLEY PUBLISHING GROUP
THIS EDITION PUBLISHED BY AGREEMENT WITH THE BERKLEY PUBLISHING GROUP

PRINTED IN GREAT BRITAIN BY
GUERNSEY PRESS CO. LTD
GUERNSEY C.I.
ISBN 0 09 970810 8

NOTE TO THE CUSP-BORN

First find the year of your birth, and then find the sign under which you were born according to your day of birth. Thus, you can determine if you are a true Sagittarius (or Scorpio or Capricorn), according to the variations of the dates of the Zodiac. (See also page 7.)

Are you *really* a Sagittarius? If your birthday falls around the fourth week in November, at the very beginning of Sagittarius, will you still retain the traits of Scorpio, the sign of the Zodiac before Sagittarius? And what if you were born near Christmas—are you more Capricorn than Sagittarius? Many people born at the edge, or cusp, of a sign have great difficulty determining exactly what sign they are. If you are one of these people, here's how you can figure it out once and for all.

Consult the following table. It will tell you the precise days on which the Sun entered and left your sign. If you were born at the beginning or end of Sagittarius, yours is a lifetime reflecting a process of subtle transformation. Your life on Earth will symbolize a significant change in consciousness, for you are about to enter a whole new way of living or are leaving one behind.

If you were born at the beginning of Sagittarius, you may want to read the horoscope for Scorpio as well as Sagittarius, for Scorpio holds the key to many of your hidden weaknesses, sexual uncertainties, wishes, fantasies, and spiritual potentials. You are the symbol of the human mind awakening to its higher capabilities. You are preparing the way for the liberation of your soul into the realms of wisdom and truth. You leave behind greed, blind desire and shallow lust, as you learn to create and understand yourself. You travel, see new places, see how people live, figure yourself out, acquire knowledge.

You may hide a stubborn and dangerous extremism and you may rely too much on luck, but at some crisis point in your life, a change of consciousness will occur to shift your behavior patterns. New worlds open up, as you become aware of immortality and the infinite possiblities of your own mind.

If you were born at the end of Sagittarius, you may want to read the horoscope book for Capricorn as well as Sagittarius, for Capricorn is a deep part of your materialistic values. You were born with the need to bring your dreams into reality and put your talents and ambitions to practical use.

You need to find a balance between believing nothing and believing too much—between cynicism and blind idealism.

DATES SUN ENTERS SAGITTARIUS (LEAVES SCORPIO)

November 22 every year from 1900 to 2000, except for the following:

November 21:		November 23:		
1976	1992	1902	1915	1931
80	93	03	19	35
84	96	07	23	39
88		10	27	43
		11		

DATES SUN LEAVES SAGITTARIUS (ENTERS CAPRICORN)

December 22 every year from 1900 to 2000, except for the following:

December 21:				
1912	1944	1964	1977	1989
16	48	65	80	92
20	52	68	81	93
23	53	69	84	94
28	56	72	85	96
32	57	73	86	97
36	60	76	88	98
40	61			

HISTORY AND USES
OF ASTROLOGY

Does astrology have a place in the fast-moving, ultra-scientific world we live in today? Can it be justified in a sophisticated society whose outriders are already preparing to step off the moon into the deep space of the planets themselves? Or is it just a hangover of ancient superstition, a psychological dummy for neurotics and dreamers of every historical age?

These are the kind of questions that any inquiring person can be expected to ask when they approach a subject like astrology which goes beyond, but never excludes, the materialistic side of life.

The simple, single answer is that astrology works. It works for tens of millions of people in the western world alone. In the United States there are 10 million followers and in Europe, an estimated 25 million. America has more than 4000 practicing astrologers, Europe nearly three times as many. Even down-under Australia has its hundreds of thousands of adherents. The importance of such vast numbers of people from diverse backgrounds and cultures is recognized by the world's biggest newspapers and magazines who probably devote more of their space to this subject in a year than to any other. In the eastern countries, astrology has enormous followings, again, because it has been proved to work. In countries like India, brides and grooms for centuries have been chosen on the basis of astrological compatibility. The low divorce rate there, despite today's heavy westernizing influence, is attributed largely to this practice.

In the western world, astrology today is more vital than ever before; more practicable because it needs a sophisticated society like ours to understand and develop its contribution to the full; more valid because science itself is confirming the precepts of astrological knowledge with every new exciting step. The ordinary person who daily applies astrology intelligently does not have to wonder whether it is true nor believe in it blindly. He can see it working for himself. And, if he can use it—and this book is designed to help the reader to do just that—he can make living a far richer experience, and become a more developed personality and a better person.

Astrology is the science of relationships. It is not just a study of planetary influences on man and his environment. It is the study of man himself.

We are at the center of our personal universe, of all our relationships. And our happiness or sadness depends on how we act, how we relate to the people and things that surround us. The emotions that we generate have a distinct affect—for better or worse—on the world around us. Our friends and our enemies will confirm this. Just look in the mirror the next time you are angry. In other words, each of us is a kind of sun or planet or star and our influence on our personal universe, whether loving, helpful or destructive, varies with our changing moods, expressed through our individual character.

And to an extent that includes the entire galaxy, this is true of the planetary bodies. Their radiations affect each other, including the earth and all the things on it. And in comparatively recent years, giant constellations called "quasars" have been discovered. These exist far beyond the night stars that we can observe, and science says these quasars are emitting radiating influences more powerful and different than ever recorded on earth. Their effect on man from an astrological point of view is under deep study. Compared with these inter-stellar forces, our personal "radiations" are negligible on the planetary scale. But ours are just as potent in the way they affect our moods, and our ability to control them. To this extent they determine much of the happiness and satisfaction in our lives. For instance, if we were bound and gagged and had to hold some strong emotion within us without being able to move, we would soon start to feel very uncomfortable. We are obviously pretty powerful radiators inside, in our own way. But usually, we are able to throw off our emotion in some sort of action—we have a good cry, walk it off, or tell someone our troubles—before it can build up too far and make us physically ill. Astrology helps us to understand the universal forces working on us, and through this understanding, we can become more properly adjusted to our surroundings and find ourselves coping where others may flounder.

Closely related to our emotions is the "other side" of our personal universe, our physical welfare. Our body, of course, is largely influenced by things around us over which we have very little control. The phone rings, we hear it. The train runs late. We snag our stocking or cut our face shaving. Our body is under a constant bombardment of events that influence our lives to varying degrees.

The question that arises from all this is, what makes each of us act so that we have to involve other people and keep the ball of activity and evolution rolling? This is the question that both science and astrology are involved with. The scientists have attacked it from different angles: anthropology, the study of human evolution as body, mind and response to environment; anatomy, the study of bodily structure; psychology, the science of the human mind; and so on. These studies have produced very impressive classifications and valuable information, but because the approach to the problem is fragmented, so is the result. They remain "branches" of science. Science generally studies effects. It keeps turning up wonderful answers but no lasting solutions. Astrology, on the other hand approaches the question from the broader viewpoint. Astrology began its inquiry with the totality of human experience and saw it as an effect. It then looked to find the cause, or at least the prime movers, and during thousands of years of observation of man and his *universal* environment, came up with the extraordinary principle of planetary influence—or astrology, which, from the Greek, means the science of the stars.

Modern science, as we shall see, has confirmed much of astrology's foundations—most of it unintentionally, some of it reluctantly, but still, indisputably.

It is not difficult to imagine that there must be a connection between outer space and the earth. Even today, scientists are not too sure how our earth was created, but it is generally agreed that it is only a tiny part of the universe. And as a part of the universe, people on earth see and feel the influence of heavenly bodies in almost every aspect of our existence. There is no doubt that the sun has the greatest influence on life on this planet. Without it there would be no life, for without it there would be no warmth, no division into day and night, no cycles of time or season at all. This is clear and easy to see. The influence of the moon, on the other hand, is more subtle, though no less definite.

There are many ways in which the influence of the moon manifests itself here on earth, both on human and animal life. It is a well-known fact, for instance, that the large movements of water on our planet—that is the ebb and flow of the tides—are caused by the moon's gravitational pull. Since this is so, it follows that these water movements do not occur only in the oceans, but that all bodies of water are affected, even down to the tiniest puddle.

The human body, too, which consists of about 70 percent water, falls within the scope of this lunar influence. For example the menstrual cycle of most women corresponds to the lunar month; the period of pregnancy in humans is 273 days, or equal to nine lunar months. Similarly, many illnesses reach a crisis at the change of the moon, and statistics in many countries have shown that the crime rate is highest at the time of the full moon. Even human sexual desire has been associated with the phases of the moon. But, it is in the movement of the tides that we get the clearest demonstration of planetary influence, and the irresistible correspondence between the so-called metaphysical and the physical.

Tide tables are prepared years in advance by calculating the future positions of the moon. Science has known for a long time that the moon is the main cause of tidal action. But only in the last few years has it begun to realize the possible extent of this influence on mankind. To begin with, the ocean tides do not rise and fall as we might imagine from our personal observations of them. The moon as it orbits around the earth, sets up a circular wave of attraction which pulls the oceans of the world after it, broadly in an east to west direction. This influence is like a phantom wave crest, a loop of power stretching from pole to pole which passes over and around the earth like an invisible shadow. It travels with equal effect across the land masses and, as scientists were recently amazed to observe, caused oysters placed in the dark in the middle of the United States where there is no sea, to open their shells to receive the non-existent tide. If the land-locked oysters react to this invisible signal, what effect does it have on us who not so long ago in evolutionary time, came out of the sea and still have its salt in our blood and sweat?

Less well known is the fact that the moon is also the primary force behind the circulation of blood in human beings and animals, and the movement of sap in trees and plants. Agriculturists have established that the moon has a distinct influence on crops, which explains why for centuries people have planted according to moon cycles. The habits of many animals, too, are directed by the movement of the moon. Migratory birds, for instance, depart only at or near the time of the full moon. Just as certain fish, eels in particular, move only in accordance with certain phases of the moon.

Know Thyself—Why?

In today's fast-changing world, everyone still longs to know what the future holds. It is the one thing that everyone has in common: rich and poor, famous and infamous, all are deeply concerned about tomorrow.

But the key to the future, as every historian knows, lies in the past. This is as true of individual people as it is of nations. You cannot understand your future without first understanding your past, which is simply another way of saying that you must first of all know yourself.

The motto "know thyself" seems obvious enough nowadays, but it was originally put forward as the foundation of wisdom by the ancient Greek philosophers. It was then adopted by the "mystery religions" of the ancient Middle East, Greece and Rome, and is still used in all genuine schools of mind training or mystical discipline, both in those of the East, based on yoga, and those of the West. So it is universally accepted now, and has been through the ages.

But how do you go about discovering what sort of person you are? The first step is usually classification into some sort of system of types. Astrology did this long before the birth of Christ. Psychology has also done it. So has modern medicine, in its way.

One system classifies men according to the source of the impulses they respond to most readily: the muscles, leading to direct bodily action; the digestive organs, resulting in emotion, or the brain and nerves. Another such system says that character is determined by the endocrine glands, and gives us labels like "pituitary," "thyroid" and "hyperthyroid" types. These different systems are neither contradictory nor mutually exclusive. In fact, they are very often different ways of saying the same thing.

Very popular and useful classifications were devised by Dr. C. G. Jung, the eminent disciple of Freud. Jung observed among the different faculties of the mind, four which have a predominant influence on character. These four faculties exist in all of us without exception, but not in perfect balance. So when we say, for instance, that a man is a "thinking type," it means that in any situation he tries to be rational. It follows that emotion, which some say is the opposite of thinking, will be his weakest function. This type can be sensible and reasonable, or calculating and unsympathetic. The emotional type, on the other hand, can often be recognized by exaggerated language—everything is either marvelous or terrible—and in extreme cases they even invent dramas and quarrels out of nothing just to make life more interesting.

The other two faculties are intuition and physical sensation. The sensation type does not only care for food and drink, nice clothes and furniture; he is also interested in all forms of physical experience. Many scientists are sensation types as are athletes and nature-lovers. Like sensation, intuition is a form of perception and we all possess it. But it works through that part of the mind which is not under conscious control—consequently it sees meanings and connections which are not obvious to thought or emotion. Inventors and original thinkers are always intuitive, but so, too, are superstitious people who see meanings where none exist.

Thus, sensation tells us what is going on in the world, feeling (that is, emotion) tells us how important it is to ourselves, thinking enables us to interpret it and work out what we should do about it, and intuition tells us what it means to ourselves and others. All four faculties are essential, and all are present in every one of us. But some people are guided chiefly by one, others by another.

Besides these four types, Jung observed a division into extrovert and introvert, which cuts across them. By and large, the introvert is one who finds truth inside himself rather than outside. He is not, therefore, ideally suited to a religion or a political party which tells him what to believe. Original thinkers are almost necessarily introverts. The extrovert, on the other hand, finds truth coming to him from outside. He believes in experts and authorities, and wants to think that nature and the laws of nature really exists, that they are what they appear to be and not just generalities made by men.

A disadvantage of all these systems of classification, is that one cannot tell very easily where to place oneself. Some people are reluctant to admit that they act to please their emotions. So they deceive themselves for years by trying to belong to whichever type they think is the "best." Of course, there is no best; each has its faults and each has its good points.

The advantage of the signs of the Zodiac is that they simplify classification. Not only that, but your date of birth is personal—it is unarguably yours. What better way to know yourself than by going back as far as possible to the very moment of your birth? And this is precisely what your horoscope is all about.

What Is a Horoscope?

If you had been able to take a picture of the heavens at the moment of your birth, that photograph would be your horoscope. Lacking such a snapshot, it is still possible to recreate the picture—and this is at the basis of the astrologer's art. In other words, your horoscope is a representation of the skies with the planets in the exact positions they occupied at the time you were born.

This information, of course, is not enough for the astrologer. He has to have a background of significance to put the photograph on. You will get the idea if you imagine two balls—one inside the other. The inner one is transparent. In the center of both is the astrologer, able to look up, down and around in all directions. The outer sphere is the Zodiac which is divided into twelve approximately equal segments, like the segments of an orange. The inner ball is our photograph. It is transparent except for the images of the planets. Looking out from the center, the astrologer sees the planets in various segments of the Zodiac. These twelve segments are known as the signs or houses.

The position of the planets when each of us is born is always different. So the photograph is always different. But the Zodiac and its signs are fixed.

Now, where in all this are you, the subject of the horoscope?

Your character is largely determined by the sign the sun is in. So that is where the astrologer looks first in your horoscope.

There are twelve signs in the Zodiac and the sun spends approximately one month in each. As the sun's motion is almost perfectly regular, the astrologers have been able to fix the dates governing each sign. There are not many people who do not know which sign of the Zodiac they were born under or who have not been amazed at some time or other at the accuracy of the description of their own character. Here are the twelve signs, the ancient zodiacal symbol, and their dates for the year 1991.*

ARIES	Ram	March 20–April 20
TAURUS	Bull	April 20–May 21
GEMINI	Twins	May 21–June 21
CANCER	Crab	June 21–July 23
LEO	Lion	July 23–August 23
VIRGO	Virgin	August 23–September 23
LIBRA	Scales	September 23–October 23
SCORPIO	Scorpion	October 23–November 22
SAGITTARIUS	Archer	November 22–December 22
CAPRICORN	Sea-Goat	December 22–January 20
AQUARIUS	Water-Bearer	January 20–February 18
PISCES	Fish	February 18–March 20

The time of birth—apart from the date—is important in advanced astrology because the planets travel at such great speed that the patterns they form change from minute to minute. For this reason, each person's horoscope is his and his alone. Further on we will see that the practicing astrologer has ways of determining and reading these minute time changes which dictate the finer character differences in us all.

However, it is still possible to draw significant conclusions and make meaningful predictions based simply on the sign of the Zodiac a person is born under. In a horoscope, the signs do not necessarily correspond with the divisions of the houses. It could be that a house begins halfway across a sign. It is the interpretation of such combinations of different influences that distinguishes the professional astrologer from the student and the follower.

However, to gain a workable understanding of astrology, it is not necessary to go into great detail. In fact, the beginner is likely to find himself confused if he attempts to absorb too much too quickly. It should be remembered that this is a science and to become proficient at it, and especially to grasp the tremendous scope of possibilities in man and his affairs and direct them into a worthwhile reading, takes a great deal of study and experience.

*These dates are fluid and change with the motion of the Earth from year to year.

If you do intend to pursue it seriously you will have to learn to figure the exact moment of birth against the degrees of longitude and latitude of the planets at that precise time. This involves adapting local time to Greenwich Mean Time (G.M.T.), reference to tables of houses to establish the Ascendant, as well as making calculations from Ephemeris—the tables of the planets' positions.

After reading this introduction, try drawing up a rough horoscope to get the "feel" of reading some elementary characteristics and natal influences.

Draw a circle with twelve equal segments. Write in counterclockwise the names of the signs—Aries, Taurus, Gemini etc.—one for each segment. Look up an ephemeris for the year of the person's birth and note down the sign each planet was in on the birthday. Do not worry about the number of degrees (although if a planet is on the edge of a sign its position obviously should be considered). Write the name of the planet in the segment/sign on your chart. Write the number 1 in the sign where the sun is. This is the first house. Number the rest of the houses, counterclockwise till you finish at 12. Now you can investigate the probable basic expectation of experience of the person concerned. This is done first of all by seeing what planet or planets is/are in what sign and house. (See also page 72.)

The 12 houses control these functions:

1st.	Individuality, body appearance, general outlook on life	(Personality house)
2nd.	Finance, business	(Money house)
3rd.	Relatives, education, correspondence	(Relatives house)
4th.	Family, neighbors	(Home house)
5th.	Pleasure, children, attempts, entertainment	(Pleasure house)
6th.	Health, employees	(Health house)
7th.	Marriage, partnerships	(Marriage house)
8th.	Death, secret deals, difficulties	(Death house)
9th.	Travel, intellectual affairs	(Travel house)
10th.	Ambition, social standing	(Business and Honor house)
11th.	Friendship, social life, luck	(Friends house)
12th.	Troubles, illness, loss	(Trouble house)

The characteristics of the planets modify the influence of the Sun according to their natures and strengths.

Sun: Source of life. Basic temperament according to sun sign. The will.
Moon: Superficial nature. Moods. Changeable. Adaptive. Mother.
Mercury: Communication. Intellect. Reasoning power. Curiosity. Short travels.
Venus: Love. Delight. Art. Beautiful possessions.
Mars: Energy. Initiative. War. Anger. Destruction. Impulse.
Jupiter: Good. Generous. Expansive. Opportunities. Protection.
Saturn: Jupiter's opposite. Contraction. Servant. Delay. Hardwork. Cold. Privation. Research. Lasting rewards after long struggle.
Uranus: Fashion. Electricity. Revolution. Sudden changes. Modern science.
Neptune: Sensationalism. Mass emotion. Devastation. Delusion.
Pluto: Creates and destroys. Lust for power. Strong obsessions.

Superimpose the characteristics of the planets on the functions of the house in which they appear. Express the result through the character of the birth (sun) sign, and you will get the basic idea of how astrology works.

Of course, many other considerations have been taken into account in producing the carefully worked out predictions in this book: The aspects of the planets to each other; their strength according to position and sign; whether they are in a house of exaltation or decline; whether they are natural enemies or not; whether a planet occupies his own sign; the position of a planet in relation to its own house or sign; whether the planet is male, female or neuter; whether the sign is a fire, earth, water or air sign. These are only a few of the colors on the astrologer's pallet which he must mix with the inspiration of the artist and the accuracy of the mathematician.

The Problem of Love

Love, of course, is never a problem. The problem lies in recognizing the difference between infatuation, emotion, sex and, sometimes, the downright deceit of the other person. Mankind, with its record of broken marriages, despair and disillusionment, is obviously not very good at making these distinctions.

Can astrology help?

Yes. In the same way that advance knowledge can usually help in any human situation. And there is probably no situation as human, as poignant, as pathetic and universal, as the failure of man's love.

Love, of course, is not just between man and woman. It involves love of children, parents, home and so on. But the big problems usually involve the choice of partner.

Astrology has established degrees of compatibility that exist between people born under the various signs of the Zodiac. Because people are individuals, there are numerous variations and modifications and the astrologer, when approached on mate and marriage matters makes allowances for them. But the fact remains that some groups of people are suited for each other and some are not and astrology has expressed this in terms of characteristics which all can study and use as a personal guide.

No matter how much enjoyment and pleasure we find in the different aspects of each other's character, if it is not an overall compatibility, the chances of our finding fulfillment or enduring happiness in each other are pretty hopeless. And astrology can help us to find someone compatible.

History of Astrology

The origins of astrology have been lost far back in history, but we do know that reference is made to it as far back as the first written records of the human race. It is not hard to see why. Even in primitive times, people must have looked for an explanation for the various happenings in their lives. They must have wanted to know why people were different from one to another. And in their search they turned to the regular movements of the sun, moon and stars to see if they could provide an answer.

It is interesting to note that as soon as man learned to use his tools in any type of design, or his mind in any kind of calculation, he turned his attention to the heavens. Ancient cave dwellings reveal dim crescents and circles representative of the sun and moon, rulers of day and night. Mesopotamia and the civilization of Chaldea, in itself the foundation of those of Babylonia and Assyria, show a complete picture of astronomical observation and well-developed astrological interpretation.

Humanity has a natural instinct for order. The study of anthropology reveals that primitive people—even as far back as prehistoric times—were striving to achieve a certain order in their lives. They tried to organize the apparent chaos of the universe. They had the desire to attach meaning to things. This demand for order has persisted throughout the history of man. So that observing the regularity of the heavenly bodies made it logical that primitive peoples should turn heavenwards in their search for an understanding of the world in which they found themselves so random and alone.

And they did find a significance in the movements of the stars. Shepherds tending their flocks, for instance, observed that when the cluster of stars now known as the constellation Aries was in sight, it was the time of fertility and they associated it with the Ram. And they noticed that the growth of plants and plant life corresponded with different phases of the moon, so that certain times were favorable for the planting of crops, and other times were not. In this way, there grew up a tradition of seasons and causes connected with the passage of the sun through the twelve signs of the Zodiac.

Astrology was valued so highly that the king was kept informed of the daily and monthly changes in the heavenly bodies, and the results of astrological studies regarding events of the future. Head astrologers were clearly men of great rank and position, and the office was said to be a hereditary one.

Omens were taken, not only from eclipses and conjunctions of the moon or sun with one of the planets, but also from storms and earthquakes. In the eastern civilizations, particularly, the reverence inspired by astrology appears to have remained unbroken since the very earliest days. In ancient China, astrology, astronomy and religion went hand in hand. The astrologer, who was also an astronomer, was part of the official government service and had his own corner in the Imperial Palace. The duties of the Imperial astrologer, whose office was one of the most important in the land, were clearly defined, as this extract from early records shows:

"This exalted gentleman must concern himself with the stars in the heavens, keeping a record of the changes and movements of the Planets, the Sun and the Moon, in order to examine the movements of the terrestial world with the object of prognosticating good and bad fortune. He divides the territories of the nine regions of the empire in accordance with their dependence on particular celestial bodies. All the fiefs and principalities are connected with the stars and from this their prosperity or misfortune should be ascertained. He makes prognostications according to the twelve years of the Jupiter cycle of good and evil of the terrestial world. From the colors of the five kinds of clouds, he determines the coming of floods or droughts, abundance or famine. From the twelve winds, he draws conclusions about the state of harmony of heaven and earth, and takes note of good and bad signs that result from their accord or disaccord. In general, he concerns himself with five kinds of phenomena so as to warn the Emperor to come to the aid of the government and to allow for variations in the ceremonies according to their circumstances."

The Chinese were also keen observers of the fixed stars, giving them such unusual names as Ghost Vehicle, Sun of Imperial Concubine, Imperial Prince, Pivot of Heaven, Twinkling Brilliance or Weaving Girl. But, great astrologers though they may have been, the Chinese lacked one aspect of mathematics that the Greeks applied to astrology—deductive geometry. Deductive geometry was the basis of much classical astrology in and after the time of the Greeks, and this explains the different methods of prognostication used in the East and West.

Down through the ages the astrologer's art has depended, not so much on the uncovering of new facts, though this is important, as on the interpretation of the facts already known. This is the essence of his skill. Obviously one cannot always tell how people will react (and this underlines the very important difference between astrology and predestination which will be discussed later on) but one can be prepared, be forewarned, to know what to expect.

But why should the signs of the zodiac have any effect at all on the formation of human character? It is easy to see why people thought they did, and even now we constantly use astrological expressions in our everyday speech. The thoughts of "lucky star," "ill-fated," "star-crossed," "mooning around," are interwoven into the very structure of our language.

In the same way that the earth has been created by influences from outside, there remains an indisputable togetherness in the working of the universe. The world, after all, is a coherent structure, for if it were not, it would be quite without order and we would never know what to expect. A dog could turn into an apple, or an elephant sprout wings and fly at any moment without so much as a by your leave. But nature, as we know, functions according to laws, not whims, and the laws of nature are certainly not subject to capricious exceptions.

This means that no part of the universe is ever arbitrarily cut off from any other part. Everything is therefore to some extent linked with everything else. The moon draws an imperceptible tide on every puddle; tiny and trivial events can be effected by outside forces (such as the fall of a feather by the faintest puff of wind). And so it is fair to think that the local events at any moment reflect to a very small extent the evolution of the world as a whole.

From this principle follows the possibility of divination, and also knowledge of events at a distance, provided one's mind were always as perfectly undisturbed, as ideally smooth, as a mirror or unruffled lake. Provided, in other words, that one did not confuse the picture with hopes, guesses, and expectations. When people try to foretell the future by cards or crystal ball gazing they find it much easier to confuse the picture with expectations than to reflect it clearly.

But the present does contain a good deal of the future to which it leads—not all, but a good deal. The diver halfway between bridge and water is going to make a splash; the train whizzing towards the station will pass through it unless interfered with; the burglar breaking a pane of glass has exposed himself to the possibility of a prison sentence. Yet this is not a doctrine of determinism, as was emphasized earlier. Clearly, there are forces already at work in the present, and any one of them could alter the situation in some way. Equally, a change of decision could alter the whole situation as well. So the future depends, not on an irresistible force, but on a small act of free will.

An individual's age, physique, and position on the earth's surface are remote consequences of his birth. Birth counts as the original cause for all that happens subsequently. The horoscope, in this case, means "this person represents the further evolution of the state of the universe pictured in this chart." Such a chart can apply equally to man or woman, dog, ship or even limited company.

If the evolution of an idea, or of a person, is to be understood as a totality, it must continue to evolve from its own beginnings, which is to say, in the terms in which it began. The brown-eyed person will be faithful to brown eyes all his life; the traitor is being faithful to some complex of ideas which has long been evolving in him; and the person born at sunset will always express, as he evolves, the psychological implications or analogies of the moment when the sun sinks out of sight.

This is the doctrine that an idea must continue to evolve in terms of its origin. It is a completely non-materialist doctrine, though it never fails to apply to material objects. And it implies, too, that the individual will continue to evolve in terms of his moment of origin, and therefore possibly of the sign of the Zodiac rising on the eastern horizon at his birth. It also implies that the signs of the Zodiac themselves will evolve in the collective mind of the human race in the same terms that they were first devised and not in the terms in which modern astrologers consciously think they ought to work.

For the human race, like every other kind of animal, has a collective mind, as Professor Jung discovered in his investigation of dreams. If no such collective mind existed, no infant could ever learn anything, for communication would be impossible. Furthermore, it is absurd to suggest that the conscious mind could be older than the "unconscious," for an infant's nervous system functions correctly before it has discovered the difference between "myself" and "something else" or discovered what eyes and hands are for. Indeed, the involuntary muscles function correctly even before birth, and will never be under conscious control. They are part of what we call the "unconscious" which is not really "unconscious" at all. To the contrary, it is totally aware of itself and everything else; it is merely that part of the mind that cannot be controlled by conscious effort.

And human experience, though it varies in detail with every individual, is basically the same for each one of us, consisting of sky and earth, day and night, waking and sleeping, man and woman, birth and death. So there is bound to be in the mind of the human race a very large number of inescapable ideas, which are called our natural archetypes.

There are also, however, artificial or cultural archetypes which are not universal or applicable to everyone, but are nevertheless inescapable within the limits of a given culture. Examples of these are the cross in Christianity, and the notion of "escape from the wheel of rebirth" in India. There was a time when these ideas did not exist. And there was a time, too, when the scheme of the Zodiac did not exist. One would not expect the Zodiac to have any influence on remote and primitive peoples, for example, who have never heard of it. If the Zodiac is only an archetype, their horoscopes probably would not work and it would not matter which sign they were born under.

But where the Zodiac is known, and the idea of it has become worked into the collective mind, then there it could well appear to have an influence, even if it has no physical existence. For ideas do not have a physical existence, anyway. No physical basis has yet been discovered for the telepathy that controls an anthill; young swallows migrate before, not after, their parents; and the weaverbird builds its intricate nest without being taught. Materialists suppose, but cannot prove, that "instinct" (as it is called, for no one knows how it works) is controlled by nucleic acid in the chromosomes. This is not a genuine explanation, though, for it only pushes the mystery one stage further back.

Does this mean, then, that the human race, in whose civilization the idea of the twelve signs of the Zodiac has long been embedded, is divided into only twelve types? Can we honestly believe that it is really as simple as that? If so, there must be pretty wide ranges of variation within each type. And if, to explain the variation, we call in heredity and environment, experiences in early childhood, the thyroid and other glands, and also the four functions of the mind mentioned at the beginning of this introduction, and extroversion and introversion, then one begins to wonder if the original classification was worth making at all. No sensible person believes that his favorite system explains everything. But even so, he will not find it much use at all if it does not even save him the trouble of bothering with the others.

Under the Jungian system, everyone has not only a dominant or principal function, but also a secondary or subsidiary one, so that the four can be arranged in order of potency. In the intuitive type, sensation is always the most inefficient function, but the second most inefficient function can be either thinking (which tends to make original thinkers such as Jung himself) or else feeling (which tends to make artistic people). Therefore, allowing for introversion and extroversion, there are at least four kinds of intuitive types, and sixteen types in all. Furthermore, one can see how the sixteen types merge into each other, so that there are no unrealistic or unconvincingly rigid divisions.

In the same way, if we were to put every person under only one sign of the Zodiac, the system becomes too rigid and unlike life. Besides, it was never intended to be used like that. It may be convenient to have only twelve types, but we know that in practice there is every possible gradation between aggressiveness and timidity, or between conscientiousness and laziness. How, then, do we account for this?

The Tyrant and the Saint

Just as the thinking type of man is also influenced to some extent by sensation and intuition, but not very much by emotion, so a person born under Leo can be influenced to some extent by one or two (but not more) of the other signs. For instance, famous persons born under the sign of Gemini include Henry VIII, whom nothing and no-one could have induced to abdicate, and Edward VIII, who did just that. Obviously, then, the sign Gemini does not fully explain the complete character of either of them.

Again, under the opposite sign, Sagittarius, were both Stalin, who was totally consumed with the notion of power, and Charles V, who freely gave up an empire because he preferred to go into a monastery. And we find under Scorpio, many uncompromising characters such as Luther, de Gaulle, Indira Gandhi and Montgomery, but also Petain, a successful commander whose name later became synonymous with collaboration.

A single sign is therefore obviously inadequate to explain the differences between people; it can only explain resemblances, such as the combativeness of the Scorpio group, or the far-reaching devotion of Charles V and Stalin to their respective ideals—the Christian heaven and the Communist utopia.

But very few people are born under one sign only. As well as the month of birth, as was mentioned earlier, the day matters, and, even more, the hour, which ought, if possible, to be noted to the nearest minute. Without this, it is impossible to have an actual horoscope, for the word horoscope means literally, "a consideration of the hour."

The month of birth tells you only which sign of the Zodiac was occupied by the sun. The day and hour tell you what sign was occupied by the moon. And the minute tells you which sign was rising on the eastern horizon. This is called the Ascendant, and it is supposed to be the most important thing in the whole horoscope.

If you were born at midnight, the sun is then in an important position, although invisible. But at one o'clock in the morning the sun is not important, so the moment of birth will not matter much. The important thing then will be the Ascendant, and possibly one or two of the planets. At a given day and hour, say, dawn on January 1st, or 9:00 p.m. on the longest day, the Ascendant will always be the same at any given place. But the moon and planets alter from day to day, at different speeds and have to be looked up in an astronomical table.

The sun is said to signify one's heart, that is to say, one's deepest desires and inmost nature. This is quite different from the moon, which, as we have seen, signifies one's superficial way of behaving. When the ancient Romans referred to the Emperor Augustus as a Capricornian, they meant that he had the moon in Capricorn; they did not pay much attention to the sun, although he was born at sunrise. Or, to take another example, a modern astrologer would call Disraeli a Scorpion because he had Scorpio rising, but most people would call him Sagittarian because he had the sun there. The Romans would have called him Leo because his moon was in Leo.

The sun, as has already been pointed out, is important if one is born near sunrise, sunset, noon or midnight, but is otherwise not reckoned as the principal influence. So if one does not seem to fit one's birth month, it is always worthwhile reading the other signs, for one may have been born at a time when any of them were rising or occupied by the moon. It also seems to be the case that the influence of the sun develops as life goes on, so that the month of birth is easier to guess in people over the age of forty. The young are supposed to be influenced mainly by their Ascendant which characterizes the body and physical personality as a whole.

It should be clearly understood that it is nonsense to assume that all people born at a certain time will exhibit the same characteristics, or that they will even behave in the same manner. It is quite obvious that, from the very moment of its birth, a child is subject to the effects of its environment, and that this in turn will influence its character and heritage to a decisive extent. Also to be taken into account are education and economic conditions, which play a very important part in the formation of one's character as well.

However, it is clearly established that people born under one sign of the Zodiac do have certain basic traits in their character which are different from those born under other signs. It is obvious to every thinking person that certain events produce different reactions in various people. For instance, if a man slips on a banana skin and falls heavily on the pavement, one passer-by may laugh and find this extremely amusing, while another may just walk on, thinking: "What a fool falling down like that. He should look where he is going." A third might also walk away saying to himself: "It's none of my business—I'm glad it wasn't me." A fourth might walk past and think: "I'm sorry for that man, but I haven't the time to be bothered with helping him." And a fifth might stop to help the fallen man to his feet, comfort him and take him home. Here is just one event which could produce entirely different reactions in different people. And, obviously, there are many more. One that comes to mind immediately is the violently opposed views to events such as wars, industrial strikes, and so on. The fact that people have different attitudes to the same event is simply another way of saying that they have different characters. And this is not something that can be put down to background, for people of the same race, religion, or class, very often express quite different reactions to happenings or events. Similarly, it is often the case that members of the same family, where there is clearly uniform background of economic and social standing, education, race and religion, often argue bitterly among themselves over political and social issues.

People have, in general, certain character traits and qualities which, according to their environment, develop in either a positive or a negative manner. Therefore, selfishness (inherent selfishness, that is) might emerge as unselfishness; kindness and consideration as cruelty and lack of consideration towards others. In the same way, a naturally constructive person, may, through frustration, become destructive, and so on. The latent characteristics with which people are born can, therefore, through environment and good or bad training, become something that would appear to be its opposite, and so give the lie to the astrologer's description of their character. But this is not the case. The true character is still there, but it is buried deep beneath these external superficialities.

Careful study of the character traits of different signs can be immeasurable help, and can render beneficial service to the intelligent person. Undoubtedly, the reader will already have discovered that, while he is able to get on very well with some people, he just "cannot stand" others. The causes sometimes seem inexplicable. At times there is intense dislike, at other times immediate sympathy. And there is, too, the phenomenon of love at first sight, which is also apparently inexplicable. People appear to be either sympathetic or unsympathetic towards each other for no apparent reason.

Now if we look at this in the light of the Zodiac, we find that people born under different signs are either compatible or incompatible with each other. In other words, there are good and bad interrelating factors among the various signs. This does not, of course, mean that humanity can be divided into groups of hostile camps. It would be quite wrong to be hostile or indifferent toward people who happen to be born under an incompatible sign. There is no reason why everybody should not, or cannot, learn to control and adjust their feelings and actions, especially after they are aware of the positive qualities of other people by studying their character analyses, among other things.

Every person born under a certain sign has both positive and negative qualities, which are developed more or less according to his free will. Nobody is entirely good or entirely bad, and it is up to each one of us to learn to control himself on the one hand, and at the same time to endeavor to learn about himself and others.

It cannot be repeated often enough that, though the intrinsic nature of man and his basic character traits are born in him, nevertheless it is his own free will that determines whether he will make really good use of his talents and abilities—whether, in other words, he will overcome his vices or allow them to rule him. Most of us are born with at least a streak of laziness, irritability, or some other fault in our nature, and it is up to each one of us to see that we exert sufficient willpower to control our failings so that they do not harm ourselves or others.

Astrology can reveal our inclinations and tendencies. Our weaknesses should not be viewed as shortcomings that are impossible to change. The horoscope of a man may show him to have criminal leanings, for instance, but this does not mean he will definitely become a criminal.

The ordinary man usually finds it difficult to know himself. He is often bewildered. Astrology can frequently tell him more about himself than the different schools of psychology are able to do. Knowing his failings and shortcomings, he will do his best to overcome them, and make himself a better and more useful member of society and a helpmate to his family and friends. It can also save him a great deal of unhappiness and remorse.

And yet it may seem absurd that an ancient philosophy, something that is known as a "pseudo-science," could be a prop to the men and women of the twentieth century. But below the material-istic surface of modern life, there are hidden streams of feeling and thought. Symbology is reappearing as a study worthy of the schol-ar; the psychosomatic factor in illness has passed from the writings of the crank to those of the specialist; spiritual healing in all its forms is no longer a pious hope but an accepted phenomenon. And it is into this context that we consider astrology, in the sense that it is an analysis of human types.

Astrology and medicine had a long journey together, and only parted company a couple of centuries ago. There still remain in medical language such astrological terms as "saturnine," "choleric," and "mercurial," used in the diagnosis of physical ten-dencies. The herbalist, for long the handyman of the medical pro-fession, has been dominated by astrology since the days of the Greeks. Certain herbs traditionally respond to certain planetary in-fluences, and diseases must therefore be treated to ensure harmony between the medicine and the disease.

No one expects the most eccentric of modern doctors to go back to the practices of his predecessors. We have come a long way since the time when phases of the moon were studied in illness. Those days were a medical nightmare, with epidemics that were beyond control, and an explanation of the Black Death sought in conjunc-tion with the planets. Nowadays, astrological diagnosis of disease has literally no parallel in modern life. And yet, age-old symbols of types and of the vulnerability of, say, the Saturnian to chronic dis-eases or the choleric to apoplexy and blood pressure and so on, are still applicable.

But the stars are expected to foretell and not only to diagnose. The astrological forecaster has a counterpart on a highly conven-tional level in the shape of the weather prophet, racing tipster and stock market forecaster, to name just three examples. All in their own way are aiming at the same result. They attempt to look a little further into the pattern of life and also try to determine future pat-terns accurately.

Astrological forecasting has been remarkably accurate, but often it is wide of the mark. The brave man who cares to predict world events takes dangerous chances. Individual forecasting is less clear cut; it can be a help or a disillusionment. Then welcome to the nagging question: if it is possible to foreknow, is it right to foretell? A complex point of ethics on which it is hard to pronounce judgment. The doctor faces the same dilemma if he finds that symp-toms of a mortal disease are present in his patient and that he can only prognosticate a steady decline. How much to tell an individual in a crisis is a problem that has perplexed many distinguished scholars. Honest and conscientious astrologers in this modern world, where so many people are seeking guidance, face the same problem.

The ancient cults, the symbols of old religions, are eclipsed for the moment. They may return with their old force within a decade or two. But at present the outlook is dark. Human beings badly need assurance, as they did in the past, that all is not chaos. Somewhere, somehow, there is a pattern that must be worked out. As to the why and wherefore, the astrologer is not expected to give judgment. He is just someone who, by dint of talent and training, can gaze into the future.

Five hundred years ago it was customary to call in a learned man who was an astrologer who was probably also a doctor and a philosopher. By his knowledge of astrology, his study of planetary influences, he felt himself qualified to guide those in distress. The world has moved forward at a fantastic rate since then, and in this twentieth century speed has been the keyword everywhere. Tensions have increased, the spur of ambition has been applied indiscriminately. People are uncertain of themselves. At first sight it seems fantastic in the light of modern thinking that they turn to the most ancient of all studies, and get someone to calculate a horoscope for them. But is it *really* so fantastic if you take a second look? For astrology is concerned with tomorrow, with survival. And in a world such as ours, those two things are the keywords of the time in which we live.

HOW TO USE
THESE PREDICTIONS

A person reading the predictions in this book should understand that they are produced from the daily position of the planets for a group of people and are not, of course, individually specialized. To get the full benefit of them he should relate the predictions to his own character and circumstances, co-ordinate them, and draw his own conclusions from them.

If he is a serious observer of his own life he should find a definite pattern emerge that will be a helpful and reliable guide.

The point is that we always retain our free will. The stars indicate certain directional tendencies but we are not compelled to follow. We can do or not do, and wisdom must make the choice.

We all have our good and bad days. Sometimes they extend into cycles of weeks. It is therefore advisable to study daily predictions in a span ranging from the day before to several days ahead; also to re-read the monthly predictions for similar cycles.

Daily predictions should be taken very generally. The word "difficult" does not necessarily indicate a whole day of obstruction or inconvenience. It is a warning to you to be cautious. Your caution will often see you around the difficulty before you are involved. This is the correct use of astrology.

In another section, detailed information is given about the influence of the moon as it passes through the various signs of the Zodiac. It includes instructions on how to use the Moon Tables. This information should be used in conjunction with the daily forecasts to give a fuller picture of the astrological trends.

THE MOON

Moon is the nearest planet to the earth. It exerts more observable influence on us from day to day than any other planet. The effect is very personal, very intimate, and if we are not aware of how it works it can make us quite unstable in our ideas. And the annoying thing is that at these times we often see our own instability but can do nothing about it. A knowledge of what can be expected may help considerably. We can then be prepared to stand strong against the moon's negative influences and use its positive ones to help us to get ahead. Who has not heard of going with the tide?

Moon reflects, has no light of its own. It reflects the sun—the life giver—in the form of vital movement. Moon controls the tides, the blood rhythm, the movement of sap in trees and plants. Its nature is inconstancy and change so it signifies our moods, our superficial behavior—walking, talking and especially thinking. Being a true reflector of other forces, moon is cold, watery like the surface of a still lake, brilliant and scintillating at times, but easily ruffled and disturbed by the winds of change.

The moon takes 28½ days to circle the earth and the Zodiac. It spends just over 2¼ days in each sign. During that time it reflects the qualities, energies and characteristics of the sign and, to a degree, the planet which rules the sign. While the moon in its transit occupies a sign incompatible with our own birth sign, we can expect to feel a vague uneasiness, perhaps a touch of irritableness. We should not be discouraged nor let the feeling get us down, or, worse still, allow ourselves to take the discomfort out on others. Try to remember that the moon has to change signs within 55 hours and, provided you are not physically ill, your mood will probably change with it. It is amazing how frequently depression lifts with the shift in the moon's position. And, of course, when the moon is transiting a sign compatible or sympathetic to yours you will probably feel some sort of stimulation or just plain happy to be alive.

In the horoscope, the moon is such a powerful indicator that competent astrologers often use the sign it occupied at birth as the birth sign of the person. This is done particularly when the sun is on the cusp, or edge, of two signs. Most experienced astrologers, however, coordinate both sun and moon signs by reading and confirming from one to the other and secure a far more accurate and personalized analysis.

For these reasons, the moon tables which follow this section (see pages 28–35) are of great importance to the individual. They show the days and the exact times the moon will enter each sign of the Zodiac for the year. Remember, you have to adjust the indicated times to local time. The corrections, already calculated for most of the main cities, are at the beginning of the tables. What follows now is a guide to the influences that will be reflected to the earth by the moon while it transits each of the twelve signs. The influence is at its peak about 26 hours after the moon enters a sign.

MOON IN ARIES

This is a time for action, for reaching out beyond the usual self-imposed limitations and faint-hearted cautions. If you have plans in your head or on your desk, put them into practice. New ventures, applications, new jobs, new starts of any kind—all have a good chance of success. This is the period when original and dynamic impulses are being reflected onto the earth. The energies are extremely vital and favor the pursuit of pleasure and adventure in practically every form. Sick people should feel an improvement. Those who are well will probably find themselves exuding confidence and optimism. People fond of physical exercise should find their bodies growing with tone and well-being. Boldness, strength, determination should characterize most of your activities with a readiness to face up to old challenges. Yesterday's problems may seem petty and exaggerated—so deal with them. Strike out alone. Self-reliance will attract others to you. This is a good time for making friends. Business and marriage partners are more likely to be impressed with the man and woman of action. Opposition will be overcome or thrown aside with much less effort than usual. CAUTION: Be dominant but not domineering.

MOON IN TAURUS

The spontaneous, action-packed person of yesterday gives way to the cautious, diligent, hardworking "thinker." In this period ideas will probably be concentrated on ways of improving finances. A great deal of time may be spent figuring out and going over schemes and plans. It is the right time to be careful with detail. People will find themselves working longer than usual at their desks. Or devoting more time to serious thought about the future. A strong desire to put order into business and financial arrangements may cause extra work. Loved ones may complain of being neglected and may fail to appreciate that your efforts are for their ultimate benefit. Your desire for system may extend to criticism of arrangements in the home and lead to minor upsets. Health may be affected through overwork. Try to secure a reasonable amount of rest and relaxation, although the tendency will be to "keep going" despite good advice. Work done conscientiously in this period should result in a solid contribution to your future security. CAUTION: Try not to be as serious with people as the work you are engaged in.

MOON IN GEMINI

The humdrum of routine and too much work should suddenly end. You are likely to find yourself in an expansive, quicksilver world of change and self-expression. Urges to write, to paint, to experience the freedom of some sort of artistic outpouring, may be very strong. Take full advantage of them. You may find yourself finishing something you began and put aside long ago. Or embarking on something new which could easily be prompted by a chance meeting, a new acquaintance, or even an advertisement. There may be a yearning for a change of scenery, the feeling to visit another country (not too far away), or at least to get away for a few days. This may result in short, quick journeys. Or, if you are planning a single visit, there may be some unexpected changes or detours on the way. Familiar activities will seem to give little satisfaction unless they contain a fresh element of excitement or expectation. The inclination will be towards untried pursuits, particularly those that allow you to express your inner nature. The accent is on new faces, new places. CAUTION: Do not be too quick to commit yourself emotionally.

MOON IN CANCER

Feelings of uncertainty and vague insecurity are likely to cause problems while the moon is in Cancer. Thoughts may turn frequently to the warmth of the home and the comfort of loved ones. Nostalgic impulses could cause you to bring out old photographs and letters and reflect on the days when your life seemed to be much more rewarding and less demanding. The love and understanding of parents and family may be important, and, if it is not forthcoming you may have to fight against a bit of self-pity. The cordiality of friends and the thought of good times with them that are sure to be repeated will help to restore you to a happier frame of mind. The feeling to be alone may follow minor setbacks or rebuffs at this time, but solitude is unlikely to help. Better to get on the telephone or visit someone. This period often causes peculiar dreams and up-surges of imaginative thinking which can be very helpful to authors of occult and mystical works. Preoccupation with the more personal world of simple human needs should overshadow any material strivings. CAUTION: Do not spend too much time thinking—seek the company of loved ones or close friends.

MOON IN LEO

New horizons of exciting and rather extravagant activity open up. This is the time for exhilarating entertainment, glamorous and lavish parties, and expensive shopping sprees. Any merrymaking that relies upon your generosity as a host has every chance of being a spectacular success. You should find yourself right in the center of the fun, either as the life of the party or simply as a person whom happy people like to be with. Romance thrives in this heady at-mosphere and friendships are likely to explode unexpectedly into serious attachments. Children and younger people should be at-tracted to you and you may find yourself organizing a picnic or a visit to a fun-fair, the cinema or the seaside. The sunny company and vitality of youthful companions should help you to find some unsuspected energy. In career, you could find an opening for pro-motion or advancement. This should be the time to make a direct approach. The period favors those engaged in original research. CAUTION: Bask in popularity but not in flattery.

MOON IN VIRGO

Off comes the party cap and out steps the busy, practical worker. He wants to get his personal affairs straight, to rearrange them, if necessary, for more efficiency, so he will have more time for more work. He clears up his correspondence, pays outstanding bills, makes numerous phone calls. He is likely to make inquiries, or sign up for some new insurance and put money into gilt-edged invest-ment. Thoughts probably revolve around the need for future secur-ity—to tie up loose ends and clear the decks. There may be a ten-dency to be "finicky," to interfere in the routine of others, particu-larly friends and family members. The motive may be a genuine desire to help with suggestions for updating or streamlining their affairs, but these will probably not be welcomed. Sympathy may be felt for less fortunate sections of the community and a flurry of some sort of voluntary service is likely. This may be accompanied by strong feelings of responsibility on several fronts and health may suffer from extra efforts made. CAUTION: Everyone may not want your help or advice.

MOON IN LIBRA

These are days of harmony and agreement and you should find yourself at peace with most others. Relationships tend to be smooth and sweet-flowing. Friends may become closer and bonds deepen in mutual understanding. Hopes will be shared. Progress by cooperation could be the secret of success in every sphere. In business, established partnerships may flourish and new ones get off to a good start. Acquaintances could discover similar interests that lead to congenial discussions and rewarding exchanges of some sort. Love, as a unifying force, reaches its optimum. Marriage partners should find accord. Those who wed at this time face the prospect of a happy union. Cooperation and tolerance are felt to be stronger than dissension and impatience. The argumentative are not quite so loud in their bellowings, nor as inflexible in their attitudes. In the home, there should be a greater recognition of the other point of view and a readiness to put the wishes of the group before selfish insistence. This is a favorable time to join an art group. CAUTION: Do not be too independent—let others help you if they want to.

MOON IN SCORPIO

Driving impulses to make money and to economize are likely to cause upsets all round. No area of expenditure is likely to be spared the axe, including the household budget. This is a time when the desire to cut down on extravagance can become near fanatical. Care must be exercised to try to keep the aim in reasonable perspective. Others may not feel the same urgent need to save and may retaliate. There is a danger that possessions of sentimental value will be sold to realize cash for investment. Buying and selling of stock for quick profit is also likely. The attention may turn to having a good clean up round the home and at the office. Neglected jobs could suddenly be done with great bursts of energy. The desire for solitude may intervene. Self-searching thoughts could disturb. The sense of invisible and mysterious energies at work could cause some excitability. The reassurance of loves ones may help. CAUTION: Be kind to the people you love.

MOON IN SAGITTARIUS

These are days when you are likely to be stirred and elevated by discussions and reflections of a religious and philosophical nature. Ideas of far-away places may cause unusual response and excitement. A decision may be made to visit someone overseas, perhaps a person whose influence was important to your earlier character development. There could be a strong resolution to get away from present intellectual patterns, to learn new subjects and to meet more interesting people. The superficial may be rejected in all its forms. An impatience with old ideas and unimaginative contacts could lead to a change of companions and interests. There may be an upsurge of religious feeling and metaphysical inquiry. Even a new insight into the significance of astrology and other occult studies is likely under the curious stimulus of the moon in Sagittarius. Physically, you may express this need for fundamental change by spending more time outdoors: sports, gardening or going for long walks. CAUTION: Try to channel any restlessness into worthwhile study.

MOON IN CAPRICORN

Life in these hours may seem to pivot around the importance of gaining prestige and honor in the career, as well as maintaining a spotless reputation. Ambitious urges may be excessive and could be accompanied by quite acquisitive drives for money. Effort should be directed along strictly ethical lines where there is no possibility of reproach or scandal. All endeavors are likely to be characterized by great earnestness, and an air of authority and purpose which should impress those who are looking for leadership or reliability. The desire to conform to accepted standards may extend to sharp criticism of family members. Frivolity and unconventional actions are unlikely to amuse while the moon is in Capricorn. Moderation and seriousness are the orders of the day. Achievement and recognition in this period could come through community work or organizing for the benefit of some amateur group. CAUTION: Dignity and esteem are not always self-awarded.

MOON IN AQUARIUS

Moon in Aquarius is in the second last sign of the Zodiac where ideas can become disturbingly fine and subtle. The result is often a mental "no-man's land" where imagination cannot be trusted with the same certitude as other times. The dangers for the individual are the extremes of optimism and pessimism. Unless the imgination is held in check, situations are likely to be misread, and rosy conclusions drawn where they do not exist. Consequences for the unwary can be costly in career and business. Best to think twice and not speak or act until you think again. Pessimism can be a cruel self-inflicted penalty for delusion at this time. Between the two extremes are strange areas of self-deception which, for example, can make the selfish person think he is actually being generous. Eerie dreams which resemble the reality and even seem to continue into the waking state are also possible. CAUTION: Look for the fact and not just for the image in your mind.

MOON IN PISCES

Everything seems to come to the surface now. Memory may be crystal clear, throwing up long-forgotten information which could be valuable in the career or business. Flashes of clairvoyance and intuition are possible along with sudden realizations of one's own nature, which may be used for self-improvement. A talent, never before suspected, may be discovered. Qualities not evident before in friends and marriage partners are likely to be noticed. As this is a period in which the truth seems to emerge, the discovery of false characteristics is likely to lead to disenchantment or a shift in attachments. However, where qualities are realized it should lead to happiness and deeper feeling. Surprise solutions could bob up for old problems. There may be a public announcement of the solving of a crime or mystery. People with secrets may find someone has "guessed" correctly. The secrets of the soul or the inner self also tend to reveal themselves. Religious and philosophical groups may make some interesting discoveries. CAUTION: Not a time for activities that depend on secrecy.

MOON TABLES

TIME CORRECTIONS FOR
GREENWICH MOON TABLES

London, Glasgow, Dublin, Dakar.................Same time

Vienna, Prague, Rome, Kinshasa, Frankfurt,
Stockholm, Brussels, Amsterdam, Warsaw,
Zurich..Add 1 hour

Bucharest, Istanbul, Beirut, Cairo, Johannesburg,
Athens, Cape Town, Helsinki, Tel Aviv........Add 2 hours

Dhahran, Baghdad, Moscow, Leningrad, Nairobi,
Addis Ababa, Zanzibar.......................Add 3 hours

Delhi, Calcutta, Bombay, Colombo ....Add 5½ hours

Rangoon ....Add 6½ hours

Saigon, Bangkok, Chungking...................Add 7 hours

Canton, Manila, Hong Kong, Shanghai, Peking ...Add 8 hours

Tokyo, Pusan, Seoul, Vladivostok, Yokohama ....Add 9 hours

Sydney, Melbourne, Guam, Port Moresby.......Add 10 hours

Azores, Reykjavik...........................Deduct 1 hour

Rio de Janeiro, Montevideo, Buenos Aires,
Sao Paulo, Recife ....Deduct 3 hours

LaPaz, San Juan, Santiago, Bermuda, Caracas,
Halifax ....Deduct 4 hours

New York, Washington, Boston, Detroit, Lima,
Havana, Miami, Bogota....................Deduct 5 hours

Mexico, Chicago, New Orleans, Houston ......Deduct 6 hours

San Francisco, Seattle, Los Angeles, Hollywood,
Ketchikan, Juneau.........................Deduct 8 hours

Honolulu, Fairbanks, Anchorage, Papeete.....Deduct 10 hours

1991 MOON TABLES—GREENWICH TIME

JANUARY		FEBRUARY		MARCH	
Day Moon Enters		**Day Moon Enters**		**Day Moon Enters**	
1. Cancer		1. Virgo		1. Virgo	
2. Leo	3:19 am	2. Libra	7:59 pm	2. Libra	5:50 am
3. Leo		3. Libra		3. Libra	
4. Virgo	5:24 am	4. Libra		4. Scorpio	0:58 pm
5. Virgo		5. Scorpio	4:23 am	5. Scorpio	
6. Libra	10:43 am	6. Scorpio		6. Sagitt.	11:48 pm
7. Libra		7. Sagitt.	4:06 pm	7. Sagitt.	
8. Scorpio	8:32 pm	8. Sagitt.		8. Sagitt.	
9. Scorpio		9. Sagitt.		9. Capric.	0:37 pm
10. Scorpio		10. Capric.	4:57 am	10. Capric.	
11. Sagitt.	8:56 am	11. Capric.		11. Capric.	
12. Sagitt.		12. Aquar.	4:39 pm	12. Aquar.	0:47 am
13. Capric.	9:29 pm	13. Aquar.		13. Aquar.	
14. Capric.		14. Aquar.		14. Pisces	10:07 am
15. Capric.		15. Pisces	2:06 am	15. Pisces	
16. Aquar.	9:25 am	16. Pisces		16. Aries	4:34 pm
17. Aquar.		17. Aries	9:07 am	17. Aries	
18. Pisces	7:15 pm	18. Aries		18. Taurus	8:49 pm
19. Pisces		19. Taurus	2:38 pm	19. Taurus	
20. Pisces		20. Taurus		20. Taurus	
21. Aries	3:27 am	21. Gemini	6:28 pm	21. Gemini	0:06 am
22. Aries		22. Gemini		22. Gemini	
23. Taurus	9:04 am	23. Cancer	9:03 pm	23. Cancer	2:46 am
24. Taurus		24. Cancer		24. Cancer	
25. Gemini	0:10 pm	25. Leo	11:01 pm	25. Leo	5:53 am
26. Gemini		26. Leo		26. Leo	
27. Cancer	1:10 pm	27. Leo		27. Virgo	9:31 am
28. Cancer		28. Virgo	1:33 am	28. Virgo	
29. Leo	1:58 pm			29. Libra	2:44 pm
30. Leo				30. Libra	
31. Virgo	3:27 pm			31. Scorpio	10:02 pm

Summer time to be considered where applicable.

1991 MOON TABLES—GREENWICH TIME

APRIL		MAY		JUNE	
Day Moon Enters		**Day Moon Enters**		**Day Moon Enters**	
1. Scorpio		1. Sagitt.		1. Aquar.	11:42 pm
2. Scorpio		2. Sagitt.		2. Aquar.	
3. Sagitt.	8:14 am	3. Capric.	4:04 am	3. Aquar.	
4. Sagitt.		4. Capric.		4. Pisces	11:48 am
5. Capric.	8:39 pm	5. Aquar.	4:48 pm	5. Pisces	
6. Capric.		6. Aquar.		6. Aries	8:37 pm
7. Capric.		7. Aquar.		7. Aries	
8. Aquar.	9:14 am	8. Pisces	4:04 am	8. Aries	
9. Aquar.		9. Pisces		9. Taurus	1:12 am
10. Pisces	7:18 pm	10. Aries	11:29 am	10. Taurus	
11. Pisces		11. Aries		11. Gemini	2:46 am
12. Pisces		12. Taurus	3:09 pm	12. Gemini	
13. Aries	1:40 am	13. Taurus		13. Cancer	2:28 am
14. Aries		14. Gemini	4:03 pm	14. Cancer	
15. Taurus	5:10 am	15. Gemini		15. Leo	2:21 am
16. Taurus		16. Cancer	4:23 pm	16. Leo	
17. Gemini	7:05 am	17. Cancer		17. Virgo	4:00 am
18. Gemini		18. Leo	5:40 pm	18. Virgo	
19. Cancer	8:41 am	19. Leo		19. Libra	8:56 am
20. Cancer		20. Virgo	9:04 pm	20. Libra	
21. Leo	11:29 am	21. Virgo		21. Scorpio	5:31 pm
22. Leo		22. Virgo		22. Scorpio	
23. Virgo	3:49 pm	23. Libra	3:09 am	23. Scorpio	
24. Virgo		24. Libra		24. Sagitt.	4:57 am
25. Libra	9:44 pm	25. Scorpio	0:12 pm	25. Sagitt.	
26. Libra		26. Scorpio		26. Capric.	5:18 pm
27. Libra		27. Sagitt.	10:54 pm	27. Capric.	
28. Scorpio	5:57 am	28. Sagitt.		28. Capric.	
29. Scorpio		29. Sagitt.		29. Aquar.	5:57 am
30. Sagitt.	3:50 pm	30. Capric.	10:49 am	30. Aquar.	
		31. Capric.			

Summer time to be considered where applicable.

1991 MOON TABLES—GREENWICH TIME

JULY		AUGUST		SEPTEMBER	
Day Moon Enters		**Day Moon Enters**		**Day Moon Enters**	
1. Pisces	5:31 pm	1. Aries		1. Gemini	3:19 am
2. Pisces		2. Taurus	4:42 pm	2. Gemini	
3. Pisces		3. Taurus		3. Cancer	6:44 am
4. Aries	3:40 am	4. Gemini	9:09 pm	4. Cancer	
5. Aries		5. Gemini		5. Leo	8:15 am
6. Taurus	10:13 am	6. Cancer	11:12 pm	6. Leo	
7. Taurus		7. Cancer		7. Virgo	9:52 am
8. Gemini	0:59 pm	8. Leo	11:11 pm	8. Virgo	
9. Gemini		9. Leo		9. Libra	Noon
10. Cancer	1:17 pm	10. Virgo	11:39 pm	10. Libra	
11. Cancer		11. Virgo		11. Scorpio	5:06 pm
12. Leo	0:39 pm	12. Virgo		12. Scorpio	
13. Leo		13. Libra	1:49 am	13. Scorpio	
14. Virgo	1:12 pm	14. Libra		14. Sagitt.	1:23 am
15. Virgo		15. Scorpio	7:34 am	15. Sagitt.	
16. Libra	4:29 pm	16. Scorpio		16. Capric.	1:25 pm
17. Libra		17. Sagitt.	5:21 pm	17. Capric.	
18. Scorpio	11:38 pm	18. Sagitt.		18. Capric.	
19. Scorpio		19. Sagitt.		19. Aquar.	1:56 am
20. Scorpio		20. Capric.	6:00 am	20. Aquar.	
21. Sagitt.	10:48 am	21. Capric.		21. Pisces	1:21 pm
22. Sagitt.		22. Aquar.	6:25 pm	22. Pisces	
23. Capric.	11:24 pm	23. Aquar.		23. Aries	9:48 pm
24. Capric.		24. Aquar.		24. Aries	
25. Capric.		25. Pisces	5:49 am	25. Aries	
26. Aquar.	11:48 am	26. Pisces		26. Taurus	4:11 am
27. Aquar.		27. Aries	3:01 pm	27. Taurus	
28. Pisces	11:25 pm	28. Aries		28. Gemini	9:00 am
29. Pisces		29. Taurus	10:02 pm	29. Gemini	
30. Pisces		30. Taurus		30. Cancer	0:31 pm
31. Aries	9:23 am	31. Taurus			

Summer time to be considered where applicable.

1991 MOON TABLES—GREENWICH TIME

OCTOBER		NOVEMBER		DECEMBER	
Day Moon Enters		**Day Moon Enters**		**Day Moon Enters**	
1. Cancer		1. Virgo		1. Libra	
2. Leo	2:44 pm	2. Virgo		2. Scorpio	4:56 pm
3. Leo		3. Libra	4:21 am	3. Scorpio	
4. Virgo	5:40 pm	4. Libra		4. Scorpio	
5. Virgo		5. Scorpio	10:33 am	5. Sagitt.	2:01 am
6. Libra	9:20 pm	6. Scorpio		6. Sagitt.	
7. Libra		7. Sagitt.	6:45 pm	7. Capric.	1:00 pm
8. Libra		8. Sagitt.		8. Capric.	
9. Scorpio	2:15 am	9. Sagitt.		9. Capric.	
10. Scorpio		10. Capric.	5:24 am	10. Aquar.	1:07 am
11. Sagitt.	10:17 am	11. Capric.		11. Aquar.	
12. Sagitt.		12. Aquar.	5:45 pm	12. Pisces	2:23 pm
13. Capric.	9:10 pm	13. Aquar.		13. Pisces	
14. Capric.		14. Aquar.		14. Pisces	
15. Capric.		15. Pisces	6:25 am	15. Aries	0:57 am
16. Aquar.	10:00 am	16. Pisces		16. Aries	
17. Aquar.		17. Aries	4:15 pm	17. Taurus	8:14 am
18. Pisces	9:52 pm	18. Aries		18. Taurus	
19. Pisces		19. Taurus	10:06 pm	19. Gemini	11:31 am
20. Pisces		20. Taurus		20. Gemini	
21. Aries	8:24 am	21. Taurus		21. Cancer	0:10 pm
22. Aries		22. Gemini	0:50 am	22. Cancer	
23. Taurus	0:11 pm	23. Gemini		23. Leo	11:41 am
24. Taurus		24. Cancer	1:58 am	24. Leo	
25. Gemini	3:42 pm	25. Cancer		25. Virgo	0:41 pm
26. Gemini		26. Leo	3:02 am	26. Virgo	
27. Cancer	6:03 pm	27. Leo		27. Libra	3:56 pm
28. Cancer		28. Virgo	5:28 am	28. Libra	
29. Leo	8:17 pm	29. Virgo		29. Scorpio	10:30 pm
30. Leo		30. Libra	9:51 am	30. Scorpio	
31. Virgo	11:49 pm			31. Scorpio	

Summer time to be considered where applicable.

1991 PHASES OF THE MOON—GREENWICH TIME

New Moon	First Quarter	Full Moon	Last Quarter
(Dec. 17, 1990)	(Dec. 25, 1990)	(Dec. 31, 1990)	Jan. 7, 1991
Jan. 16	Jan. 23	Jan. 30	Feb. 6
Feb. 14	Feb. 21	Feb. 28	Mar. 8
Mar. 16	Mar. 23	Mar. 30	Apr. 7
Apr. 14	Apr. 21	Apr. 28	May 7
May 14	May 20	May 28	June 5
June 12	June 19	June 27	July 5
July 11	July 18	July 26	Aug. 3
Aug. 10	Aug. 17	Aug. 25	Sep. 1
Sep. 8	Sep. 15	Sep. 23	Oct. 1
Oct. 7	Oct. 15	Oct. 23	Oct. 30
Nov. 6	Nov. 14	Nov. 21	Nov. 28
Dec. 6	Dec. 14	Dec. 21	Dec. 28

Summer time to be considered where applicable.

1991 PLANTING GUIDE

	Aboveground Crops	Root Crops	Pruning	Weeds Pests
January	19-20-23-24-28	1-7-8-9-10-14-15	1-9-10	2-3-4-5-11-12-30-31
February	15-16-20-24	3-4-5-6-10-11	5-6	1-8-9-13
March	19-20-23-24	2-3-4-5-6-10-11-15-30-31	5-6-15	1-7-8-12-13
April	15-16-19-20-26-27	1-2-6-7-11-12-29	1-2-11-12-29	3-4-8-9-13
May	17-23-24-25-26-27	3-4-8-9-13-31	8-9	1-2-6-7-11-29
June	13-14-19-20-21-22-23	1-5-9-10-27-28	5	2-3-7-8-11-29-30
July	17-18-19-20-24-25	2-3-7-29-30	2-3-29-30	4-5-9-27-28-31
August	13-14-15-16-20-21	3-7-8-25-26-30-31	7-8-25-26	1-5-9-28-29
September	10-11-12-13-17-18-22	3-4-26-27	3-4	1-2-5-6-7-24-25-28-29
October	8-9-10-14-15-19-20	1-7-24-28	1-28	3-4-5-26-30-31
November	10-11-15-16-20-21	3-4-5-24-25-30	24-25	1-2-22-23-26-27-28-29
December	8-9-13-14-17-18	1-2-3-4-22-28-29-30-31	3-4-22-30-31	5-24-25-26

1991 FISHING GUIDE

	Good	Best
January	2-3-16-27-29-30-31	1-7-23-28
February	1-2-14-21-26-27-28	6-25
March	1-8-16-27-28-29	2-3-23-30-31
April	14-21-25-30	1-2-7-26-27-28-29
May	1-7-14-20-28-29-30	25-26-27-31
June	12-24-25-26-29-30	5-19-27-28
July	5-23-26-27-28	11-18-24-25-29
August	10-17-22-23-24-27-28	3-25-26
September	1-8-15-20-21-23-24-25	22-26
October	21-22-23-25-26-30	1-7-15-20-24
November	14-18-19-22-23-28	6-20-21-24
December	6-19-20-21-23-24	14-18-22-28

MOON'S INFLUENCE OVER DAILY AFFAIRS

The Moon makes a complete transit of the Zodiac every 27 days 7 hours and 43 minutes. In making this transit the Moon forms different aspects with the planets and consequently has favorable or unfavorable bearings on affairs and events for persons according to the sign of the Zodiac under which they were born. Whereas the Sun exclusively represents fire, the Moon rules water. The action of the Moon may be described as fluctuating, variable, absorbent and receptive.

When the Moon is in conjunction with the Sun it is called a New Moon; when the Moon and Sun are in opposition it is called a Full Moon. From New Moon to Full Moon, first and second quarter—which takes about two weeks—the Moon is increasing or waxing. From Full Moon to New Moon, third and fourth quarter, the Moon is decreasing or waning. The Moon Table indicates the New Moon and Full Moon and the quarters.

ACTIVITY	MOON IN
Business:	
buying and selling	Sagittarius, Aries, Gemini, Virgo
new, requiring public support	1st and 2nd quarter
meant to be kept quiet	3rd and 4th quarter
Investigation	3rd and 4th quarter
Signing documents	1st & 2nd quarter, Cancer, Scorpio, Pisces
Advertising	2nd quarter, Sagittarius
Journeys and trips	1st & 2nd quarter, Gemini, Virgo
Renting offices, etc.	Taurus, Leo, Scorpio, Aquarius
Painting of house/apartment	3rd & 4th quarter, Taurus, Scorpio, Aquarius
Decorating	Gemini, Libra, Aquarius
Buying clothes and accessories	Taurus, Virgo
Beauty salon or barber shop visit	1st & 2nd quarter, Taurus, Leo, Libra, Scorpio, Aquarius
Weddings	1st & 2nd quarter

MOON'S INFLUENCE OVER YOUR HEALTH

ARIES	Head, brain, face, upper jaw
TAURUS	Throat, neck, lower jaw
GEMINI	Hands, arms, lungs, shoulders, nervous system
CANCER	Esophagus, stomach, breasts, womb, liver
LEO	Heart, spine
VIRGO	Intestines, liver
LIBRA	Kidneys, lower back
SCORPIO	Sex and eliminative organs
SAGITTARIUS	Hips, thighs, liver
CAPRICORN	Skin, bones, teeth, knees
AQUARIUS	Circulatory system, lower legs
PISCES	Feet, tone of being

Try to avoid work being done on that part of the body
when the Moon is in the sign governing that part.

MOON'S INFLUENCE OVER PLANTS

Centuries ago it was established that seeds planted when the Moon is
in certain signs and phases called Fruitful will produce more growth
than seeds planted when the Moon is in a Barren sign.

FRUITFUL SIGNS	BARREN SIGNS	DRY SIGNS
Taurus	Aries	Aries
Cancer	Gemini	Gemini
Libra	Leo	Sagittarius
Scorpio	Virgo	Aquarius
Capricorn	Sagittarius	
Pisces	Aquarius	

ACTIVITY	MOON IN
Mow lawn, trim plants	**Fruitful sign:** 1st & 2nd quarter
Plant flowers	**Fruitful sign:** 2nd quarter; best in Cancer and Libra
Prune	**Fruitful sign:** 3rd & 4th quarter
Destroy pests; spray	**Barren sign:** 4th quarter
Harvest potatoes, root crops	**Dry sign:** 3rd & 4th quarter; Taurus, Leo, and Aquarius

THE SIGNS: DOMINANT CHARACTERISTICS

March 21–April 20

The Positive Side of Aries

The Arien has many positive points to his character. People born under this first sign of the Zodiac are often quite strong and enthusiastic. On the whole, they are forward-looking people who are not easily discouraged by temporary setbacks. They know what they want out of life and they go out after it. Their personalities are strong. Others are usually quite impressed by the Arien's way of doing things. Quite often they are sources of inspiration for others traveling the same route. Aries men and women have a special zest for life that is often contagious; for others, they are often the example of how life should be lived.

The Aries person usually has a quick and active mind. He is imaginative and inventive. He enjoys keeping busy and active. He generally gets along well with all kinds of people. He is interested in mankind, as a whole. He likes to be challenged. Some would say he thrives on opposition, for it is when he is set against that he often does his best. Getting over or around obstacles is a challenge he generally enjoys. All in all, the Arien is quite positive and young-thinking. He likes to keep abreast of new things that are happening in the world. Ariens are often fond of speed. They like things to be done quickly and this sometimes aggravates their slower colleagues and associates.

The Aries man or woman always seems to remain young. Their whole approach to life is youthful and optimistic. They never say die, no matter what the odds. They may have an occasional setback, but it is not long before they are back on their feet again.

The Negative Side of Aries

Everybody has his less positive qualities—and Aries is no exception. Sometimes the Aries man or woman is not very tactful in communicating with others; in his hurry to get things done he is apt to

be a little callous or inconsiderate. Sensitive people are likely to find him somewhat sharp-tongued in some situations. Often in his eagerness to achieve his aims, he misses the mark altogether. At times the Arien is too impulsive. He can occasionally be stubborn and refuse to listen to reason. If things do not move quickly enough to suit the Aries man or woman, he or she is apt to become rather nervous or irritable. The uncultivated Arien is not unfamiliar with moments of doubt and fear. He is capable of being destructive if he does not get his way. He can overcome some of his emotional problems by steadily trying to express himself as he really is, but this requires effort.

April 21–May 20

The Positive Side of Taurus

The Taurus person is known for his ability to concentrate and for his tenacity. These are perhaps his strongest qualities. The Taurus man or woman generally has very little trouble in getting along with others; it's his nature to be helpful toward people in need. He can always be depended on by his friends, especially those in trouble.

The Taurean generally achieves what he wants through his ability to persevere. He never leaves anything unfinished but works on something until it has been completed. People can usually take him at his word; he is honest and forthright in most of his dealings. The Taurus person has a good chance to make a success of his life because of his many positive qualities. The Taurean who aims high seldom falls short of his mark. He learns well by experience. He is thorough and does not believe in short-cuts of any kind. The Taurean's thoroughness pays off in the end, for through his deliberateness he learns how to rely on himself and what he has learned. The Taurus person tries to get along with others, as a rule. He is not overly critical and likes people to be themselves. He is a tolerant person and enjoys peace and harmony—especially in his home life.

The Taurean is usually cautious in all that he does. He is not a person who believes in taking unnecessary risks. Before adopting any one line of action, he will weigh all of the pros and cons. The

Taurus person is steadfast. Once his mind is made up it seldom changes. The person born under this sign usually is a good family person—reliable and loving.

The Negative Side of Taurus

Sometimes the Taurus man or woman is a bit too stubborn. He won't listen to other points of view if his mind is set on something. To others, this can be quite annoying. The Taurean also does not like to be told what to do. He becomes rather angry if others think him not too bright. He does not like to be told he is wrong, even when he is. He dislikes being contradicted.

Some people who are born under this sign are very suspicious of others—even of those persons close to them. They find it difficult to trust people fully. They are often afraid of being deceived or taken advantage of. The Taurean often finds it difficult to forget or forgive. His love of material things sometimes makes him rather avaricious and petty.

May 21–June 20

The Positive Side of Gemini

The person born under this sign of the Heavenly Twins is usually quite bright and quick-witted. Some of them are capable of doing many different things. The Gemini person very often has many different interests. He keeps an open mind and is always anxious to learn new things.

The Geminian is often an analytical person. He is a person who enjoys making use of his intellect. He is governed more by his mind than by his emotions. He is a person who is not confined to one view; he can often understand both sides to a problem or question. He knows how to reason; how to make rapid decisions if need be.

He is an adaptable person and can make himself at home almost anywhere. There are all kinds of situations he can adapt to. He is a person who seldom doubts himself; he is sure of his talents and his

ability to think and reason. The Geminian is generally most satisfied when he is in a situation where he can make use of his intellect. Never short of imagination, he often has strong talents for invention. He is rather a modern person when it comes to life; the Geminian almost always moves along with the times—perhaps that is why he remains so youthful throughout most of his life.

Literature and art appeal to the person born under this sign. Creativity in almost any form will interest and intrigue the Gemini man or woman.

The Geminian is often quite charming. A good talker, he often is the center of attraction at any gathering. People find it easy to like a person born under this sign because he can appear easygoing and usually has a good sense of humor.

The Negative Side of Gemini

Sometimes the Gemini person tries to do too many things at one time—and as a result, winds up finishing nothing. Some Geminians are easily distracted and find it rather difficult to concentrate on one thing for too long a time. Sometimes they give in to trifling fancies and find it rather boring to become too serious about any one thing. Some of them are never dependable, no matter what they promise.

Although the Gemini man or woman often appears to be well-versed on many subjects, this is sometimes just a veneer. His knowledge may be only superficial, but because he speaks so well he gives people the impression of erudition. Some Geminians are sharp-tongued and inconsiderate; they think only of themselves and their own pleasure.

June 21–July 20

The Positive Side of Cancer

The Cancerians's most positive point is his understanding nature. On the whole, he is a loving and sympathetic person. He would never go out of his way to hurt anyone. The Cancer man or woman

is often very kind and tender; they give what they can to others. They hate to see others suffering and will do what they can to help someone in less fortunate circumstances than themselves. They are often very concerned about the world. Their interest in people generally goes beyond that of just their own families and close friends; they have a deep sense of brotherhood and respect humanitarian values. The Cancerian means what he says, as a rule; he is honest about his feelings.

The Cancer man or woman is a person who knows the art of patience. When something seems difficult, he is willing to wait until the situation becomes manageable again. He is a person who knows how to bide his time. The Cancerian knows how to concentrate on one thing at a time. When he has made his mind up he generally sticks with what he does, seeing it through to the end.

The Cancerian is a person who loves his home. He enjoys being surrounded by familiar things and the people he loves. Of all the signs, Cancer is the most maternal. Even the men born under this sign often have a motherly or protective quality about them. They like to take care of people in their family—to see that they are well loved and well provided for. They are usually loyal and faithful. Family ties mean a lot to the Cancer man or woman. Parents and in-laws are respected and loved. The Cancerian has a strong sense of tradition. He is very sensitive to the moods of others.

The Negative Side of Cancer

Sometimes the Cancerian finds it rather hard to face life. It becomes too much for him. He can be a little timid and retiring, when things don't go too well. When unfortunate things happen, he is apt to just shrug and say, "Whatever will be will be." He can be fatalistic to a fault. The uncultivated Cancerian is a bit lazy. He doesn't have very much ambition. Anything that seems a bit difficult he'll gladly leave to others. He may be lacking in initiative. Too sensitive, when he feels he's been injured, he'll crawl back into his shell and nurse his imaginary wounds. The Cancer woman often is given to crying when the smallest thing goes wrong.

Some Cancerians find it difficult to enjoy themselves in environments outside their homes. They make heavy demands on others, and need to be constantly reassured that they are loved.

July 21–August 21

The Positive Side of Leo

Often Leos make good leaders. They seem to be good organizers and administrators. Usually they are quite popular with others. Whatever group it is that he belongs to, the Leo man is almost sure to be or become the leader.

The Leo person is generous most of the time. It is his best characteristic. He or she likes to give gifts and presents. In making others happy, the Leo person becomes happy himself. He likes to splurge when spending money on others. In some instances it may seem that the Leo's generosity knows no boundaries. A hospitable person, the Leo man or woman is very fond of welcoming people to his house and entertaining them. He is never short of company.

The Leo person has plenty of energy and drive. He enjoys working toward some specific goal. When he applies himself correctly, he gets what he wants most often. The Leo person is almost never unsure of himself. He has plenty of confidence and aplomb. He is a person who is direct in almost everything he does. He has a quick mind and can make a decision in a very short time.

He usually sets a good example for others because of his ambitious manner and positive ways. He knows how to stick to something once he's started. Although the Leo person may be good at making a joke, he is not superficial or glib. He is a loving person, kind and thoughtful.

There is generally nothing small or petty about the Leo man or woman. He does what he can for those who are deserving. He is a person others can rely upon at all times. He means what he says. An honest person, generally speaking, he is a friend that others value.

The Negative Side of Leo

Leo, however, does have his faults. At times, he can be just a bit too arrogant. He thinks that no one deserves a leadership position except him. Only he is capable of doing things well. His opinion of himself is often much too high. Because of his conceit, he is sometimes rather unpopular with a good many people. Some Leos are too materialistic; they can only think in terms of money and profit.

Some Leos enjoy lording it over others—at home or at their place of business. What is more, they feel they have the right to. Egocentric to an impossible degree, this sort of Leo cares little about how others think or feel. He can be rude and cutting.

August 22–September 22

The Positive Side of Virgo

The person born under the sign of Virgo is generally a busy person. He knows how to arrange and organize things. He is a good planner. Above all, he is practical and is not afraid of hard work.

The person born under this sign, Virgo, knows how to attain what he desires. He sticks with something until it is finished. He never shirks his duties, and can always be depended upon. The Virgo person can be thoroughly trusted at all times.

The man or woman born under this sign tries to do everything to perfection. He doesn't believe in doing anything half-way. He always aims for the top. He is the sort of a person who is constantly striving to better himself—not because he wants more money or glory, but because it gives him a feeling of accomplishment.

The Virgo man or woman is a very observant person. He is sensitive to how others feel, and can see things below the surface of a situation. He usually puts this talent to constructive use.

It is not difficult for the Virgoan to be open and earnest. He believes in putting his cards on the table. He is never secretive or under-handed. He's as good as his word. The Virgo person is generally plain-spoken and down-to-earth. He has no trouble in expressing himself.

The Virgo person likes to keep up to date on new developments in his particular field. Well-informed, generally, he sometimes has a keen interest in the arts or literature. What he knows, he knows well. His ability to use his critical faculties is well-developed and sometimes startles others because of its accuracy.

The Virgoan adheres to a moderate way of life; he avoids excesses. He is a responsible person and enjoys being of service.

The Negative Side of Virgo

Sometimes a Virgo person is too critical. He thinks that only he can do something the way it should be done. Whatever anyone else does is inferior. He can be rather annoying in the way he quibbles over insignificant details. In telling others how things should be done, he can be rather tactless and mean.

Some Virgos seem rather emotionless and cool. They feel emo-

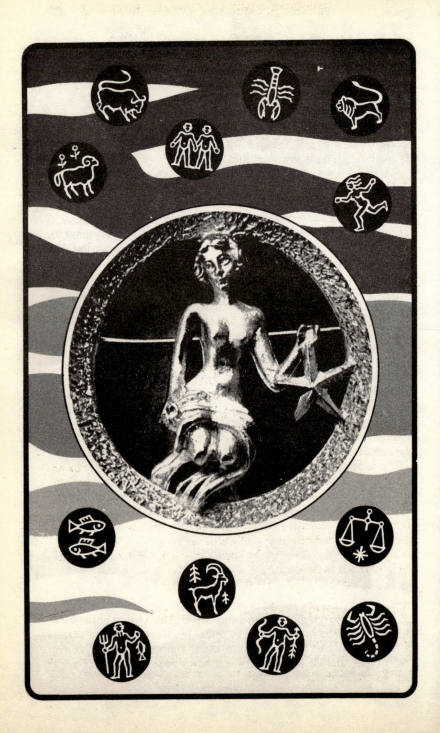

tional involvement is beneath them. They are sometimes too tidy, too neat. With money they can be rather miserly. Some try to force their opinions and ideas on others.

September 23–October 22

The Positive Side of Libra

Librans love harmony. It is one of their most outstanding character traits. They are interested in achieving balance; they admire beauty and grace in things as well as in people. Generally speaking, they are kind and considerate people. Librans are usually very sympathetic. They go out of their way not to hurt another person's feelings. They are outgoing and do what they can to help those in need.

People born under the sign of Libra almost always make good friends. They are loyal and amiable. They enjoy the company of others. Many of them are rather moderate in their views; they believe in keeping an open mind, however, and weighing both sides of an issue fairly before making a decision.

Alert and often intelligent, the Libran, always fair-minded, tries to put himself in the position of the other person. They are against injustice; quite often they take up for the underdog. In most of their social dealings, they try to be tactful and kind. They dislike discord and bickering, and most Libras strive for peace and harmony in all their relationships.

The Libra man or woman has a keen sense of beauty. They appreciate handsome furnishings and clothes. Many of them are artistically inclined. Their taste is usually impeccable. They know how to use color. Their homes are almost always attractively arranged and inviting. They enjoy entertaining people and see to it that their guests always feel at home and welcome.

The Libran gets along with almost everyone. He is well-liked and socially much in demand.

The Negative Side of Libra

Some people born under this sign tend to be rather insincere. So eager are they to achieve harmony in all relationships that they will even go so far as to lie. Many of them are escapists. They find facing

the truth an ordeal and prefer living in a world of make-believe.

In a serious argument, some Librans give in rather easily even when they know they are right. Arguing, even about something they believe in, is too unsettling for some of them.

Librans sometimes care too much for material things. They enjoy possessions and luxuries. Some are vain and tend to be jealous.

October 23–November 22

The Positive Side of Scorpio

The Scorpio man or woman generally knows what he or she wants out of life. He is a determined person. He sees something through to the end. The Scorpion is quite sincere, and seldom says anything he doesn't mean. When he sets a goal for himself he tries to go about achieving it in a very direct way.

The Scorpion is brave and courageous. They are not afraid of hard work. Obstacles do not frighten them. They forge ahead until they achieve what they set out for. The Scorpio man or woman has a strong will.

Although the Scorpion may seem rather fixed and determined, inside he is often quite tender and loving. He can care very much for others. He believes in sincerity in all relationships. His feelings about someone tend to last; they are profound and not superficial.

The Scorpio person is someone who adheres to his principles no matter what happens. He will not be deterred from a path he believes to be right.

Because of his many positive strengths, the Scorpion can often achieve happiness for himself and for those that he loves.

He is a constructive person by nature. He often has a deep understanding of people and of life, in general. He is perceptive and unafraid. Obstacles often seem to spur him on. He is a positive person who enjoys winning. He has many strengths and resources; challenge of any sort often brings out the best in him.

The Negative Side of Scorpio

The Scorpio person is sometimes hypersensitive. Often he imagines injury when there is none. He feels that others do not bother to

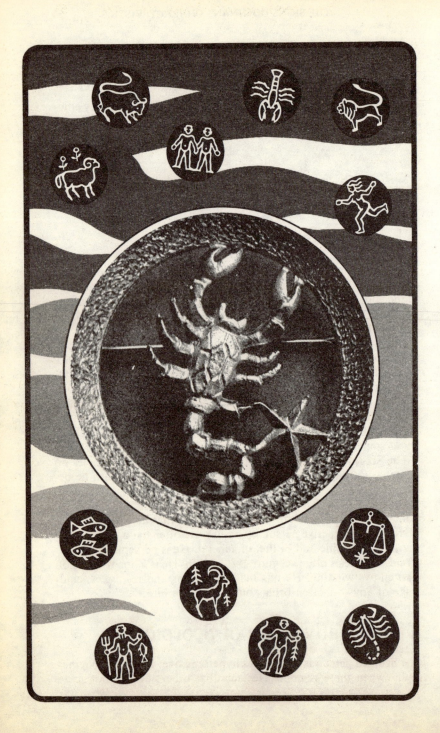

recognize him for his true worth. Sometimes he is given to excessive boasting in order to compensate for what he feels is neglect

The Scorpio person can be rather proud and arrogant. They can be rather sly when they put their minds to it and they enjoy outwitting persons or institutions noted for their cleverness.

Their tactics for getting what they want are sometimes devious and ruthless. They don't care too much about what others may think. If they feel others have done them an injustice, they will do their best to seek revenge. The Scorpion often has a sudden, violent temper; and this person's interest in sex is sometimes quite unbalanced or excessive.

November 23–December 20

The Positive Side of Sagittarius

People born under this sign are often honest and forthright. Their approach to life is earnest and open. The Sagittarian is often quite adult in his way of seeing things. They are broadminded and tolerant people. When dealing with others the person born under the sign of Sagittarius is almost always open and forthright. He doesn't believe in deceit or pretension. His standards are high. People who associate with the Sagittarian, generally admire and respect him.

The Sagittarian trusts others easily and expects them to trust him. He is never suspicious or envious and almost always thinks well of others. People always enjoy his company because he is so friendly and easy-going. The Sagittarius man or woman is often good-humored. He can always be depended upon by his friends, family, and co-workers.

The person born under this sign of the Zodiac likes a good joke every now and then; he is keen on fun and this makes him very popular with others.

A lively person, he enjoys sports and outdoor life. The Sagittarian is fond of animals. Intelligent and interesting, he can begin an animated conversation with ease. He likes exchanging ideas and discussing various views.

He is not selfish or proud. If someone proposes an idea or plan that is better than his, he will immediately adopt it. Imaginative yet practical, he knows how to put ideas into practice.

He enjoys sport and game, and it doesn't matter if he wins or loses. He is a forgiving person, and never sulks over something that has not worked out in his favor.

He is seldom critical, and is almost always generous.

The Negative Side of Sagittarius

Some Sagittarians are restless. They take foolish risks and seldom learn from the mistakes they make. They don't have heads for money and are often mismanaging their finances. Some of them devote much of their time to gambling.

Some are too outspoken and tactless, always putting their feet in their mouths. They hurt others carelessly by being honest at the wrong time. Sometimes they make promises which they don't keep. They don't stick close enough to their plans and go from one failure to another. They are undisciplined and waste a lot of energy.

December 21–January 19

The Positive Side of Capricorn

The person born under the sign of Capricorn is usually very stable and patient. He sticks to whatever tasks he has and sees them through. He can always be relied upon and he is not averse to work.

An honest person, the Capricornian is generally serious about whatever he does. He does not take his duties lightly. He is a practical person and believes in keeping his feet on the ground.

Quite often the person born under this sign is ambitious and knows how to get what he wants out of life. He forges ahead and never gives up his goal. When he is determined about something, he almost always wins. He is a good worker—a hard worker. Although things may not come easy to him, he will not complain, but continue working until his chores are finished.

He is usually good at business matters and knows the value of money. He is not a spendthrift and knows how to put something away for a rainy day; he dislikes waste and unnecessary loss.

The Capricornian knows how to make use of his self-control. He

can apply himself to almost anything once he puts his mind to it. His ability to concentrate sometimes astounds others. He is diligent and does well when involved in detail work.

The Capricorn man or woman is charitable, generally speaking, and will do what is possible to help others less fortunate. As a friend, he is loyal and trustworthy. He never shirks his duties or responsibilities. He is self-reliant and never expects too much of the other fellow. He does what he can on his own. If someone does him a good turn, then he will do his best to return the favor.

The Negative Side of Capricorn

Like everyone, the Capricornian, too, has his faults. At times, he can be over-critical of others. He expects others to live up to his own high standards. He thinks highly of himself and tends to look down on others.

His interest in material things may be exaggerated. The Capricorn man or woman thinks too much about getting on in the world and having something to show for it. He may even be a little greedy.

He sometimes thinks he knows what's best for everyone. He is too bossy. He is always trying to organize and correct others. He may be a little narrow in his thinking.

January 20–February 18

The Positive Side of Aquarius

The Aquarius man or woman is usually very honest and forthright. These are his two greatest qualities. His standards for himself are generally very high. He can always be relied upon by others. His word is his bond.

The Aquarian is perhaps the most tolerant of all the Zodiac personalities. He respects other people's beliefs and feels that everyone is entitled to his own approach to life.

He would never do anything to injure another's feelings. He is never unkind or cruel. Always considerate of others, the Aquarian is always willing to help a person in need. He feels a very strong tie between himself and all the other members of mankind.

The person born under this sign is almost always an individualist. He does not believe in teaming up with the masses, but prefers going his own way. His ideas about life and mankind are often quite advanced. There is a saying to the effect that the average Aquarian is fifty years ahead of his time.

He is broadminded. The problems of the world concern him greatly. He is interested in helping others no matter what part of the globe they live in. He is truly a humanitarian sort. He likes to be of service to others.

Giving, considerate, and without prejudice, Aquarians have no trouble getting along with others.

The Negative Side of Aquarius

The Aquarian may be too much of a dreamer. He makes plans but seldom carries them out. He is rather unrealistic. His imagination has a tendency to run away with him. Because many of his plans are impractical, he is always in some sort of a dither.

Others may not approve of him at all times because of his unconventional behavior. He may be a bit eccentric. Sometimes he is so busy with his own thoughts, that he loses touch with the realities of existence.

Some Aquarians feel they are more clever and intelligent than others. They seldom admit to their own faults, even when they are quite apparent. Some become rather fanatic in their views. Their criticism of others is sometimes destructive and negative.

February 19–March 20

The Positive Side of Pisces

The Piscean can often understand the problems of others quite easily. He has a sympathetic nature. Kindly, he is often dedicated in the way he goes about helping others. The sick and the troubled often turn to him for advice and assistance.

He is very broadminded and does not criticize others for their faults. He knows how to accept people for what they are. On the whole, he is a trustworthy and earnest person. He is loyal to his

friends and will do what he can to help them in time of need. Generous and good-natured, he is a lover of peace; he is often willing to help others solve their differences. People who have taken a wrong turn in life often interest him and he will do what he can to persuade them to rehabilitate themselves.

He has a strong intuitive sense and most of the time he knows how to make it work for him; the Piscean is unusually perceptive and often knows what is bothering someone before that person, himself, is aware of it. The Pisces man or woman is an idealistic person, basically, and is interested in making the world a better place in which to live. The Piscean believes that everyone should help each other. He is willing to do more than his share in order to achieve cooperation with others.

The person born under this sign often is talented in music or art. He is a receptive person; he is able to take the ups and downs of life with philosophic calm.

The Negative Side of Pisces

Some Pisceans are often depressed; their outlook on life is rather glum. They may feel that they have been given a bad deal in life and that others are always taking unfair advantage of them. The Piscean sometimes feel that the world is a cold and cruel place. He is easily discouraged. He may even withdraw from the harshness of reality into a secret shell of his own where he dreams and idles away a good deal of his time.

The Piscean can be rather lazy. He lets things happen without giving the least bit of resistance. He drifts along, whether on the high road or on the low. He is rather short on willpower.

Some Pisces people seek escape through drugs or alcohol. When temptation comes along they find it hard to resist. In matters of sex, they can be rather permissive.

THE SIGNS AND
THEIR KEY WORDS

		POSITIVE	NEGATIVE
ARIES	self	courage, initiative, pioneer instinct	brash rudeness, selfish impetuosity
TAURUS	money	endurance, loyalty, wealth	obstinacy, gluttony
GEMINI	mind	versatility	capriciousness, unreliability
CANCER	family	sympathy, homing instinct	clannishness, childishness
LEO	children	love, authority, integrity	egotism, force
VIRGO	work	purity, industry, analysis	fault-finding, cynicism
LIBRA	marriage	harmony, justice	vacillation, superficiality
SCORPIO	sex	survival, regeneration	vengeance, discord
SAGITTARIUS	travel	optimism, higher learning	lawlessness
CAPRICORN	career	depth	narrowness, gloom
AQUARIUS	friends	human fellowship, genius	perverse unpredictability
PISCES	confine-ment	spiritual love, universality	diffusion, escapism

THE ELEMENTS AND QUALITIES OF THE SIGNS

ELEMENT	SIGN	QUALITY	SIGN
FIRE..................	ARIES LEO SAGITTARIUS	CARDINAL.........	ARIES LIBRA CANCER CAPRICORN
EARTH...............	TAURUS VIRGO CAPRICORN	FIXED................	TAURUS LEO SCORPIO AQUARIUS
AIR.....................	GEMINI LIBRA AQUARIUS	MUTABLE.........	GEMINI VIRGO SAGITTARIUS PISCES
WATER..............	CANCER SCORPIO PISCES		

Every sign has both an element and a quality associated with it. The element indicates the basic makeup of the sign, and the quality describes the kind of activity associated with each.

Signs can be grouped together according to their *element* and *quality*. Signs of the same element share many basic traits in common. They tend to form stable configurations and ultimately harmonious relationships. Signs of the same quality are often less harmonious, but they share many dynamic potentials for growth as well as profound fulfillment.

THE FIRE SIGNS

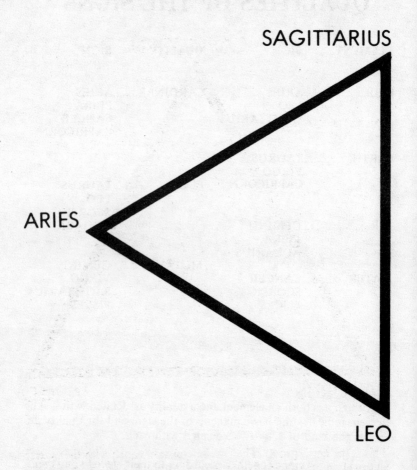

This is the fire group. On the whole these are emotional, volatile types, quick to anger, quick to forgive. They are adventurous, powerful people and.act as a source of inspiration for everyone. They spark into action with immediate exuberant impulses. They are intelligent, self-involved, creative and idealistic. They all share a certain vibrancy and glow that outwardly reflects an inner flame and passion for living.

THE EARTH SIGNS

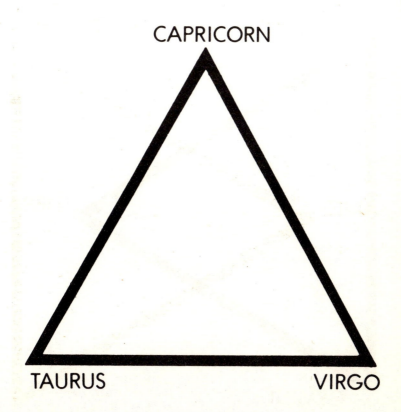

This is the earth group. They are in constant touch with the material world and tend to be conservative. Although they are all capable
of spartan self-discipline, they are earthy, sensual people who are
stimulated by the tangible, elegant and luxurious. The thread of
their lives is always practical, but they do fantasize and are often
attracted to dark, mysterious, emotional people. They are like great
cliffs overhanging the sea, forever married to the ocean but always
resisting erosion from the dark, emotional forces that thunder at
their feet.

THE AIR SIGNS

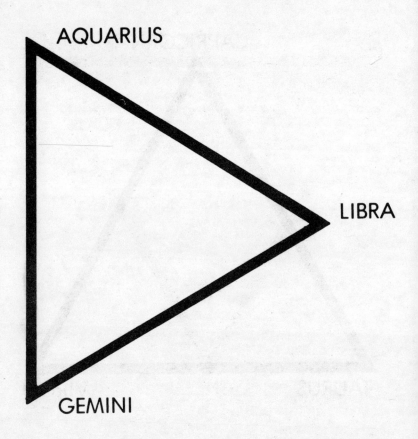

This is the air group. They are light, mental creatures desirous of contact, communication and relationship. They are involved with people and the forming of ties on many levels. Original thinkers, they are the bearers of human news. Their language is their sense of word, color, style and beauty. They provide an atmosphere suitable and pleasant for living. They add change and versatility to the scene, and it is through them that we can explore new territory of human intelligence and experience.

THE WATER SIGNS

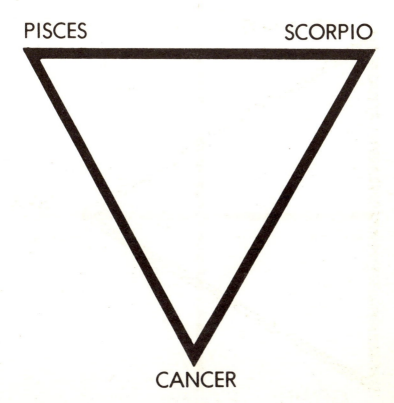

PISCES　　　　　SCORPIO

CANCER

This is the water group. Through the water people, we are all joined together on emotional, non-verbal levels. They are silent, mysterious types whose magic hypnotizes even the most determined realist. They have uncanny perceptions about people and are as rich as the oceans when it comes to feeling, emotion or imagination. They are sensitive, mystical creatures with memories that go back beyond time. Through water, life is sustained. These people have the potential for the depths of darkness or the heights of mysticism and art.

THE CARDINAL SIGNS

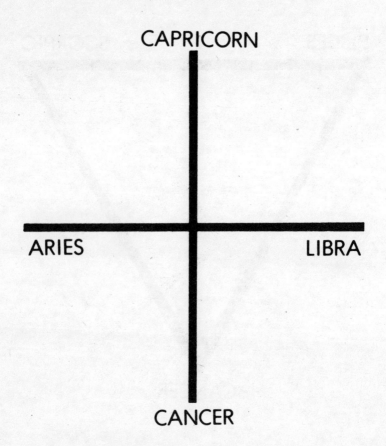

Put together, this is a clear-cut picture of dynamism, activity, tremendous stress and remarkable achievement. These people know the meaning of great change since their lives are often characterized by significant crises and major successes. This combination is like a simultaneous storm of summer, fall, winter and spring. The danger is chaotic diffusion of energy; the potential is irrepressible growth and victory.

THE FIXED SIGNS

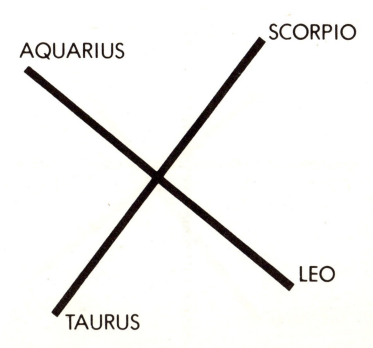

Fixed signs are always establishing themselves in a given place or area of experience. Like explorers who arrive and plant a flag, these people claim a position from which they do not enjoy being deposed. They are staunch, stalwart, upright, trusty, honorable people, although their obstinacy is well-known. Their contribution is fixity, and they are the angels who support our visible world.

THE MUTABLE SIGNS

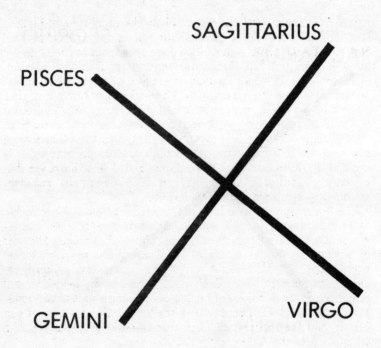

Mutable people are versatile, sensitive, intelligent, nervous and deeply curious about life. They are the translators of all energy. They often carry out or complete tasks initiated by others. Combinations of these signs have highly developed minds; they are imaginative and jumpy and think and talk a lot. At worst their lives are a Tower of Babel. At best they are adaptable and ready creatures who can assimilate one kind of experience and enjoy it while anticipating coming changes.

HOW TO APPROXIMATE YOUR RISING SIGN

Apart from the month and day of birth, the exact *time* of birth is another vital factor in the determination of an accurate horoscope. Not only do the planets move with great speed, but one must know how far the Earth has turned during the day. That way you can determine exactly where the planets are located with respect to the precise birthplace of an individual. This makes *your* horoscope *your* horoscope. In addition to these factors, another grid is laid upon that of the Zodiac and the planets: the houses. After all three have been considered, specific planetary relationships can be measured and analyzed in accordance with certain ordered procedures. It is the skillful translation of all this complex astrological language that a serious astrologer strives for in his attempt at coherent astrological synthesis. Keep this in mind.

The horoscope sets up a kind of framework around which the life of an individual grows like wild ivy, this way and that, weaving its way around the trellis of the natal positions of the planets. The year of birth tells us the positions of the distant, slow-moving planets like Jupiter, Saturn, Uranus and Pluto. The month of birth indicates the Sun sign, or birth sign as it is commonly called, as well as indicating the positions of the rapidly moving planets like Venus, Mercury and Mars. The day of birth locates the position of our Moon, and the moment of birth determines the houses through what is called the Ascendant, or Rising Sign.

As the Earth rotates on its axis once every 24 hours, each one of the twelve signs of the Zodiac appears to be "rising" on the horizon, with a new one appearing about every two hours. Actually it is the turning of the Earth that exposes each sign to view, but you will remember that in much of our astrological work we are discussing "apparent" motion. This *Rising Sign* marks the Ascendant and it colors the whole orientation of a horoscope. It indicates the sign governing the first house of the chart, and will thus determine which signs will govern all the other houses. The idea is a bit complicated at first, and we needn't dwell on complications in this introduction, but if you can imagine two color wheels with twelve divisions superimposed upon each other, one moving slowly and the other remaining still, you will have some idea of how the signs keep shifting the "color" of the houses as the Rising Sign continues to change every two hours.

The important point is that the birth chart, or horoscope, actually does define specific factors of a person's makeup. It contains a picture of being, much the way the nucleus of a tiny cell contains the potential for an entire elephant, or a packet of seeds contains a rosebush. If there were no order or continuity to the world, we could plant roses and get elephants. This same order that gives continuous flow to our lives often annoys people if it threatens to determine too much of their lives. We must grow from what we were planted, and there's no reason why we can't do that magnificently. It's all there in the horoscope. Where there is limitation, there is breakthrough; where there is crisis, there is transformation. Accurate analysis of a horoscope can help you find these points of breakthrough and transformation, and it requires knowledge of subtleties and distinctions that demand skillful judgment in order to solve even the simplest kind of personal question.

It is still quite possible, however, to draw some conclusions based upon the sign occupied by the Sun alone. In fact, if you're just being introduced to this vast subject, you're better off keeping it simple. Otherwise it seems like an impossible jumble, much like trying to read a novel in a foreign language without knowing the basic vocabulary. As with anything else, you can progress in your appreciation and understanding of astrology in direct proportion to your interest. To become really good at it requires study, experience, patience and above all—and maybe simplest of all—a fundamental understanding of what is actually going on right up there in the sky over your head. It is a vital living process you can observe, contemplate and ultimately understand. You can start by observing sunrise, or sunset, or even the full Moon.

In fact you can do a simple experiment after reading this introduction. You can erect a rough chart by following the simple procedure below:

1. Draw a circle with twelve equal segments.

2. Starting at what would be the nine o'clock position on a clock, number the segments, or houses, from 1 to 12 in a *counterclockwise direction.*

3. Label house number 1 in the following way: 4 A.M.-6 A.M.

4. In a counterclockwise direction, label the rest of the houses: 2 A.M.-4 A.M., MIDNIGHT-2 A.M., 10 P.M-MIDNIGHT, 8 P.M.-10 P.M., 6 P.M.-8 P.M., 4 P.M.-6 P.M., 2 P.M.-4 P.M., NOON-2 P.M., 10 A.M.-NOON, 8 A.M.-10 A.M., and 6 A.M.-8 A.M.

5. Now find out what time you were born and place the sun in the appropriate house.

6. Label the edge of that house with your Sun sign. You now have a description of your basic character and your fundamental drives. You can also see in what areas of life on Earth you will be most likely to focus your constant energy and center your activity.

7. If you are really feeling ambitious, label the rest of the houses with the signs, starting with your Sun sign, in order, still in a *counterclockwise direction*. When you get to Pisces, start over with Aries and keep going until you reach the house behind the Sun.

8. Look to house number 1. The sign that you have now labeled and attached to house number 1 is your Rising sign. It will color your self-image, outlook, physical constitution, early life and whole orientation to life. Of course this is a mere approximation, since there are many complicated calculations that must be made with respect to adjustments for birth time, but if you read descriptions of the sign preceding and the sign following the one you have calculated in the above manner, you may be able to identify yourself better. In any case, when you get through labeling all the houses, your drawing should look something like this:

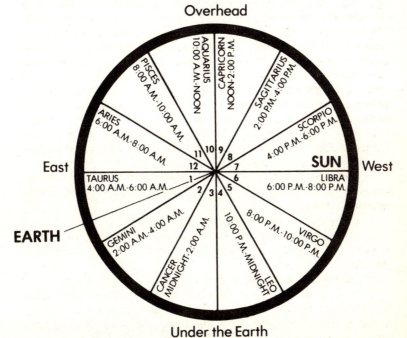

Basic chart illustrating the position of the Sun in Scorpio,
with the Ascendant Taurus as the Rising Sign.

This individual was born at 5:15 P.M. on October 31 in New York City. The Sun is in Scorpio and is found in the 7th house. The Rising sign, or the sign governing house number 1, is Taurus, so this person is a blend of Scorpio and Taurus.

Any further calculation would necessitate that you look in an ephemeris, or table of planetary motion, for the positions of the rest of the planets for your particular birth year. But we will take the time to define briefly all the known planets of our Solar System and the Sun to acquaint you with some more of the astrological vocabulary that you will be meeting again and again. (See page 21 for a full explanation of the Moon in all the Signs.)

THE PLANETS AND SIGNS THEY RULE

The signs of the Zodiac are linked to the planets in the following way. Each sign is governed or ruled by one or more planets. No matter where the planets are located in the sky at any given moment, they still rule their respective signs, and when they travel through the signs they rule, they have special dignity and their effects are stronger.

Following is a list of the planets and the signs they rule. After looking at the list, go back over the definitions of the planets and see if you can determine how the planet ruling *your* Sun sign has affected your life.

SIGNS	RULING PLANETS
Aries	Mars, Pluto
Taurus	Venus
Gemini	Mercury
Cancer	Moon
Leo	Sun
Virgo	Mercury
Libra	Venus
Scorpio	Mars, Pluto
Sagittarius	Jupiter
Capricorn	Saturn
Aquarius	Saturn, Uranus
Pisces	Jupiter, Neptune

THE PLANETS
OF THE
SOLAR SYSTEM

Here are the planets of the Solar System. They all travel around the Sun at different speeds and different distances. Taken with the Sun, they all distribute individual intelligence and ability throughout the entire chart.

The planets modify the influence of the Sun in a chart according to their own particular natures, strengths and positions. Their positions must be calculated for each year and day, and their function and expression in a horoscope will change as they move from one area of the Zodiac to another.

Following, you will find brief statements of their pure meanings.

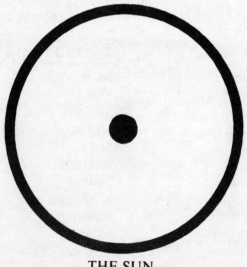

THE SUN

SUN

This is the center of existence. Around this flaming sphere all the planets revolve in endless orbits. Our star is constantly sending out its beams of light and energy without which no life on Earth would be possible. In astrology it symbolizes everything we are trying to become, the center around which all of our activity in life will always revolve. It is the symbol of our basic nature and describes the natural and constant thread that runs through everything that we do from birth to death on this planet.

To early astrologers, the sun seemed to be another planet because it crossed the heavens every day, just like the rest of the bodies in the sky.

It is the only star near enough to be seen well—it is, in fact, a dwarf star. Approximately 860,000 miles in diameter, it is about ten times as wide as the giant planet Jupiter. The next nearest star is nearly 300,000 times as far away, and if the Sun were located as far away as most of the bright stars, it would be too faint to be seen without a telescope.

Everything in the horoscope ultimately revolves around this singular body. Although other forces may be prominent in the charts of some individuals, still the Sun is the total nucleus of being and symbolizes the complete potential of every human being alive. It is vitality and the life force. Your whole essence comes from the position of the Sun.

You are always trying to express the Sun according to its position by house and sign. Possibility for all development is found in the Sun, and it marks the fundamental character of your personal radiations all around you.

It is the symbol of strength, vigor, wisdom, dignity, ardor and generosity, and the ability for a person to function as a mature individual. It is also a creative force in society. It is consciousness of the gift of life.

The underdeveloped solar nature is arrogant, pushy, undependable and proud, and is constantly using force.

MERCURY

Mercury is the planet closest to the Sun. It races around our star, gathering information and translating it to the rest of the system. Mercury represents your capacity to understand the desires of your own will and to translate those desires into action.

In other words it is the planet of Mind and the power of communication. Through Mercury we develop an ability to think, write, speak and observe—to become aware of the world around us. It colors our attitudes and vision of the world, as well as our capacity to communicate our inner responses to the outside world. Some people who have serious disabilities in their power of verbal communication have often wrongly been described as people lacking intelligence.

Although this planet (and its position in the horoscope) indicates your power to communicate your thoughts and perceptions to the world, intelligence is something deeper. Intelligence is distributed throughout all the planets. It is the relationship of the planets to each other that truly describes what we call intelligence. Mercury rules speaking, language, mathematics, draft and design, students, messengers, young people, offices, teachers and any pursuits where the mind of man has wings.

VENUS

Venus is beauty. It symbolizes the harmony and radiance of a rare and elusive quality: beauty itself. It is refinement and delicacy, softness and charm. In astrology it indicates grace, balance and the aesthetic sense. Where Venus is we see beauty, a gentle drawing in of energy and the need for satisfaction and completion. It is a special touch that finishes off rough edges. It is sensitivity, and affection, and it is always the place for that other elusive phenomenon: love. Venus describes our sense of what is beautiful and loving. Poorly developed, it is vulgar, tasteless and self-indulgent. But its ideal is the flame of spiritual love—Aphrodite, goddess of love, and the sweetness and power of personal beauty.

MARS

This is raw, crude energy. The planet next to Earth but outward from the Sun is a fiery red sphere that charges through the horoscope with force and fury. It represents the way you reach out for new adventure and new experience. It is energy and drive, initiative, courage and daring. The power to start something and see it through. It can be thoughtless, cruel and wild, angry and hostile, causing cuts, burns, scalds and wounds. It can stab its way through a chart, or it can be the symbol of healthy spirited adventure, well-channeled constructive power to begin and keep up the drive. If you have trouble starting things, if you lack the get-up-and-go to start the ball rolling, if you lack aggressiveness and self-confidence, chances are there's another planet influencing your Mars. Mars rules soldiers, butchers, surgeons, salesmen—any field that requires daring, bold skill, operational technique or self-promotion.

JUPITER

This is the largest planet of the Solar System. Scientists have recently learned that Jupiter reflects more light than it receives from the Sun. In a sense it is like a star itself. In astrology it rules good luck and good cheer, health, wealth, optimism, happiness, success and joy. It is the symbol of opportunity and always opens the way for new possibilities in your life. It rules exuberance, enthusiasm, wisdom, knowledge, generosity and all forms of expansion in general. It rules actors, statesmen, clerics, professional people, religion, publishing and the distribution of many people over large areas.

Sometimes Jupiter makes you think you deserve everything, and you become sloppy, wasteful, careless and rude, prodigal and lawless, in the illusion that nothing can ever go wrong. Then there is the danger of over-confidence, exaggeration, undependability and over-indulgence.

Jupiter is the minimization of limitation and the emphasis on spirituality and potential. It is the thirst for knowledge and higher learning.

SATURN

Saturn circles our system in dark splendor with its mysterious rings, forcing us to be awakened to whatever we have neglected in the past. It will present real puzzles and problems to be solved, causing delays, obstacles and hindrances. By doing so, Saturn stirs our own sensitivity to those areas where we are laziest.

Here we must patiently develop *method,* and only through painstaking effort can our ends be achieved. It brings order to a horoscope and imposes reason just where we are feeling least reasonable. By creating limitations and boundary, Saturn shows the consequences of being human and demands that we accept the changing cycles inevitable in human life. Saturn rules time, old age and sobriety. It can bring depression, gloom, jealousy and greed, or serious acceptance of responsibilities out of which success will develop. With Saturn there is nothing to do but face facts. It rules laborers, stones, granite, rocks and crystals of all kinds.

The Outer Planets

The following three are the outer planets. They liberate human beings from cultural conditioning, and in that sense are the law breakers. In early times it was thought that Saturn was the last planet of the system—the outer limit beyond which we could never go. The discovery of the next three planets ushered in new phases of human history, revolution and technology.

URANUS

Uranus rules unexpected change, upheaval, revolution. It is the symbol of total independence and asserts the freedom of an individual from all restriction and restraint. It is a breakthrough planet and indicates talent, originality and genius in a horoscope. It usually causes last-minute reversals and changes of plan, unwanted separations, accidents, catastrophes and eccentric behavior. It can add irrational rebelliousness and perverse bohemianism to a personality or a streak of unaffected brilliance in science and art. It rules technology, aviation and all forms of electrical and electronic advancement. It governs great leaps forward and topsy-turvy situations, and *always* turns things around at the last minute. Its effects are difficult to ever really predict, since it rules sudden last-minute decisions and events that come like lightning out of the blue.

NEPTUNE

Neptune dissolves existing reality the way the sea erodes the cliffs beside it. Its effects are subtle like the ringing of a buoy's bell in the fog. It suggests a reality higher than definition can usually describe. It awakens a sense of higher responsibility often causing guilt, worry, anxieties or delusions. Neptune is associated with all forms of escape and can make things seem a certain way so convincingly that you are absolutely sure of something that eventually turns out to be quite different.

It is the planet of illusion and therefore governs the invisible realms that lie beyond our ordinary minds, beyond our simple factual ability to prove what is "real." Treachery, deceit, disillusionment and disappointment are linked to Neptune. It describes a vague reality that promises eternity and the divine, yet in a manner so complex that we cannot really fathom it at all. At its worst Neptune is a cheap intoxicant; at its best it is the poetry, music and inspiration of the higher planes of spiritual love. It has dominion over movies, photographs and much of the arts.

PLUTO

Pluto lies at the outpost of our system and therefore rules finality in a horoscope—the final closing of chapters in your life, the passing of major milestones and points of development from which there is no return. It is a final wipeout, a closeout, an evacuation. It is a distant, subtle but powerful catalyst in all transformations that occur. It creates, destroys, then recreates. Sometimes Pluto starts its influence with a minor event or insignificant incident that might even go unnoticed. Slowly but surely, little by little, everything changes, until at last there has been a total transformation in the area of your life where Pluto has been operating. It rules mass thinking and the trends that society first rejects, then adopts and finally outgrows.

Pluto rules the dead and the underworld—all the powerful forces of creation and destruction that go on all the time beneath, around and above us. It can bring a lust for power with strong obsessions.

It is the planet that rules the metamorphoses of the caterpillar into a butterfly, for it symbolizes the capacity to change totally and forever a person's life style, way of thought and behavior.

FAMOUS PERSONALITIES

ARIES: Hans Christian Andersen, Pearl Bailey, Marlon Brando, Wernher Von Braun, Charlie Chaplin, Joan Crawford, Da Vinci, Bette Davis, Doris Day, W. C. Fields, Alec Guinness, Adolf Hitler, William Holden, Thomas Jefferson, Nikita Khrushchev, Elton John, Arturo Toscanini, J. P. Morgan, Paul Robeson, Gloria Steinem, Lowell Thomas, Vincent van Gogh, Tennessee Williams

TAURUS: Fred Astaire, Charlote Brontë, Carol Burnett, Irving Berlin, Bing Crosby, Salvador Dali, Tchaikovsky, Queen Elizabeth II, Duke Ellington, Ella Fitzgerald, Henry Fonda, Sigmund Freud, Orson Welles, Joe Louis, Lenin, Karl Marx, Golda Meir, Eva Peron, Bertrand Russell, Shakespeare, Kate Smith, Benjamin Spock, Barbra Streisand, Shirley Temple, Harry Truman

GEMINI: Mikhail Baryshnikov, Boy George, Igor Stravinsky, Carlos Chavez, Walt Whitman, Bob Dylan, Ralph Waldo Emerson, Judy Garland, Paul Gauguin, Allen Ginsberg, Benny Goodman, Bob Hope, Burl Ives, John F. Kennedy, Peggy Lee, Marilyn Monroe, Joe Namath, Cole Porter, Laurence Olivier, Harriet Beecher Stowe, Queen Victoria, John Wayne, Frank Lloyd Wright

CANCER: "Dear Abby," David Brinkley, Yul Brynner, Pearl Buck, Marc Chagall, Jack Dempsey, Mildred (Babe) Zaharias, Mary Baker Eddy, Henry VIII, John Glenn, Ernest Hemingway, Lena Horne, Oscar Hammerstein, Helen Keller, Ann Landers, George Orwell, Nancy Reagan, Rembrandt, Richard Rodgers, Ginger Rogers, Rubens, Jean-Paul Sartre, O. J. Simpson

LEO: Neil Armstrong, Russell Baker, James Baldwin, Emily Brontë, Wilt Chamberlain, Julia Child, Cecil B. De Mille, Ogden Nash, Amelia Earhart, Edna Ferber, Arthur Goldberg, Dag Hammarskjöld, Alfred Hitchcock, Mick Jagger, George Meany, George Bernard Shaw, Napoleon, Jacqueline Onassis, Henry Ford, Francis Scott Key, Andy Warhol, Mae West, Orville Wright

VIRGO: Ingrid Bergman, Warren Burger, Maurice Chevalier, Agatha Christie, Sean Connery, Lafayette, Peter Falk, Greta Garbo, Althea Gibson, Arthur Godfrey, Goethe, Buddy Hackett, Michael Jackson, Lyndon Johnson, D. H. Lawrence, Sophia Loren, Grandma Moses, Arnold Palmer, Queen Elizabeth I, Walter Reuther, Peter Sellers, Lily Tomlin, George Wallace

LIBRA: Brigitte Bardot, Art Buchwald, Truman Capote, Dwight D. Eisenhower, William Faulkner, F. Scott Fitzgerald, Gandhi, George Gershwin, Micky Mantle, Helen Hayes, Vladimir Horowitz, Doris Lessing, Martina Navratalova, Eugene O'Neill, Luciano Pavarotti, Emily Post, Eleanor Roosevelt, Bruce Springsteen, Margaret Thatcher, Gore Vidal, Barbara Walters, Oscar Wilde

SCORPIO: Vivien Leigh, Richard Burton, Art Carney, Johnny Carson, Billy Graham, Grace Kelly, Walter Cronkite, Marie Curie, Charles de Gaulle, Linda Evans, Indira Gandhi, Theodore Roosevelt, Rock Hudson, Katherine Hepburn, Robert F. Kennedy, Billie Jean King, Martin Luther, Georgia O'Keeffe, Pablo Picasso, Jonas Salk, Alan Shepard, Robert Louis Stevenson

SAGITTARIUS: Jane Austen, Louisa May Alcott, Woody Allen, Beethoven, Willy Brandt, Mary Martin, William F. Buckley, Maria Callas, Winston Churchill, Noel Coward, Emily Dickinson, Walt Disney, Benjamin Disraeli, James Doolittle, Kirk Douglas, Chet Huntley, Jane Fonda, Chris Evert Lloyd, Margaret Mead, Charles Schulz, John Milton, Frank Sinatra, Steven Spielberg

CAPRICORN: Muhammad Ali, Isaac Asimov, Pablo Casals, Dizzy Dean, Marlene Dietrich, James Farmer, Ava Gardner, Barry Goldwater, Cary Grant, J. Edgar Hoover, Howard Hughes, Joan of Arc, Gypsy Rose Lee, Martin Luther King, Jr., Rudyard Kipling, Mao Tse-tung, Richard Nixon, Gamal Nasser, Louis Pasteur, Albert Schweitzer, Stalin, Benjamin Franklin, Elvis Presley

AQUARIUS: Marian Anderson, Susan B. Anthony, Jack Benny, Charles Darwin, Charles Dickens, Thomas Edison, John Barrymore, Clark Gable, Jascha Heifetz, Abraham Lincoln, John McEnroe, Yehudi Menuhin, Mozart, Jack Nicklaus, Ronald Reagan, Jackie Robinson, Norman Rockwell, Franklin D. Roosevelt, Gertrude Stein, Charles Lindbergh, Margaret Truman

PISCES: Edward Albee, Harry Belafonte, Alexander Graham Bell, Frank Borman, Chopin, Adelle Davis, Albert Einstein, Jackie Gleason, Winslow Homer, Edward M. Kennedy, Victor Hugo, Mike Mansfield, Michelangelo, Edna St. Vincent Millay, Liza Minelli, John Steinbeck, Linus Pauling, Ravel, Diana Ross, William Shirer, Elizabeth Taylor, George Washington

SAGITTARIUS

CHARACTER ANALYSIS

People born under this ninth sign of the Zodiac are quite often self-reliant and intelligent. Generally, they are quite philosophical in their outlook on life. They know how to make practical use of their imagination.

There is seldom anything narrow about a Sagittarian. He is generally very tolerant and considerate. He would never consciously do anything that would hurt another's feelings. He is gifted with a good sense of humor and believes in being honest in his relationships with others. At times he is a little short of tact. He is so intent on telling the truth that sometimes he is a bit blunt. At any rate, he means well, and people who enjoy their relationship with him are often willing to overlook this flaw. He may even tell people true things about themselves that they do not wish to hear. At times this can cause a strain in the relationship. The Sagittarian often wishes that others were as forthright and honest as he is—no matter what the consequences.

The person born under this sign is often positive and optimistic. He likes life. He often helps others to snap out of an ill mood. His joie de vivre is often infectious. People enjoy being around the Sagittarian because he is almost always in a good mood. Quite often people born under the sign of Sagittarius are fond of the outdoors. They enjoy sporting events and often excel in them. Many of them are fond of animals—especially horses. Generally speaking they are healthy—in mind and limb. They have pluck; they enjoy the simple things of life. Fresh air and good comradeship are important to them. On the other hand, they are fond of developing their minds. Many Sagittarians cannot read or study enough. They like to keep abreast of things. They are interested in theater and the arts in general. Some of them are rather religious. Some choose a religious life.

Because they are outgoing for the most part, they sometimes come in touch with situations that others are never confronted with. In the long run this tends to make their life experiences quite rich and varied. They are well-balanced. They like to be active; they enjoy using their intellects.

It is important to the person born under this sign that justice prevails. They dislike seeing anyone treated unfairly. If the Sagittarian feels that the old laws are out-of-date or unrealistic he will fight to have them changed. At times he can be quite a rebel. It is important to him that law is carried out impartially. In matters of law, he often excels.

Sagittarians are almost always fond of travel. It seems to be imbedded in their natures. At times, they feel impelled to get away from familiar surroundings and people. Far away places have a magical attraction for someone born under this sign. They enjoy reading about foreign lands and strange customs. Many people who are Sagittarians are not terribly fond of living in big cities; they prefer the quiet and greenery of the countryside. Of all the signs of the Zodiac the Sign of Sagittarius is closest to mother nature. They can usually build a trusting relationship with animals.

The Sagittarian is quite clever in conversation. He has a definite way with words. He is fond of a good argument. He knows how to phrase things exactly; his sense of humor often has a cheerful effect on his manner of speech. He is seldom without a joke of some sort. At times he is apt to hurt others with his wit, but this is never done intentionally. A slip of the tongue sometimes gets him into social difficulties. The person born under this sign often angers quite easily; however, they cool down quickly and are not given to holding grudges. They are willing to forgive and forget.

On the whole, the Sagittarian is good-natured and fun-loving. He finds it easy to take up with people of all sorts. In most cases, his social circle is rather large. People enjoy his company. Many of his friends share his interest in outdoor life and intellectual pursuits.

At times, he can be rather impulsive. He is not afraid of risk; on the contrary, at times he can be rather foolhardy in the way he courts danger. However, he is very sporting in all that he does, and if he should wind up the loser, he is not apt to waste much time grieving about it. He can be fairly optimistic—he believes in good luck.

Health

Often people born under the sign of Sagittarius are quite athletic. They are healthy-looking—quite striking in a robust way. Often they are rather tall and well-built. They are enthusiastic people and like being active or involved. Exercise may interest them a great deal. The Sagittarian cannot stand not being active. He has to be on the go. As he grows older, he seems to increase his strength and physical ability. At times he may have worries, but he never allows them to affect his humor or health.

It is important to the Sagittarian to remain physically sound. He is usually very physically fit, but his nervous system may be somewhat sensitive. Too much activity—even while he finds action attractive—may put a severe strain upon him after a time. The Sagittarian should try to concentrate his energies on as few objects as possible. However, usually he has his projects scattered here and there, and as a result he is easily exhausted. At times illnesses fall upon him rather suddenly. Some Sagittarians are accident-prone. They are not afraid of taking risks and as a result are sometimes careless in the way they do things. Injuries often come to them by way of sports or other vigorous activities.

At times, people of this sign try to ignore signs of illness —especially if they are engaged in some activity that has captured their interest. This results in a severe setback at times.

In later life, the Sagittarian sometimes suffers from stomach disorders. High blood pressure is another ailment that might affect him; he should also be on guard for signs of arthritis and sciatica. In spite of these possible dangers, the average Sagittarian manages to stay quite youthful and alert through his interest in life.

Occupation

The Sagittarian is someone who can be relied upon in a work situation. He is loyal and dependable. He is an energetic worker, anxious to please his superiors. He is forward-looking by nature and enjoys working in modern surroundings and toward progressive goals. Challenges do not frighten him. He is rather flexible and can work in confining situations even though he may not enjoy it. Work which gives him a chance to move about and meet new people is well suited to his character. If he has to stay in one locale he is apt to become sad and ill-humored. He can take orders but he would rather be in a situation where he does not have to. He is difficult to please at times, and may hop from job to job before feeling that it is really time to settle down. He does his best work when he is allowed to work on his own.

The Sagittarian is interested in expressing himself in the work he does. If he occupies a position which does not allow him to do this, he will seek outside activities that give him a chance to develop in a direction which interests him.

Some Sagittarians do well in the field of journalism; others make good teachers and public speakers. They are generally quite flexible and would do well in many different positions. Some excel as foreign ministers or in music; others do well in government work or in publishing.

The person born under this sign is often more intelligent than the average man. The cultivated Sagittarian knows how to employ his intellectual gifts to their best advantage. In politics and religion, the Sagittarian often displays considerable brilliance.

He is generally pleasant to work with; he is considerate of his colleagues and would do nothing that might upset their working relationship. Because he is so self-reliant he often inspires others. He likes to work with detail. His ideas are often quite practical and intelligent. The Sagittarian is curious by nature and is always looking for ways of increasing his knowledge.

The people born under this sign are almost always generous. They rarely refuse someone in need, but are always willing to share what they have. Whether he is up or down, the Sagittarian can always be relied upon to help someone in dire straits. His attitude toward life may be happy-go-lucky in general. He is difficult to depress no matter what his situation. He is optimistic and forward-looking. Money always seems to fall into his hands; it's seldom a problem for him.

The average Sagittarian is interested in expansion and promotion. Sometimes these concerns weaken his projects rather than strengthen them.

He is interested in large profit and is sometimes willing to take risks to secure it. In the long run he is successful. He has a flair for carrying off business deals well. It is the cultivated Sagittarian who prepares himself well in business matters so that he is well-supported in his interests by knowledge, as well as by experience.

The average person born under this sign is more interested in contentment and joy than in material gain. However he will do his best to make the most of profit when it comes his way.

Home and Family

Not all Sagittarians are very interested in home life. Many of them set great store in being mobile. Their activities outside the home may attract them more than those inside the home. Not exactly homebodies, Sagittarians, however, can adjust themselves to a stable domestic life if they put their minds to it.

People born under this sign are not keen on luxuries and other displays of wealth. They prefer the simple things. Anyone entering their home should be able to discern this. They are generally neat; they like a place that has plenty of space—not too cluttered with imposing furniture.

Even when he settles down, the Sagittarian likes to keep a small corner of his life just for himself; independence is important to him. If necessary, he'll insist upon it, no matter what the situation. He likes a certain amount of beauty in his home, but he may not be too interested in keeping things looking nice—his interests lead him elsewhere. Housekeeping may bore him to distraction. If he is forced to stick to a domestic routine he is liable to become somewhat disagreeable.

Children bring him a great deal of happiness. He is fond of family life. Friends generally drop in any old time to visit a Sagittarian for they know they will always be welcomed and properly entertained. The Sagittarian's love of his fellow man is well known.

When children are small, he may not understand them too well, even though he tries. He may feel he is a bit too clumsy to handle them properly—although this may be far from the case. As they begin to grow up and develop definite personalities, the Sagittarian's interest grows. There is always a strong tie between children and the Sagittarian parent.

Children are especially drawn to Sagittarians because they seem to understand them better than other adults.

One is apt to find children born under this sign a little restless and disorganized at times. They are usually quite independent in their ways and may ask for quite a bit of freedom while still young. They don't like being fussed over by adults. They like to feel that their parents believe in them and trust them on their own.

Social Relationships

The Sagittarian enjoys having people around. It is not difficult for him to make friends. He is very sociable by nature. Most of the friends he makes, he keeps for life. As a rule, the person born under this sign is rather broadminded; he is apt to have all sorts of friends. He appreciates people for their good qualities, however few they may have. He is not quick to judge and is often very forgiving. He is not impressed by what a friend has in the way of material goods.

The Sagittarian is generally quite popular. He is much in demand socially; people like him for his easy disposition and his good humor. His friendship is valued by others. Quite often in spite of his chumminess, the Sagittarian is rather serious; light conversation may be somewhat difficult for him.

He believes in speaking his mind—in saying what he feels—yet at times, he can appear rather quiet and retiring. It all depends on his mood. Others may feel that there are two sides to his personality because of this quirk in his nature; for this reason it may be difficult for some people to get to know him. In some instances, he employs his silence as a sort of protection. When people pierce through however and don't leave him in peace, he can become rather angry.

On the whole, he is a kind and considerate person. His nature is gentle and unassuming. With the wrong people though, he can become somewhat disagreeable. He can become angry quite easily at times; however, he cools down quickly and is willing to let bygones be bygones. He never holds a grudge against anyone. Companionship and harmony in all social relationships is quite necessary for the Sagittarian; he is willing to make some sacrifices for it. The partner for someone born under this sign must be a good listener. There are times when the Sagittarian feels it is necessary to pour his heart out. He is willing to listen to another's problems, too. His mate or loved one should be able to take an interest in his hobbies and such. If not, the Sagittarian may be tempted to go his own way even more.

The Sagittarian says what he means; he doesn't beat around the bush. Being direct is one of his strongest qualities. Sometimes it pays off; sometimes it doesn't. He is often forgetful that the one he loves may be more sensitive than she allows herself to appear—even to him. He has a tendency to put his foot in his mouth at times. However, his mate should be able to overlook this flaw in his character or else try to correct it in some subtle way. At times, when joking broadly he has the ability to strike a sensitive chord in his loved one and this may result in a serious misunderstanding. The cultivated Sagittarian learns his boundaries; he knows when not to go too far. Understanding his partner's viewpoint is also an important thing for someone born under this sign to learn.

LOVE AND MARRIAGE

Sagittarians are faithful to their loved ones. They are affectionate in nature and not at all possessive. Love is important for them spiritually as well as physically. For some people born under this sign, romance is a chance to escape reality—it is a chance for adventure. Quite often, the Sagittarian's mate finds it difficult to keep up with him—he is so active and energetic. When Sagittarians fall in love, however, they are quite easy to handle.

Sagittarians do like having freedom. They will make concessions in a steady relationship; still there will be a part of themselves that they keep from others. He or she is very keen on preserving his individual rights, no matter what sort of relationship he is engaged in. The Sagittarian's ideals are generally high and they are important to him. He is looking for someone with similar standards, not someone too lax or conventional.

In love, the Sagittarian may be a bit childlike at times. As a result of this he is apt to encounter various disappointments before he has found the one meant for him. At times he or she says things he really shouldn't and this causes the end of a romantic relationship. The person born under this sign may have many love affairs before he feels he is ready to settle down with just one person. If the person he loves does not exactly measure up to his standards, the Sagittarian is apt to overlook this—depending on how strong his love is—and accept the person for what that person is.

On the whole, the Sagittarian is not an envious person. He is willing to allow his or her partner needed freedoms—within reason. The Sagittarian does this so that he will not have to jeopardize his own liberties. Live and let live could easily be his motto. If his ideals and freedom are threatened, the Sagittarian fights hard to protect what he believes is just and fair.

He does not want to make any mistakes in love, so he takes his time when choosing someone to settle down with. He is direct and positive when he meets the right one; he does not waste time.

95

The average Sagittarian may be a bit altar-shy. It may take a bit of convincing before Sagittarians agree that married life is right for them. This is generally because they do not want to lose their freedom. The Sagittarian is an active person who enjoys being around a lot of other people. Sitting quietly at home does not interest him at all. At times it may seem that he or she wants to have things his own way, even in marriage. It may take some doing to get him to realize that in marriage, as in other things, give and take plays a great role.

Romance and the Sagittarius Woman

The Sagittarian woman is often kind and gentle. Most of the time she is very considerate of others and enjoys being of help in some way to her friends. She can be quite active and, as a result, be rather difficult to catch. On the whole, she is optimistic and friendly. She believes in looking on the bright side of things. She knows how to make the best of situations that others feel are not worth salvaging. She has plenty of pluck.

Men generally like her because of her easy-going manner. Quite often she becomes friends with a man before venturing on to romance. There is something about her that makes her more of a companion than a lover. She can best be described as sporting and broad-minded.

She is almost never possessive; she enjoys her own freedom too much to want to make demands on that of another person.

She is always youthful in her disposition. She may seem rather guileless at times. Generally it takes her longer really to mature than it does others. She tends to be impulsive and may easily jump from one thing to another. If she has an unfortunate experience in love early in life, she may shy away from fast or intimate contacts for a while. She is usually very popular. Not all the men who are attracted to her see her as a possible lover, but more as a friend or companion.

The woman born under this sign generally believes in true love. She may have several romances before she decides to settle down. For her there is no particular rush. She is willing to have a long romantic relationship with the man she loves before making marriage plans.

The Sagittarius woman is often the outdoors type and has a strong liking for animals—especially dogs and horses. Quite often she excels in sports. She is not generally someone who is content to stay at home and cook and take care of the house. She would rather be out attending to her other interests. When she does household work, however, she does it well.

She makes a good companion as well as a wife. She usually enjoys participating with her husband in his various interests and affairs. Her sunny disposition often brightens up the dull moments of a love affair.

At times her temper may flare, but she is herself again after a few moments. She would never butt into her husband's business affairs, but she does enjoy being asked for her opinion from time to time. Generally she is up to date on all that her husband is doing and can offer him some pretty sound advice.

The Sagittarius woman is seldom jealous of her husband's interest in other people—even if some of them are of the opposite sex. If she has no reason to doubt his love, she never questions it.

She makes a loving and sympathetic mother. Quite often she will play with her children. Her cheerful manner makes her an invaluable playmate.

Romance and the Sagittarius Man

The. Sagittarius man is often an adventurer. He likes taking chances in love as well as in life. He may hop around quite a bit—from one romance to another—before really thinking about settling down. Many men born under this sign feel that marriage would mean the end of their freedom—so they avoid it as much as possible. Whenever a romance becomes too serious, they move on. Many Sagittarians are rather impulsive in love. Early marriages for some often end unpleasantly. The Sagittarian is not a very mature person—even at an age when most others are. He takes a bit more time. He may not always make a wise choice in a love partner.

He is affectionate and loving but not at all possessive. Because he is rather lighthearted in love, he sometimes gets into trouble.

Most Sagittarius men find romance an exciting adventure. They make attentive lovers and are never cool or indifferent. Love should also have a bit of fun in it for him too. He likes to keep things light and gay. Romance without humor—at times—is difficult for him to accept. The woman he loves should also be a good sport. She should have as open and fun-loving a disposition as he has—if she is to understand him properly.

He wants his mate to share his interest in the outdoor life and animals. If she is good at sports, she is likely to win his heart, for the average Sagittarian generally has an interest in athletics of various sorts—from bicycling to baseball.

His mate must also be a good intellectual companion; someone who can easily discuss those matters which interest her Sagittarian. Physical love is important to him—but so is spiritual love. A good romance will contain these in balance.

His sense of humor may sometimes seem a little unkind to someone who is not used to being laughed at. He enjoys playing jokes now and again; it is the child in his nature that remains a part of his character even when he grows old and gray.

He is not a homebody. He is responsible, however, and will do what is necessary to keep a home together. Still and all, the best wife for him is one who can manage household matters single-handedly if need be.

He loves children—especially as they grow older and begin to take on definite personalities.

Woman—Man

SAGITTARIUS WOMAN
ARIES MAN

In some ways, the Aries man resembles an intellectual mountain goat leaping from crag to crag. He has an insatiable thirst for knowledge. He's ambitious and is apt to have his finger in many pies. He can do with a woman like you—someone attractive, quick-witted, and smart.

He is not interested in a clinging vine kind of wife, but someone who is there when he needs her; someone who listens and understands what he says; someone who can give advice if he should ever need it . . . which is not likely to be often. The Aries man wants a woman who will look good on his arm without hanging on it too heavily. He is looking for a woman who has both feet on the ground and yet is mysterious and enticing . . . a kind of domestic Helen of Troy whose face or fine dinner can launch a thousand business deals if need be. That woman he's in search of sounds a little like you, doesn't she? If the shoe fits, put it on. You won't regret it.

The Aries man makes a good husband. He is faithful and attentive. He is an affectionate kind of man. He'll make you feel needed and loved. Love is a serious matter for the Aries man. He does not believe in flirting or playing the field—especially after he's found the woman of his dreams. He'll expect you to be as constant in your affection as he is in his. He'll expect you to be one hundred percent his; he won't put up with any nonsense while romancing you.

The Aries man may be pretty progressive and modern about many things; however, when it comes to pants wearing, he's downright conventional: it's strictly male attire. The best position you can take in the relationship is a supporting one. He's the boss and that's that. Once you have learned to accept that, you'll find the going easy.

The Aries man, with his endless energy and drive, likes to relax in the comfort of his home at the end of the day. The good home-maker can be sure of holding his love. He's keen on slippers and pipe and a comfortable armchair. If you see to it that everything in the house is where he expects to find it, you'll have no difficulty keeping the relationship on an even keel.

Life and love with an Aries man may be just the medicine you need. He'll be a good provider. He'll spoil you if he's financially able.

He's young at heart and can get along with children easily. He'll spoil them every chance he gets.

SAGITTARIUS WOMAN
TAURUS MAN

If you've got your heart set on a man born under the sign of Taurus, you'll have to learn the art of being patient. Taureans take their time about everything—even love.

The steady and deliberate Taurus man is a little slow on the draw; it may take him quite a while before he gets around to popping that question. For the woman who doesn't mind twiddling her thumbs, the waiting and anticipating almost always pays off in the end. Taurus men want to make sure that every step they take is a good one—particularly, if they feel that the path they're on is one that leads to the altar.

If you are in the mood for a whirlwind romance, you had better cast your net in shallower waters. Moreover, most Taureans prefer to do the angling themselves. They are not keen on a woman taking the lead; once she does, they are liable to drop her like a dead fish. If you let yourself get caught on a Taurean's terms, you'll find that he's fallen for you—hook, line, and sinker.

The Taurus man is fond of a comfortable homelife. It is very important to him. If you keep those home fires burning you will have no trouble keeping that flame in your Taurean's heart aglow. You have a talent for homemaking; use it. Your taste in furnishings is excellent. You know how to make a house come to life with colors and decorations.

Taurus, the strong, steady, and protective Bull may not be your idea of a man on the move, still he's reliable. Perhaps he could be the anchor for your dreams and plans. He could help you to acquire a more balanced outlook and approach to your life. If you're given to impulsiveness, he could help you to curb it. He's the man who is always there when you need him.

When you tie the knot with a man born under Taurus, you can put away fears about creditors pounding on the front door. Taureans are practical about everything including bill-paying. When he carries you over that threshold, you can be certain that the entire house is paid for, not only the doorsill.

As a housewife, you won't have to worry about putting aside your many interests for the sake of back-breaking house chores. Your Taurus husband will see to it that you have all the latest time-saving appliances and comforts.

Your children will be obedient and orderly. Your Taurus husband will see to that.

SAGITTARIUS WOMAN
GEMINI MAN

The Gemini man is quite a catch. Many a woman has set her cap for him and failed to bag him. Generally, Gemini men are intelligent, witty, and outgoing. Many of them tend to be versatile.

On the other hand, some of them seem to lack that sort of common sense that you set so much store in. Their tendency to start a half-dozen projects, then toss them up in the air out of boredom may do nothing more than exasperate you.

One thing that causes a Twin's mind and affection to wander is a bore, but it is unlikely that an active woman like you would ever allow herself to be accused of dullness. The Gemini man that has caught your heart will admire you for your ideas and intellect—perhaps even more than for your homemaking talents and good looks.

A strong willed woman could easily fill the role of rudder for her Gemini's ship-without-a-sail. The intelligent Gemini is often aware of his shortcomings and doesn't mind if someone with better bearings gives him a shove in the right direction—when it's needed. The average Gemini doesn't have serious ego-hangups and will even accept a well-deserved chewing out from his mate or girlfriend gracefully.

A successful and serious-minded Gemini could make you a very happy woman, perhaps, if you gave him half the chance. Although he may give you the impression that he has a hole in his head, the Gemini man generally has a good head on his shoulders and can make efficient use of it when he wants. Some of them, who have learned the art of being steadfast, have risen to great heights in their professions. President Kennedy was a Gemini as was Thomas Mann and William Butler Yeats.

Once you convince yourself that not all people born under the sign of the Twins are witless grasshoppers, you won't mind dating a few—to test your newborn conviction. If you do wind up walking down the aisle with one, accept the fact that married life with him will mean your taking the bitter with the sweet.

Life with a Gemini man can be more fun than a barrel of clowns. You'll never be allowed to experience a dull moment. But don't leave money matters to him or you'll both wind up behind the eight ball.

Gemini men are always attractive to the opposite sex. You'll perhaps have to allow him an occasional harmless flirt—it will seldom amount to more than that if you're his proper mate.

The Gemini father is a pushover for children. See to it that you keep them in line; otherwise they'll be running the house.

SAGITTARIUS WOMAN
CANCER MAN

Chances are you won't hit it off too well with the man born under Cancer if your plans concern love, but then, Cupid has been known to do some pretty unlikely things. The Cancerian is a very sensitive man—thin-skinned and occasionally moody. You've got to keep on your toes—and not step on his—if you're determined to make a go of the relationship.

The Cancer man may be lacking in some of the qualities you seek in a man, but when it comes to being faithful and being a good provider, he's hard to beat.

The perceptive woman will not mistake the Crab's quietness for sullenness or his thriftiness for penny-pinching. In some respects, he is like that wise old owl out on a limb; he may look like he's dozing but actually he hasn't missed a thing. Cancerians often possess a well of knowledge about human behavior; they can come across with some pretty helpful advice to those in trouble or in need. He can certainly guide you in making investments both in time and money. He may not say much, but he's always got his wits about him.

The Crab may not be the match or catch for a woman like you; at times, you are likely to find him downright dull. True to his sign, he can be fairly cranky and crabby when handled the wrong way. He is perhaps more sensitive than he should be.

If you're smarter than your Cancer friend, be smart enough

not to let him know. Never give him the idea that you think he's a little short on brain power. It would send him scurrying back into his shell—and all that ground lost in the relationship will perhaps never be recovered.

The Crab is most content at home. Once settled down for the night or the weekend, wild horses couldn't drag him any farther than the gatepost—that is, unless those wild horses were dispatched by his mother. The Crab is sometimes a Momma's boy. If his mate does not put her foot down, he will see to it that his mother always comes first. No self-respecting wife would ever allow herself to play second fiddle—even if it's to her old gray-haired mother-in-law. With a little bit of tact, however, she'll find that slipping into that number-one position is as easy as pie (that legendary one his mother used to bake).

If you pamper your Cancer man, you'll find that "Mother" turns up increasingly less—at the front door as well as in conversations.

Cancerians make protective, proud, and patient fathers.

SAGITTARIUS WOMAN
LEO MAN

For the woman who enjoys being swept off her feet in a romantic whirlwind fashion, Leo is the sign of such love. When the Lion puts his mind to romancing, he doesn't stint. It's all wining and dining and dancing till the wee hours of the morning.

Leo is all heart and knows how to make his woman feel like a woman. The girl in constant search of a man she can look up to need go no farther: Leo is ten-feet tall—in spirit if not in stature. He's a man not only in full control of his faculties but in full control of just about any situation he finds himself in. He's a winner.

The Leo man may not look like Tarzan, but he knows how to roar and beat his chest if he has to. The woman who has had her fill of weak-kneed men finds in a Leo someone she can at last lean upon. He can support you not only physically but spiritually as well. He's good at giving advice that pays off.

Leos are direct people. They don't believe in wasting time or effort. They almost never make unwise investments.

Many Leos rise to the top of their professions; through example, they often prove to be a source of great inspiration to others.

Although he's a ladies' man, the Leo man is very particular about his ladies. His standards are high when it comes to love interests. The idealistic and cultivated woman should have no trouble keeping her balance on the pedestal the Lion sets her on. Leo believes that romance should be played on a fair give-and-take basis. He won't stand for any monkey business in a love relationship. It's all or nothing.

You'll find him a frank, off-the-shoulder person; he generally says what is on his mind.

If you decide upon a Leo man for a mate, you must be prepared to stand behind him full-force. He expects it—and usually deserves it. He's the head of the house and can handle that position without a hitch. He knows how to go about breadwinning and, if he has his way (and most Leos do have their own way), he'll see to it that you'll have all the luxuries you crave and the comforts you need.

It's unlikely that the romance in your marriage will ever die out. Lions need love like flowers need sunshine. They're ever amorous and generally expect similar attention and affection from their mates. Leos are fond of going out on the town; they love to give parties, as well as to go to them.

Leos make strict fathers, generally. They love their children but won't spoil them.

SAGITTARIUS WOMAN
VIRGO MAN

Although the Virgo man may be a bit of a fussbudget at times, his seriousness and dedication to common sense may help you to overlook his tendency to sometimes be overcritical about minor things.

Virgo men are often quiet, respectable types who set great store in conservative behavior and levelheadedness. He'll admire you for your practicality and tenacity . . . perhaps even more than for your good looks. He's seldom bowled over by a glamour-puss. When he gets his courage up, he turns to a serious and reliable girl for romance. He'll be far from a Valentino while dating. In fact, you may wind up making all the passes. Once he does get his motor running, however, he can be a warm and wonderful fellow—to the right girl.

He's gradual about love. Chances are your romance with him will start out looking like an ordinary friendship. Once he's sure you're no fly-by-night flirt and have no plans of taking him for a ride, he'll open up and rain sunshine all over your heart.

Virgo men tend to marry late in life. The Virgo believes in holding out until he's met the right girl. He may not have many names in his little black book; in fact, he may not even have a black book. He's not interested in playing the field; leave that to men of the more flamboyant signs. The Virgo man is so particular that he may remain romantically inactive for a long period. His girl has to be perfect or it's no go. If you find yourself feeling weak-kneed for a Virgo, do your best to convince him that perfect is not so important when it comes to love; help him to realize that he's missing out on a great deal by not considering the near perfect or whatever it is you consider yourself to be. With your surefire perseverance, you will most likely be able to make him listen to reason and he'll wind up reciprocating your romantic interests.

The Virgo man is no block of ice. He'll respond to what he feels to be the right feminine flame. Once your love-life with a Virgo man starts to bubble, don't give it a chance to fall flat. You may never have a second chance at winning his heart.

If you should ever have a falling out with him, forget about patching it up. He'd prefer to let the pieces lie scattered. Once married, though, he'll stay that way—even if it hurts. He's too conscientious to try to back out of a legal deal of any sort.

The Virgo man is as neat as a pin. He's thumbs down on sloppy housekeeping. Keep everything bright, neat, and shiny . . . and that goes for the children, too, at least by the time he gets home from work. Chocolate-coated kisses from Daddy's little girl go over like a lead balloon with him.

SAGITTARIUS WOMAN
LIBRA MAN

If there's a Libran in your life, you are most likely a very happy woman. Men born under this sign have a way with women. You'll always feel at ease in a Libran's company; you can be yourself when you're with him.

The Libra man can be moody at times. His moodiness is often puzzling. One moment he comes on hard and strong with declarations of his love, the next moment you find that he's left you like yesterday's mashed potatoes. He'll come back, though; don't worry. Librans are like that. Deep down inside he really knows what he wants even though he may not appear to.

You'll appreciate his admiration of beauty and harmony. If you're dressed to the teeth and never looked lovelier, you'll get a ready compliment—and one that's really deserved. Librans don't indulge in idle flattery. If they don't like something, they are tactful enough to remain silent.

Librans will go to great lengths to preserve peace and harmony—they will even tell a fat lie if necessary. They don't like showdowns or disagreeable confrontations. The frank woman is all for getting whatever is bothering her off her chest and out into the open, even if it comes out all wrong. To the Libran, making a clean breast of everything seems like sheer folly sometimes.

You may lose your patience while waiting for your Libra friend to make up his mind. It takes him ages sometimes to make a decision. He weighs both sides carefully before comitting himself to anything. You seldom dillydally—at least about small things—and so it's likely that you will find it difficult to see eye to eye with a hesitating Libran when it comes to decision-making methods.

All in all, though, he is kind, considerate, and fair. He is interested in the "real" truth; he'll try to balance everything out until he has all the correct answers. It's not difficult for him to see both sides of a story.

He's a peace-loving man. The sight of blood is apt to turn his stomach.

Librans are not show-offs. Generally, they are well-balanced, modest people. Honest, wholesome, and affectionate, they are serious about every love encounter they have. If one should find that the girl he's dating is not really suited to him, he will end the relationship in such a tactful manner that no hard feelings will come about.

The Libra father is firm, gentle, and patient.

SAGITTARIUS WOMAN
SCORPIO MAN

Many find the Scorpio's sting a fate worse than death. When his anger breaks loose, you had better clear out of the vicinity.

The average Scorpio may strike you as a brute. He'll stick pins into the balloons of your plans and dreams if they don't line up with what he thinks is right. If you do anything to irritate him—just anything—you'll wish you hadn't. He'll give you a sounding out that would make you pack your bags and go back to Mother—if you were that kind of a girl.

The Scorpio man hates being tied down to homelife—he would rather be out on the battlefield of life, belting away at whatever he feels is a just and worthy cause, instead of staying home nestled in a comfortable armchair with the evening paper. If you are a girl who has a homemaking streak—don't keep those home fires burning too brightly too long; you may just run out of firewood.

As passionate as he is in business affairs and politics, the Scorpio man still has plenty of pep and ginger stored away for lovemaking.

Most women are easily attracted to him—perhaps you are no exception. Those who allow a man born under this sign to sweep them off their feet, shortly find that they're dealing with a pepper pot of seething excitement. The Scorpio man is passionate with a capital P, you can be sure of that. But he's capable of dishing out as much pain as pleasure. Damsels with fluttering hearts who, when in the embrace of a Scorpio, think "This is it," had better be in a position moments later to realize that "Perhaps this isn't it."

Scorpios are blunt. An insult is likely to whiz out of their mouths quicker than a compliment.

If you're the kind of woman who can keep a stiff upper lip, take it on the chin, turn a deaf ear, and all of that, because you feel you are still under his love spell in spite of everything: lots of luck.

If you have decided to take the bitter with the sweet, prepare yourself for a lot of ups and downs. Chances are you won't have as much time for your own affairs and interests as you'd like. The Scorpio's love of power may cause you to be at his constant beck and call.

Scorpios like fathering large families. They love children but quite often they fail to live up to their responsibilities as a parent.

SAGITTARIUS WOMAN
SAGITTARIUS MAN

The woman who has set her cap for a man born under the sign of Sagittarius may have to apply an awful amount of strategy before she can get him to drop down on bended knee. Although some Sagittarians may be marriage-shy, they're not ones to skitter away from romance. A high-spirited woman may find a relationship with a Sagittarian—whether a fling or "the real thing"—a very enjoyable experience.

As a rule, Sagittarians are bright, happy, and healthy people. They have a strong sense of fair play. Often they're a source of inspiration to others. They're full of ideas and drive.

You'll be taken by the Sagittarian's infectious grin and his lighthearted friendly nature. If you do wind up being the woman in his life, you'll find that he's apt to treat you more like a buddy than the love of his life. It's just his way. Sagittarians are often chummy instead of romantic.

You'll admire his broadmindedness in most matters—including those of the heart. If, while dating you, he claims that he still wants to play the field, he'll expect you to enjoy the same liberty. Once he's promised to love, honor, and obey, however, he does just that. Marriage for him, once he's taken that big step, is very serious business.

A woman who has a keen imagination and a great love of freedom will not be disappointed if she does tie up with a Sagittarian. The Sagittarius man is often quick-witted. Men of this sign have a genuine interest in equality. They hate prejudice and injustice.

If he does insist on a night out with the boys once a week, he won't scowl if you decide to let him shift for himself in the kitchen once a week while you pursue some of your own interests. He believes in fairness.

He's not much of a homebody. Quite often he's occupied with faraway places either in his dreams or in reality. He enjoys—just as you do—being on the go or on the move. He's got ants in his pants and refuses to sit still for long stretches at a time. Humdrum routine—especially at home—bores him. At the drop of a hat, he may ask you to whip off your apron and dine out for a change. He likes surprising people. He'll take great pride in showing you off to his friends. He'll always be a considerate mate; he will never embarrass or disappoint you intentionally.

He's very tolerant when it comes to friends and you'll most likely spend a lot of time entertaining people.

Sagittarians become interested in their children when the children are out of the baby stage.

SAGITTARIUS WOMAN
CAPRICORN MAN

A with-it girl like you is likely to find the average Capricorn man a bit of a drag. The man born under this sign is often a closed up person and difficult to get to know. Even if you do get to know him, you may not find him very interesting.

In romance, Capricorn men are a little on the rusty side. You'll probably have to make all the passes.

You may find his plodding manner irritating and his conservative, traditional ways downright maddening. He's not one to take a chance on anything. "If it was good enough for my father, it's good enough for me" may be his motto. He follows a way that is tried and true.

Whenever adventure rears its tantalizing head, the Goat will turn the other way; he's just not interested.

He may be just as ambitious as you are—perhaps even more so—but his ways of accomplishing his aims are more subterranean or, at least, seem so. He operates from the background a good deal of the time. At a gathering you may never even notice him, but he's there, taking everything in, sizing everyone up, planning his next careful move.

Although Capricorns may be intellectual to a degree, it is not generally the kind of intelligence you appreciate. He may not be as quick or as bright as you; it may take him ages to understand a simple joke.

If you do decide to take up with a man born under this sign of the Goat, you ought to be pretty good in the "Cheering Up" department. The Capricorn man often acts as though he's constantly being followed by a cloud of gloom.

The Capricorn man is most himself when in the comfort and privacy of his own home. The security possible within four walls can make him a happy man. He'll spend as much time as he can at home. If he is loaded down with extra work, he'll bring it home instead of finishing it up at the office.

You'll most likely find yourself frequently confronted by his relatives. Family is very important to the Capricorn—*his* family that is. They had better take an important place in your life, too, if you want to keep your home a happy one.

Although his caution in most matters may all but drive you up the wall, you'll find that his concerned way with money is justified most of the time. He'll plan everything right down to the last penny.

He can be quite a scolder with children. You'll have to step in and smooth things out.

SAGITTARIUS WOMAN
AQUARIUS MAN

Aquarians love everybody—even their worst enemies sometimes. Through your love relationship with an Aquarian you'll find yourself running into all sorts of people, ranging from near-genius to downright insane . . . and they're all friends of his.

As a rule, Aquarians are extremely friendly and open. Of all the signs, they are perhaps the most tolerant. In the thinking department, they are often miles ahead of others.

You'll most likely find your relationship with this man a challenging one. Your high respect for intelligence and imagination may be reason enough for you to set your heart on a Water Bearer. You'll find that you can learn a lot from him.

In the holding-hands phase of your romance, you may find that your Water Bearing friend has cold feet. Aquarians take quite a bit of warming up before they are ready to come across with that first goodnight kiss. More than likely, he'll just want to be your pal in the beginning. For him, that's an important first step in any relationship—love, included. The "poetry and flowers" stage—if it ever comes—will come later. The Aquarian is all heart; still, when it comes to tying himself down to one person and for keeps, he is almost always sure to hesitate. He may even try to get out of it if you breathe down his neck too heavily.

The Aquarius man is no Valentino and wouldn't want to be. The kind of love-life he's looking for is one that's made up mainly of companionship. Although he may not be very romantic, the memory of his first romance will always hold an important position in his heart. Some Aquarians wind up marrying their childhood sweethearts.

You won't find it difficult to look up to a man born under the sign of the Water Bearer, but you may find the challenge of trying to keep up with him dizzying. He can pierce through the most complicated problem as if it were a matter of 2 + 2. You may find him a little too lofty and high-minded—but don't judge him too harshly if that's the case; he's way ahead of his time—your time, too, most likely.

If you marry this man, he'll stay true to you. Don't think that once the honeymoon is over, you'll be chained to the kitchen sink forever. Your Aquarius husband will encourage you to keep active in your own interests and affairs. You'll most likely have a minor tiff now and again but never anything serious.

Kids love him and vice-versa. He'll be as tolerant with them as he is with adults.

SAGITTARIUS WOMAN
PISCES MAN

The man born under Pisces is quite a dreamer. Sometimes he's so wrapped up in his dreams that he's difficult to reach. To the average, active woman, he may seem a little sluggish.

He's easygoing most of the time. He seems to take things in his stride. He'll entertain all kinds of views and opinions from just about everyone, nodding or smiling vaguely, giving the impression that he's with them one hundred percent while that may not be the case at all. His attitude may be "why bother" when he's confronted with someone wrong who thinks he's right. The Pisces man will seldom speak his mind if he thinks he'll be rigidly opposed.

The Pisces man is oversensitive at times—he's afraid of getting his feelings hurt. He'll sometimes imagine a personal affront when none's been made. Chances are you'll find this complex of his maddening; at times you may feel like giving him a swift kick where it hurts the most. It wouldn't do any good, though. It would just add fuel to the fire of his complex.

One thing you'll admire about this man is his concern for people who are sickly or troubled. He'll make his shoulder available to anyone in the mood for a good cry. He can listen to one hard-luck story after another without seeming to tire. When his advice is asked, he is capable of coming across with some words of wisdom. He often knows what is bugging someone before that person is aware of it himself. It's almost intuitive with Pisceans, it seems.

Still, at the end of the day, this man will want some peace and quiet. If you've got a problem when he comes home, don't unload it in his lap. If you do, you are liable to find him short-tempered. He's a good listener but he can only take so much.

Pisceans are not aimless although they may seem so at times. The positive sort of Pisces man is quite often successful in his profession and is likely to wind up rich and influential. Material gain, however, is never a direct goal for a man born under this sign.

The weaker Pisces are usually content to stay on the level where they find themselves. They won't complain too much if the roof leaks or if the fence is in need of repair.

Because of their seemingly laissez-faire manner, people under this sign—needless to say—are immensely popular with children. For tots they play the double role of confidant and playmate. It will never enter the mind of a Pisces to discipline a child, no matter how spoiled or incorrigible that child becomes.

Man—Woman

SAGITTARIUS MAN
ARIES WOMAN

The Aries woman is quite a charmer. When she tugs at the strings of your heart, you'll know it. She's a woman who's in search of a knight in shining armor. She is a very particular person with very high ideals. She won't accept anyone but the man of her dreams.

The Aries woman never plays around with passion; she means business when it comes to love.

Don't get the idea that she's a dewy-eyed Miss. She isn't. In fact, she can be pretty practical and to-the-point when she wants. She's a girl with plenty of drive and ambition. With an Aries woman behind you, you are liable to go far in life. She knows how to help her man get ahead. She's full of wise advice; you only have to ask. In some cases, the Aries woman has a keen business sense; many of them become successful career women. There is nothing backward or retiring about her. She is equipped with a good brain and she knows how to use it.

Your union with her could be something strong, secure, and romantic. If both of you have your sights fixed in the same direction, there is almost nothing that you could not accomplish.

The Aries woman is proud and capable of being quite jealous. While you're with her, never cast your eye in another woman's direction. It could spell disaster for your relationship. The Aries woman won't put up with romantic nonsense when her heart is at stake.

If the Aries woman backs you up in your business affairs, you can be sure of succeeding. However, if she only is interested in advancing her own career and puts her interests before yours, she can be sure to rock the boat. It will put a strain on the relationship. The over-ambitious Aries woman can be a pain in the neck and make you forget that you were in love with her once.

The cultivated Aries woman makes a wonderful wife and mother. She has a natural talent for homemaking. With a pot of paint and some wallpaper, she can transform the dreariest domicile into an abode of beauty and snug comfort. The perfect hostess—even when friends just happen by—she knows how to make guests feel at home.

You'll also admire your Arien because she knows how to stand on her own two feet. Hers is an independent nature. She won't break down and cry when things go wrong, but will pick herself up and try to patch up matters.

The Aries woman makes a fine, affectionate mother.

SAGITTARIUS MAN
TAURUS WOMAN

The woman born under the sign of Taurus may lack a little of the sparkle and bubble you often like to find in a woman. The Taurus woman is generally down-to-earth and never flighty. It's important to her that she keep both feet flat on the ground. She is not fond of bounding all over the place, especially if she's under the impression that there's no profit in it.

On the other hand, if you hit it off with a Taurus woman, you won't be disappointed in the romance area. The Taurus woman is all woman and proud of it, too. She can be very devoted and loving once she decides that her relationship with you is no fly-by-night romance. Basically, she's a passionate person. In sex, she's direct and to-the-point. If she really loves you, she'll let you know she's yours—and without reservations.

Better not flirt with other women once you've committed yourself to her. She's capable of being very jealous and possessive.

She'll stick by you through thick and thin. It's almost certain that if the going ever gets rough, she won't go running home to her mother. She can adjust to the hard times just as graciously as she can to the good times.

Taureans are, on the whole, pretty even-tempered. They like to be treated with kindness. Pretty things and soft objects make them purr like kittens.

You may find her a little slow and deliberate. She likes to be safe and sure about everything. Let her plod along if she likes;

don't coax her, but just let her take her own sweet time. Everything she does is done thoroughly and, generally, without mistakes.

Don't deride her for being a slow-poke. It could lead to flying pots and pans and a fireworks display that could put Bastille Day to shame. The Taurus woman doesn't anger readily but when prodded often enough, she's capable of letting loose with a cyclone of ill-will. If you treat her with kindness and consideration, you'll have no cause for complaint.

The Taurean loves doing things for her man. She's a whiz in the kitchen and can whip up feasts fit for a king if she thinks they'll be royally appreciated. She may not fully understand you, but she'll adore you and be faithful to you if she feels you're worthy of it.

The Taurus woman makes a wonderful mother. She knows how to keep her children well-loved, cuddled, and warm. She may have some difficult times with them when they reach adolescence, though.

SAGITTARIUS MAN
GEMINI WOMAN

You may find a romance with a woman born under the sign of the Twins a many splendoured thing. In her you can find the intellectual companionship you often look for in a friend or mate. A Gemini girl friend can appreciate your aims and desires because she travels pretty much the same road as you do intellectually . . . that is, at least part of the way. She may share your interests but she will lack your tenacity.

She suffers from itchy feet. She can be here, there . . . all over the place and at the same time, or so it would seem. Her eagerness to move about may make you dizzy, still you'll enjoy and appreciate her liveliness and mental agility.

Geminians often have sparkling personalities; you'll be attracted by her warmth and grace. While she's on your arm you'll probably notice that many male eyes are drawn to her—she may even return a gaze or two, but don't let that worry you. All women born under this sign have nothing against a harmless flirt once in a while. They enjoy this sort of attention; if the Gemini feels she is already spoken for, however, she will never let such attention get out of hand.

Although she may not be as handy as you'd like in the kitchen, you'll never go hungry for a filling and tasty meal. The Gemini girl is always in a rush; she won't feel like she's cheating by breaking out the instant mashed potatoes or the frozen peas. She may not be much of a good cook but she is clever; with a dash of this and a suggestion of that, she can make an uninteresting TV dinner taste like something out of a Jim Beard cookbook. Then, again, maybe you've struck it rich and have a Gemini girl friend who finds complicated recipes a challenge to her intellect. If so, you'll find every meal a tantalizing and mouth-watering surprise.

When you're beating your brains out over the Sunday crossword puzzle and find yourself stuck, just ask your Gemini girl; she'll give you all the right answers without batting an eyelash.

Like you, she loves all kinds of people. You may even find that you're a bit more particular than she. Often all that a Geminian requires is that her friends be interesting . . . and stay interesting. One thing she's not able to abide is a dullard.

Leave the party-organizing to your Gemini sweetheart or mate and you'll never have a chance to know a dull moment. She'll bring out the swinger in you if you give her half the chance.

A Gemini mother enjoys her children. Like them, she's often restless, adventurous, and easily bored.

SAGITTARIUS MAN
CANCER WOMAN

If you fall in love with a Cancer woman, be prepared for anything. The Cancerian is sometimes difficult to understand when it comes to love. In one hour, she can unravel a whole gamut of emotions that will leave you in a tizzy. She'll undoubtedly keep you guessing.

You may find her a little too uncertain and sensitive for your liking. You'll most likely spend a good deal of time encouraging her—helping her to erase her foolish fears. Tell her she's a living doll a dozen times a day and you'll be well loved in return.

Be careful of the jokes you make when in her company—don't let any of them revolve around her, her personal interests, or her family. If you do, you'll most likely reduce her to tears. She can't stand being made fun of. It will take bushels of roses and tons of chocolates—not to mention the apologies—to get her to come back out of her shell.

In matters of money-managing, she may not easily come around to your way of thinking. Money will never burn a hole in her pocket. You may get the notion that your Cancerian sweetheart or mate is a direct descendent of Scrooge. If she has her way, she'll hang onto that first dollar you earned. She's not only that way with money, but with everything right on up from bakery string to jelly jars. She's a saver; she never throws anything away, no matter how trivial.

Once she returns your "I love you," you'll find you have an affectionate, self-sacrificing, and devoted woman on your hands. Her love for you will never alter unless you want it to. She'll put you high upon a pedestal and will do everything—even if it's against your will—to keep you up there.

Cancer women love homelife. For them, marriage is an easy step. They're domestic with a capital D. The Cancerian will do her best to make your home comfortable and cozy. She, herself, is more at ease at home than anywhere else. She makes an excellent hostess. The best in her comes out when she is in her own environment.

Cancer women make the best mothers. Each will consider every complaint of her child a major catastrophe. With her, children always come first. If you're lucky, you'll run a close second. You'll perhaps see her as too devoted to the children. You may have a hard time convincing her that her apron strings are a little too tight.

SAGITTARIUS MAN
LEO WOMAN

If you can manage a girl who likes to kick up her heels every now and again, then the Leo woman was made for you. You'll have to learn to put away jealous fears when you take up with a woman born under this sign, as she's often the kind that makes heads turn and tongues wag. You don't necessarily have to believe any of what you hear—it's most likely just jealous gossip or wishful thinking.

The Leo girl has more than a fair share of grace and glamour. She knows it, generally, and knows how to put it to good use. Needless to say, other women in her vicinity turn green with envy and will try anything short of shoving her into the nearest lake in order to put her out of the running.

If she's captured your heart and fancy, woo her full-force—if your intention is eventually to win her. Shower her with expensive gifts and promise her the moon—if you're in a position to go that far—then you'll find her resistance beginning to weaken. It's not that she's such a difficult cookie—she'll probably make a lot over you once she's decided you're the man for her—but she does enjoy a lot of attention. What's more, she feels she's entitled to it. Her mild arrogance, however, is becoming. The Leo woman knows how to transform the crime of excessive pride into a very charming misdemeanor. It sweeps most men—or rather, all men—right off their feet. Those who do not succumb to her leonine charm are few and far between.

If you've got an important business deal to clinch and you have doubts as to whether you can bring it off as you should, take your Leo wife along to the business luncheon and it'll be a cinch that you'll have that contract—lock, stock, and barrel—in your pocket before the meeting is over. She won't have to say or do anything . . . just be there at your side. The grouchiest oil magnate can be transformed into a gushing, obedient schoolboy if there's a Leo woman in the room.

If you're rich and want to see to it that you stay that way, don't give your Leo spouse a free hand with the charge accounts and credit cards. When it comes to spending, Leo tend to overdo. If you're poor, you have no worries because the luxury-loving Leo will most likely never recognize your existence—let alone, consent to marry you.

As a mother, she's both strict and easy. She can pal around with her children and still see to it that they know their places. She won't spoil them but she'll be a loving and devoted parent.

SAGITTARIUS MAN
VIRGO WOMAN

The Virgo woman may be a little too difficult for you to understand at first. Her waters run deep. Even when you think you know her, don't take any bets on it. She's capable of keeping things hidden in the deep recesses of her womanly soul—things she'll only release when she's sure that you're the man she's been looking for. It may take her some time to come around to this decision. Virgo girls are finnicky about almost everything; everything has to be letter-perfect before they're satisfied. Many of them have the idea that the only people who can do things right are Virgos.

Nothing offends a Virgo woman more than slovenly dress, sloppy character, or a careless display of affection. Make sure your tie is not crooked and that your shoes sport a bright shine before you go calling on this lady. Keep your off-color jokes for the locker room; she'll have none of that. Take her arm when crossing the street. Don't rush the romance. Trying to corner her in the back of a cab may be one way of striking out. Never criticize the way she looks—in fact, the best policy would be to agree with her as much as possible. Still, there's just so much a man can take; all those dos and don'ts you'll have to observe if you want to get to first base with a Virgo may be just a little too much to ask of you. After a few dates, you may come to the conclusion that she just isn't worth all that trouble. However, the Virgo woman is mysterious enough, generally speaking, to keep her men running back for more. Chances are you'll be intrigued by her airs and graces.

If lovemaking means a lot to you, you'll be disappointed at first in the cool ways of your Virgo girl. However, under her glacial facade there lies a hot cauldron of seething excitement. If you're patient and artful in your romantic approach, you'll find that all that caution was well worth the trouble. When Virgos love, they don't stint. It's all or nothing as far as they're concerned. Once they're convinced that they love you, they go all the way right off the bat—tossing all cares to the wind.

One thing a Virgo woman can't stand in love is hypocrisy. They don't give a hoot about what the neighbors say if their hearts tell them "Go ahead!" They're very concerned with human truths—so much so that if their hearts stumble upon another fancy, they're liable to be true to that new heartthrob and leave you standing in the rain. She's honest to her heart and will be as true to you as you are with her, generally. Do her wrong once, however, and it's farewell.

Both strict and tender, she tries to bring out the best in her children.

SAGITTARIUS MAN
LIBRA WOMAN

You'll probably find that the girl born under the sign of Libra is worth more than her weight in gold. She's a woman after your own heart.

With her, you'll always come first—make no mistake about that. She'll always be behind you 100 percent, no matter what you do. When you ask her advice about almost anything, you are likely to get a very balanced and realistic opinion. She is good at thinking things out and never lets her emotions run away with her when clear logic is called for.

As a homemaker she is hard to beat. She is very concerned with harmony and balance. You can be sure she'll make your house a joy to live in; she'll see to it that the home is tastefully furnished and decorated. A Libran cannot stand filth or disarray—it gives her goose-bumps. Anything that does not radiate harmony, in fact, runs against her orderly grain.

She is chock-full of charm and womanly ways. She can sweep just about any man off his feet with one winning smile. When it comes to using her brains, she can out-think almost anyone and, sometimes, with half the effort. She is diplomatic enough, though, never to let this become glaringly apparent. She may even turn the conversation around so that you think you were the one who did all the brain-work. She couldn't care less, really, just as long as you wind up doing what is right.

The Libra woman will put you up on a pretty high pedestal. You are her man and her idol. She'll leave all the decision-making—large or small—up to you. She's not interested in running things and will only offer her assistance if she feels you really need it.

Some find her approach to reason masculine; however, in the areas of love and affection the Libra woman is *all* woman. She'll literally shower you with love and kisses during your romance with her. She doesn't believe in holding out. You shouldn't, either, if you want to hang onto her.

She is the kind of girl who likes to snuggle up to you in front of the fire on chilly autumn nights . . . the kind of girl who will bring you breakfast in bed on Sunday. She'll be very thoughtful about anything that concerns you. If anyone dares suggest you're not the grandest guy in the world, she'll give that person what-for. She'll defend you till her dying breath. The Libra woman will be everything you want her to be.

She'll be a sensitive and loving mother. Still, you'll always come before the children.

SAGITTARIUS MAN
SCORPIO WOMAN

The Scorpio woman can be a whirlwind of passion—perhaps too much passion to really suit you. When her temper flies, you'd better lock up the family heirlooms and take cover. When she chooses to be sweet, you're apt to think that butter wouldn't melt in her mouth . . . but, of course, it would.

The Scorpio woman can be as hot as a *tamale* or as cool as a cucumber, but whatever mood she's in, she's in it for real. She does not believe in posing or putting on airs.

The Scorpio woman is often sultry and seductive—her femme fatale charme can pierce through the hardest of hearts like a laser ray. She may not look like Mata Hari (quite often Scorpios resemble the tomboy next door) but once she's fixed you with her tantalizing eyes, you're a goner.

Life with the Scorpio woman will not be all smiles and smooth-sailing; when prompted, she can unleash a gale of venom. Generally, she'll have the good grace to keep family battles within the walls of your home. When company visits, she's apt to give the impression that married life with you is one great big joy-ride. It's just one of her ways of expressing her loyalty to you—at least in front of others. She may fight you tooth and nail in the confines of your living room, but at a ball or during an evening out, she'll hang onto your arm and have stars in her eyes.

Scorpio women are good at keeping secrets. She may even keep a few buried from you if she feels like it.

Never cross her up on even the smallest thing. When it comes to revenge, she's an eye-for-an-eye woman. She's not too keen on forgiveness—especially if she feels she's been wronged unfairly. You'd be well-advised not to give her any cause to be jealous, either. When the Scorpio woman sees green, your life will be made far from rosy. Once she's put you in the doghouse, you can be sure that you're going to stay there a while.

You may find life with a Scorpio woman too draining. Although she may be full of the old paprika, it's quite likely that she's not the kind of girl you'd like to spend the rest of your natural life with. You'd prefer someone gentler and not so hot-tempered . . . someone who can take the highs with the lows and not complain . . . someone who is flexible and understanding. A woman born under Scorpio can be heavenly, but she can also be the very devil when she chooses.

As a mother, a Scorpio is protective and encouraging.

SAGITTARIUS MAN
SAGITTARIUS WOMAN

You'll most likely never come across a more good-natured girl than the one born under the sign of Sagittarius. Generally, they're full of bounce and good cheer. Their sunny dispositions seem almost permanent and can be relied upon even on the rainiest of days.

Women born under this sign are almost never malicious. If ever they seem to be, it is only seeming. Sagittarians are often a little short on tact and say literally anything that comes into their pretty little heads—no matter what the occasion. Sometimes the words that tumble out of their mouths seem downright cutting and cruel. Still, no matter what the Sagittarian says, she means well. The Sagittarius woman is quite capable of losing some of her friends—and perhaps even some of yours—through a careless slip of the lip.

On the other hand, you are liable to appreciate her honesty and good intentions. To you, qualities of this sort play an important part in life. With a little patience and practice, you can probably help cure your Sagittarian of her loose tongue; in most cases, she'll give in to your better judgement and try to follow your advice to the letter.

Chances are, she'll be the outdoors type of girlfriend. Long hikes, fishing trips, and white-water canoeing will most likely appeal to her. She's a busy person; no one could ever call her a slouch. She sets great store in mobility. She won't sit still for one minute if she doesn't have to.

She is great company most of the time and, generally, lots of fun. Even if your buddies drop by for poker and beer, she won't have any trouble fitting in.

On the whole, she is a very kind and sympathetic woman. If she feels she's made a mistake, she'll be the first to call your attention to it. She's not afraid to own up to her own faults and short-comings.

You might lose your patience with her once or twice. After she's seen how upset her shortsightedness or tendency to blabber-mouth has made you, she'll do her best to straighten up.

The Sagittarius woman is not the kind who will pry into your business affairs. But she'll always be there, ready to offer advice if you need it.

The Sagittarius woman is seldom suspicious. Your word will almost always be good enough for her.

She is a wonderful and loving friend to her children.

SAGITTARIUS MAN
CAPRICORN WOMAN

If you are not a successful businessman or, at least, on your way to success, it's quite possible that a Capricorn woman will have no interest in entering your life. Generally speaking, she is a very se-curity-minded female; she'll see to it that she invests her time only in sure things. Men who whittle away their time with one unsuc-cessful scheme or another, seldom attract a Capricorn. Men who are interested in getting somewhere in life and keep their noses close to the grindstone quite often have a Capricorn woman behind them, helping them to get ahead.

Although she is a kind of "climber," she is not what you could call cruel or hard-hearted. Beneath that cool, seemingly calculating, exterior, there's a warm and desirable woman. She just happens to think that it is just as easy to fall in love with a rich or ambitious man as it is with a poor or lazy one. She's prac-tical.

The Capricorn woman may be keenly interested in rising to the top, but she'll never be aggressive about it. She'll seldom step on someone's feet or nudge competitors away with her elbows. She's quiet about her desires. She sits, waits, and watches. When an opening or opportunity does appear, she'll latch onto it lickety-split. For an on-the-move man, an ambitious Capricorn wife or girlfriend can be quite an asset. She can probably give you some very good advice about business matters. When you invite the boss and his wife for dinner, she'll charm them both right off the ground.

The Capricorn woman is thorough in whatever she does: cooking, cleaning, making a success out of life . . . Capricorns make excellent hostesses as well as guests. Generally, they are very well-mannered and gracious, no matter what their backgrounds are. They seem to have a built-in sense of what is right. Crude behavior or a careless faux-pas can offend them no end.

If you should marry a woman born under Capricorn, you need never worry about her going on a wild shopping spree. Capricorns are careful with every cent that comes into their hands. They understand the value of money better than most women and have no room in their lives for careless spending.

The Capricorn girl is usually very fond of family—her own, that is. With her, family ties run very deep. Don't make jokes about her relatives; she won't stand for it. You'd better check her family out before you get down on bended knee; after your marriage you'll undoubtedly be seeing a lot of them.

Capricorn mothers train their children to be polite and kind.

SAGITTARIUS MAN
AQUARIUS WOMAN

If you find that you've fallen head over heels for a woman born under the sign of the Water Bearer, you'd better fasten your safety belt. It may take you quite a while actually to discover what this girl is like—and even then, you may have nothing to go on but a string of vague hunches. The Aquarian is like a rainbow, full of bright and shining hues; she's like no other girl you've ever known. There is something elusive about her—something delightfully mysterious. You'll most likely never be able to put your finger on it. It's nothing calculated, either; Aquarians don't believe in phony charm.

There will never be a dull moment in your life with this Water Bearing woman; she seems to radiate adventure and magic. She'll most likely be the most open-minded and tolerant woman you've ever met. She has a strong dislike for injustice and prejudice. Narrow-mindedness runs against her grain.

She is very independent by nature and quite capable of shifting for herself if necessary. She may receive many proposals of marriage from all sorts of people without ever really taking them seriously. Marriage is a very big step for her; she wants to be sure she knows what she's getting into. If she thinks that it will seriously curb her independence and love of freedom, she's liable to shake her head and give the man his engagement ring back—if indeed she's let the romance get that far.

The line between friendship and romance is a pretty fuzzy one for an Aquarian. It's not difficult for her to remain buddy-buddy with an ex-lover. She's tolerant, remember? So, if you should see her on the arm of an old love, don't jump to any hasty conclusions.

She's not a jealous person herself and doesn't expect you to be, either. You'll find her pretty much of a free spirit most of the time. Just when you think you know her inside-out, you'll discover that you don't really know her at all, though.

She's a very sympathetic and warm person; she can be helpful to people in need of assistance and advice.

She'll seldom be suspicious even if she has every right to be. If she loves a man, she'll forgive him just about anything. If he allows himself a little fling, chances are she'll just turn her head the other way. Her tolerance does have its limits, however, and her man should never press his luck at hanky-panky.

She makes a big-hearted mother; her good qualities rub off on her children.

SAGITTARIUS MAN
PISCES WOMAN

Many a man dreams of a Piscean kind of girl. You're perhaps no exception. She's soft and cuddly—and very domestic. She'll let you be the brains of the family; she's contented to just lean on your shoulder and let you be the master of the household.

She can be very ladylike and proper. Your business associates and friends will be dazzled by her warmth and femininity. Although she's a charmer, there is a lot more to her than just a pretty exterior. There is a brain ticking away behind that soft, womanly facade. You may never become aware of it—that is, until you're married to her. It's no cause for alarm, however; she'll most likely never use it against you.

If she feels you're botching up your married life through careless behavior or if she feels you could be earning more money than you do, she'll tell you about it. But any wife would, really. She will never try to usurp your position as head and breadwinner of the family.

No one had better dare say an uncomplimentary word about you in her presence. It's liable to cause her to break into tears. Pisces women are usually very sensitive beings. Their reaction to adversity, frustration, or anger is just a plain, good, old-fashioned cry. They can weep buckets when so inclined.

She'll have an extra-special dinner prepared for you when you make a new conquest in your profession. Don't bother to go into details, though, at the dinner table; she doesn't have much of a head for business matters usually, and is only too happy to leave that up to you.

She can do wonders with a house. She is very fond of soft and beautiful things. There will always be plenty of fresh-cut flowers around the house. She'll see that you always have plenty of socks and underwear in that top drawer of your dresser.

Treat her with tenderness and generosity and your relationship will be an enjoyable one. She's most likely fond of chocolates. A bunch of beautiful flowers will never fail to make her eyes light up. See to it that you never forget her birthday or your anniversary. These things are very important to her. If you let them slip your mind, you'll send her into a crying fit that could last a considerable length of time. If you are patient and kind, you can keep a Pisces woman happy for a lifetime. She, however, is not without her faults. Her "sensitivity" may get on your nerves after a while; you may find her lacking in imagination and zest; you may even feel that she uses her tears as a method of getting her own way.

She makes a strong, self-sacrificing mother.

SAGITTARIUS

YEARLY FORECAST: 1991

*Forecast for 1991 Concerning Business
and Financial Matters, Job Prospects,
Travel, Health, Romance and Marriage
for Those Born with the Sun
in the Zodiacal Sign of Sagittarius
November 23–December 20.*

You people with Sagittarius for the home of your Sun are ever hopeful for the future, its prosperity and expanding prospects. Your ruling planet, Jupiter, endows you with these gifts. This year it is in a particularly helpful position to encourage you to fulfill yourself in ways that are typical, giving scope for your courage and undying optimism. Keeping options open, allowing yourself space to maneuver, seeking pastures newer and greener, these are the motivations that can ensure your progress and make life exciting. Travel on the grand scale can be of particular interest and meaning. As you widen your horizons, so will you be ever conscious that prestige and honor can be developed. The future matters a great deal, so you are conscious of the reputation you create for yourself during the year, and probably with more significance, the way you will be remembered many years from now historically. For you know that your name will live on. So you can be philosophic, futuristic and practical, all in one, to make this a year to remember. In the material sense, business should prosper hand in hand with your general feeling of hope and well-being. Some financial burdens or restrictions may be removed during the year as you change your priorities. You may find you have more scope to determine for yourself how to use your resources, and the need to be overly conservative can gradually disappear. It may be that you tend to concentrate more on ways and means of making satisfactory progress than on establishing a firm financial base, once you feel secure of your position.

It will be time to apply yourself to adopting firm techniques, establishing contacts and organizing your thinking with a view to future system and order that will last for some years. In consequence, contracts or liaisons made this year can be a structure upon which you can build, provided opportunities are accepted. Personal relationships can be of considerable importance. In a year when social status, ego and progress are all being urged to develop, you can be encouraged to share your hopes and good fortune in order to expand at double speed. Personal liberty does not necessarily mean doing it all alone. Your common sense will tell you that the future depends to a large extent on how you encourage others to cooperate and thus reach your target much sooner. This applies also to your career or business life as well as to the emotional and personal. You are by nature a friendly person, so have little difficulty in arousing any emotion you feel will help you in your contact with others. You can enthuse or banish when it suits your mood. With prospects glowing on the horizon, you are not likely to waste time on situations or people who do not match up to your standards. It is all the more reason why you may go for the main option and feel good about it.

Business success should form a large part of the overall picture of progress this year. It may evolve that things fall into place exactly as you would wish, apparently making life and social success a natural part of your development. This does not mean you can just sit and wait for renown to come to you. In your usual enthusiastic way you will be determined to try your luck and make an impact in numerous ways. The spirit of advantage can encourage you to seek business expansion. This could mean broadening your scope to take in overseas markets by setting up branches abroad. Much will depend on the way you go about this sort of expansion before mid-September. From that point on, you may be reaping the reward for your preparations and search for goodwill on a large scale. Recognition can come your way after September 12. Your advice or presence may be sought later as an inspiration to those who are seeking success. You also have the opportunity to diversify or look for the specialist market from this time. Do not be afraid to try a different approach or the unusual market.

After February 6 you may need to consider more seriously your public relations and advertising. The media will want to see the color of your money and may initially be cautious, if not hostile. Be sure you get facts straight, and cost this side of business carefully. Also be selective where you seek reliable support and service from the communications system. Rethinking can be a regular feature till you are quite satisfied. Between January 21 and April 2, look for advancement through partnership or direct dealing. It is a time for initiative; excitement and danger are possible if your judgment is awry. The period between August 23 and September 22 should be a key indication of how you are succeeding in your business or profession. Success and recognition should be apparent.

The desire to make progress can take your mind off financial affairs at times. In some respects, money matters, the correct use of resources, even the building up of funds, all can be a mixed bag. There are differing pressures, so different reasons apply as to why you should or should not do this or that with the means at hand. You may feel clearer in your thinking, or have paid a debt or cleared a backlog by the second week in February. Financial independence means a great deal and this change of conditions will ease pressure. From February 6 onward, more heavy expense can be expected. You need reliable advertising, establishment of local bases and links, purchase of transport, and necessary equipment. The day-to-day running costs go hand in hand with expanding responsibilities and interests. Investments, possibly foreign, can provide assets until September 11. Returns from expanding business can be better than outgoings. Between April 3 and May 25 you should be attentive to taxation, insurance or other such matters that are a strain on the exchequer. Do not be stampeded into hasty actions. The period between September 1 and October 15 may bring problems connected with funds that are not strictly your own. So do not do any financial dealings on hearsay. Friends can be a financial liability. After September 11, however, there is also more chance that you can benefit financially from promotion or salary increase.

If friends cause you some problems, you will not hold this as a grudge for long. In a more personal way, you may wish to consider the choice between enjoying greater freedom on your own or making life more interesting in the future through a lasting relationship. Involvement with people from afar, a desire to move abroad, or the simple need to look to the future and establish yourself, all can encourage you to break new ground, change the pattern of your life and settle down. No doubt you will enjoy the process of reaching this point, so will have your times of flirtation. Between January 5 and 28, life should be light, friendly and flirtatious. You will not want to be tied down. For some, there may be a homecoming or the establishment of a home, from January 29 to February 21. The period following this, up till about March 17, can be exciting and romantic, whether married or single. The realization of true commitment to a relationship may occur between April 13 and May 8. Another exciting period comes between June 6 and July 10. This is when romance can mean so much to the future, when you may appreciate the attraction of someone from afar or when traveling is combined with romance. The excitement may have died down between November 9 and December 5. By then you may be in a mood to be sociable without getting too deeply involved personally. Possibly you are more settled. If you remain single you could be a little skeptical during this late period.

Your attitude to life can play an important part in things functional. Health will have no hitches if you look to the future with optimism. There may be some desire to look over your shoulder, perhaps to be aware of precedent, or to have someone remind you of pitfalls rather than prevention. If you are in any situation where you are unhappy or feel restricted, break away from it when it is personally convenient. The ball is in your court if you will just accept the fact. Home life can be miserable if you feel your security is threatened. Family will notice and may remind you to be more positive. Pressure of work can be wearing if you allow it to be. A change of diet may be a help if you feel inclined that way.

Your attitude toward work can fluctuate. At the beginning of the year, for the first three weeks, you seem to be keen to get on with something and get it finished. If you start a new job, get into the routine with enthusiasm. You may need or get little free time. The reward for your efforts may be the main attraction as you are concerned at this early stage of the year in building up resources. After February 6 there may be less harmony among colleagues and fellow workers. Conditions may be the root cause. Discipline may be needed to keep up standards, or discipline may be imposed. This could cause you to look around for a better outlet for your time and talent. Up till September 11, some may be studying for higher qualifications, some can be learning a language with a view to working abroad or handling foreign labor. The more you learn, the wider your scope and potential in a competitive world. As it can be the year of opportunity, you are not likely to let the grass grow under your feet, nor to be content with grass that is less green than that over the fence. Between July 15 and August 31, you should be quite clear in your mind as to what you want from a job. This can bring to a head any dissatisfaction about remuneration or conditions of work. The end result can be more responsibility and probably more scope to use your initiative. During most of September you could impress superiors with your ability. So much depends on your foresight and sense of positive purpose. It is a year when you can truly come into your own.

DAILY FORECAST

January–December 1991

JANUARY

1. TUESDAY. Disconcerting. You could be counting the cost of early celebrations. A hangover is probable if you have overdone it. Take a brisk walk and clear your lungs. Work may seem attractive; so just for a change, do something that really extends you and gets the adrenaline flowing. Keep off the topic of money with a loved one. Your requests are likely to be denied if you push your luck with someone who is a little shy. Last-minute hitches concerning someone else's property can slow you down. Later in the day you will probably have more room to maneuver and could be thinking of making a short, return trip. Try to keep harmony until then, even though you are pressed.

2. WEDNESDAY. Lucky. Be optimistic. Refuse to look on the dark side of life. It's time to get your skates on and make a positive move. Traveling is definitely in the cards, so be sure of your destination and the object of the exercise. A relationship that has been rather suppressed of late can be charged up. You will feel like spending on the boy or girl of your dreams. There is method in your madness. Future planning should put you in a good frame of mind. You can be practical and make those vacation dreams come true if you visit the travel agency. There may be news of a promotion in the mail; or you hear about an improvement that will boost your income. Be sure to follow that up and keep close tabs on it.

3. THURSDAY. Mixed. Follow up on any romantic advantage. It's a case of making hay while the sun shines for some. Another flame may want to step in while your back is turned. Just keep your options open and don't take everything at face value. Progress can be achieved if you will make a genuine effort to express your opinion. You have the ability today to make your

127

point and have it understood. In-laws are important at this stage, so keep them as well informed of your plans as you think wise. This could counter any rumors or discontent that may otherwise be brewing. Only if you are negative will you have problems. So be of good cheer and concentrate on what the real issues are.

4. FRIDAY. Useful. Be like the three wise monkeys. Hear all, see all, know all, but say nothing! Superiors may have ideas that are difficult to fathom. Avoid rushing to conclusions as to their mental state. They could be on the ball and way ahead of their time. Don't be naive. Check facts, especially those connected with finance. Keep clear of doubtful deals that promise something for nothing. On the positive side, you may find that a parent or future in-law is ready and willing to see things your way. Look for the original outlet in business. Trust your insight. Modernize or improve your technique and encourage the enterprising to have their say. Don't feel satisfied with existing methods. Try to improve on them all the time.

5. SATURDAY. Productive. Avoid making snap decisions. It is better to think things through and take your time. Seek support from folks in the back room who keep the records. A private or secret get-together could work to your professional advantage. Ego can be shattered a bit by a careless comment or a personal mistake. So be practical and look after your job and your income. It's a good period for earning overtime or making a job on the side pay off. Look to the future. Immediate gains may be ephemeral, but that which is soundly based will eventually pay dividends. Show appreciation for staff who are prepared to work that extra bit. Your reputation could depend on the willing helper.

6. SUNDAY. Happy. Love may be right there on your doorstep. Don't travel too far in search of good company. The local talent is well above par. Time can be found for a project close to your heart. Aims can be realized. You may feel you have succeeded, but this may only be the start of a beautiful dream. There are better things to come. Neighbors should be more sociable than they have been of late. You could be glad to have someone popping in to lend a hand or a word of advice. Social activities should go with a swing. Good people give comfort and the feeling is reciprocal. Make the most of local contacts and run-of-the-mill relationships. Something rather special may be emerging.

7. MONDAY. Misleading. Be careful who you call a friend. Misjudgments will probably be your own fault. But you may try to unload blame on someone who is really trying too hard to please. But keep an open mind. Look for any advantage for making progress, because it is there. You may be tempted to take financial advice from someone who is really not on the ball. In all fairness, you are better following your own inclinations and not looking for any favors from those in positions of authority. Overseas business could be more profitable than home-based kind. Look for outlets in this direction. There may be some fiddling of accounts or expenses. If you are responsible for finances, keep your eyes and ears open.

8. TUESDAY. Disturbing. You could be feeling rather sorry for yourself today. There will be a good reason for doubts, so cheer up and make friends again. Someone may be moving away from the neighborhood. Remember the value of true friendship. Long-term plans may seem to be threatened. This could be a passing phase, so do not jump to conclusions or throw in the towel. It is time to consolidate. If you cannot make progress, at least you should not go into retreat. Whatever you do, do not bear a grudge. Quite naturally, you could be a bit more cynical than usual. This should not cloud your judgment, but it could lose friends for you today. So watch your step and try to put things in perspective.

9. WEDNESDAY. Uncertain. Keep your business affairs well hidden. There may be someone around looking for business secrets. Foreign competition may be worrying you. Just file that problem for a little while and concentrate on more favorable ways for making money fast. An unexpected revelation can put you in the right position to make a financial gain. Trust your feelings or intuition. Something, you may well feel, could be developing. Publicity at this stage will be harmful. So look out for those who would let the cat out of the bag. Put off an overseas journey. Charity begins at home. Lend a helping hand to someone in need, or join a charitable organization.

10. THURSDAY. Useful. Your feelings of yesterday could be confirmed. Family or kinship links can be very meaningful. You could be looking into your family tree. Advantage can be gained through someone with influence in the banking or financial world. A loan could be arranged to make a private purchase more easy. You are only too well aware of responsibilities, but know you have things under control. Something may have to be revealed today. It may be instigated by you or it may give you a sense of relief. Be glad that you have the understanding to cope with something others may find to be too much. A little humility will gain you a lot of respect, but don't go too far or the effect will be the opposite.

11. FRIDAY. Fortunate.   The ball is in your court today. Make the most of your charm. There is a possibility that someone is going to catch your eye. It will be a mutual attraction that could go a long way. Just relax and you'll find things are starting to happen. Pleasant neighbors are an asset when you have a lot of personal matters to handle. A child-minder can take a load off your shoulders. There may be news of a wedding among your relatives or colleagues. The invitation comes at the right time and you can fit it in nicely. Daily routine goes with a swing. If you are a bit on the romantic side the day will pass quickly. There could be a date to keep this evening and you are feeling good.

12. SATURDAY. Easygoing.   There will be a lot to keep you busy at the weekend. A journey could take you away from local surroundings. You have to be up and doing early if you hope to make it. Once things are moving, you should be able to stand back and admire your handiwork. Then it's back to essentials, and to pay attention to all those things you've left hanging fire for the previous week. Personal matters are by far the most important things today. Not till you get your own house in order can you afford to branch out or make any proposals. Give your opinion only when asked. This is something you seldom refuse, but you may not be volunteering advice. You have other things to do.

13. SUNDAY. Mixed.   It could be a stay-at-home kind of day. Plans made earlier may have to be canceled. Avoid getting too deeply involved with someone attractive who lives at a distance. It may be that a romantic outing keeps you apart. This could be a for a good reason, though you may not think so at the time. Something needs to be said. Whether or not you are asked, you will want to get something very personal sorted out. Direct action in an emergency may be needed. Get on with a job you have to do and don't talk too much. If you need to make your point, there is no need to waffle. No doubt your sharp tongue will raise a few hackles. You are unlikely to notice this till something you want is refused. So be careful in asking or giving favors.

14. MONDAY. Confusing.   Bright ideas to make money can be off target. This should not stop you from making plans. The main thing is to leave the action till later and allow the dreams and ideas to mature. You'll meet someone else today with all the answers. Honesty will pay off, but it may seem to you a rather odd way.

Romantic interests seem to be paramount. You are possibly getting bored and would like a change. Consider all offers, therefore, and don't be too hasty in your judgments. Someone really attractive is likely to come your way, so enough of the daydreaming. Get on the ball. Investment in electrical goods may appeal to you if you have some spare money to put to work. You might hit a winner.

15. TUESDAY. Erratic. It's a great day to take the bull by the horns. Responsibility is likely to come your way. Be positive and take the lead. If you refuse the opportunity you could regret it. You seem to have considerable endurance and a strong desire to work. This may be more and more obvious as the day wears on. Be considerate in your handling of affairs, particularly those involving money. Some may think you are heavy-handed or far too bossy. Cooperate with someone influential if this is necessary. A positive move will have to be made some time during the day. See that you are in on the action, not being led. It depends on your attitude as to whether you are successful or a stick-in-the-mud.

16. WEDNESDAY. Inactive. Take a breather. Decisions made yesterday may need to be followed up with more detailed attention. This may be a part of your routine, or you may leave it to others. Get in the mood to look ahead. Late in the day you may be called upon to make a decision or weigh up possibilities. A little time for reflection or getting to know the basic facts may help you come to a satisfactory conclusion. Someone from a distance may be trying to get in touch all day. If you have communication problems it may be better to wait till after business hours to be at your best. Stick to routine and you'll find things will work out. After all, you have to allow a bit of time for developments, so don't be impatient.

17. THURSDAY. Changeable. Be charming and affable. Don't let others think you are anything else. There could be an undercurrent of jealousy building up near you, but you should not get obviously upset. If you have to, make your own private inquiries about something that may be bothering you. Remember that a great deal depends on your ability to make people happy and to keep up appearances. So be prepared to take the rough with the smooth. Friends or neighbors should be very helpful if you have a moment of need. A relationship should blossom if you are prepared to play your part. Rumors could make life a bit difficult.

18. FRIDAY. Difficult. Your boss may be hard to find. A restriction could be placed on your earnings or earning power. Be careful how you react to proposals made to you today. Look after your health if you are doing manual or difficult work. Temper can rule and you may be in the mood to overreach yourself or to let things fly. Consider what the potential cost may be and remember that someone at the top is not in a very forgiving frame of mind. If you need more money, listen carefully to what your bank manager has to say. There is little going to be offered without collateral. It's up to you to make yourself a safe proposition. Be constructive, but also conservative, in using your energy.

19. SATURDAY. Enjoyable. There may be more money to spend on the home. Whatever you get up to around the home, do it with a will. You could be on the go bright and early. Advance planning will now pay off. There is some need to look to the artistic things of life. This would be a good day to write a sonnet or mail a love letter. Visitors to your home or apartment may find you in a relaxed mood. You need gentle and understanding company. Something connected with drapes or decor is likely to catch your eye. Musical interest can be stirred or you may be having thoughts that take you far away from your present surroundings. Perhaps you have plans or ideas for a domestic move and see something that appeals.

20. SUNDAY. Excellent. It may seem that the best things in life are not free. Get your sense of values in good trim. There may be a family get together on something important. Responsible actions are called for. Material conditions should be good. There should be indications of getting a square deal in whatever you do. Outdoor activity can get you into trim. Practical jobs should give added pleasure as you are aware of the possibilities that lie ahead. Adventurous and influential people may find their way to your home over the weekend. Use your judgment as well as your natural charm in making them welcome without showing that you hope they will be useful. It's a day to be practical, above all else.

21. MONDAY. Useful. Progress will be made if you are positive. Too many people may try to interfere in your affairs and make life difficult if you do not assert yourself. This will not be a day to be too concerned with money. Avoid dealing in such matters as your mind could well be on other more important things. Penny-pinching types may try to influence you and you'll be in no mood to negotiate. Look ahead over the long term. This is a year with great future potential that you will readily recognize. Creative talents are much more important at this stage than the expected material reward for their use. A true Sagittarius, your hopes, dreams and ambition need an ever adventurous mind.

22. TUESDAY. Exciting. Be lighthearted today! Make the most of your romantic chances. Be friendly and accommodating because you have nothing to lose and a lot to gain by being generous. Those interests that turn you on should be furthered. The young are to your liking. You may feel as young as you care to today, as age is really no problem. Children will generally try to please and you will be inclined to respond in a positive manner. Decide to spend if you want to please a loved one. There may be an offer made to you that you will find hard to refuse. A vacation can be decided upon, or you could have a day off in order to keep a promise to someone you love. Let things go with a swing.

23. WEDNESDAY. Difficult. Stick to routine. Do not get on your high horse or you could be in trouble. Be careful or philosophic about meeting old friends you haven't seen for a while. At some stage you are likely to go one step too far. That could mean the company you keep will decide whether you make it or are left to your own devices. There could be local problems early in the day. Take note of the observations of those in authority, even though you may feel they are taking it a bit too far. Left to your own devices, you may find you are still out on a limb and unable to focus properly. There could be a need to work something through to see if it's all that it is cracked up to be.

24. THURSDAY. Demanding. Put your best foot forward. Relationship problems can leave you out of sorts or at a loss. This will pass, so don't take life too seriously. It may be necessary to look after someone who is under the weather. Do this with a good heart. If you resent being pinned down, try to be philosophic. See to it that what you do in the line of duty is amply rewarded. At the same time, you must not become overly materialistic. Rumors can be spread quickly through the so-called bush telegraph. Things are in your favor, so don't be misled by scaremongers. It may be necessary to break a romantic appointment because of the call of duty or possibly of ill health. You may be looking for an excuse, so don't be surprised if someone pulls a fast one on you.

25. FRIDAY. Uncertain. Consider carefully the views of others. You cannot get away with some things today, even if you feel in the mood to fight. Positive action needs to be practiced in a diplomatic way. Look for the cooperation of people who matter. This applies particularly in the field of publicity or advertising. It would be better for you to be seen with the right people, or have the right contacts than for you yourself to advertise what you are. Understanding the opposition is all-important. You can expand if you have the feel of the situation, but will antagonize if you are too keen to make progress. Analyze everything well before you commit yourself to a decision. It will pay off.

26. SATURDAY. Tricky. Keep away from money transactions. Shopping can be a misery. You may be tempted to buy a pig in a poke. There are thieves abounding in the markets and shopping malls, so look after your purse or wallet. It is essential you think about others. This could make you aware of your own plight if you are feeling lonely. Don't try to kid yourself or anyone else. You know very well that a bit of peace to meditate is essential, so why get yourself in a tizzy when friends appear to let you down? There may be someone playing with your affections. Accept the fact. What is to be will be, and you may be better off doing your own thing. If you can come to terms with yourself, that is the first step up the ladder to a happier future.

27. SUNDAY. Useful. Keep out of the limelight while you have the chance. Look after family affairs and see that your dependents sample a bit of your life for a change. Time should be taken to sort out marital or joint problems. Remember you have some responsibilities that must be shouldered. A natural break such as this gives you time and space to catch up on many lost things, possibly sleep for one. Your partner will want to have a say in whatever is going on. There are potential pitfalls or temptations ahead and you should jointly be briefed for the future. Do a bit of digging or investigation if you feel you are being kept in the dark. Prepare yourself for hitches that are sure to materialize.

28. MONDAY. Misleading. Do not let the left hand know what the right is doing. It's one of those days when you can be a cheat or be cheated. So start off feeling you must be one-up on the opposition. Be prepared for sudden switches. Again, you should be prepared to initiate rather than respond; but if you are at the wrong end, just keep cool and use your intuition. Try to avoid showing your hand. More will be gained by private or clandestine arrangements than by open dealing. Nothing is what it appears at first hand, and you yourself could be putting on an act. Publishing or advertising is not in the cards at the moment. The top brass is looking for too much. Wait your time and confound the critics.

29. TUESDAY. Sensitive. All that glitters is not gold. High hopes can founder on the whim of a superior. Make your plans well in advance if you are to succeed. Be progressive in your thinking and in your attitude toward business and life in general. People with a narrow outlook will try hard to confound you. You have a moral issue to settle today and should listen to your heart. Others cannot help when it is a question of right and wrong. A partner could hold the key to the solution. Do not mind if he or she wants to take the initiative. You could learn something and benefit at the same time. A legal problem can be straightened out quickly. Marriage prospects are rosier, once you clear the air.

30. WEDNESDAY. Disconcerting. Try not to be ineffective or too casual. A good relationship could end up on the rocks if you get your values mixed. Marriage can be having its ups and downs. There is little hope of getting any agreement on home repairs or renewing curtains and household fittings. Be a bit more patient if you are to sort out basic problems. In-laws may not be very helpful. There could be rumors circulating that are a bit below the belt. Just bide your time and do not stir up trouble in the home. If you try too hard you can upset the apple cart, just as easily as you can by being noncommittal. It's a bit of a dilemma, but time will tell and it will be all right in the end.

31. THURSDAY. Confusing. Get your priorities right. If business calls, you should make it clear to your family that this is so. A reliable assistant may have to leave. The post will be difficult to fill, so you may be in a state of confusion for a little while. Remember to inform your partner if you plan to make changes. A delay at the office should be quickly passed on to those who may be waiting for your return home. It should be frustrating for you to make things easy for others when you are keen to make progress. This is one of the penalties you must accept with partnership and family responsibilities. Even if you are single, you should be sure you are not locked out if you are late in coming back to home base.

FEBRUARY

1. FRIDAY. Successful. Take control effectively. You will not be accused of wielding the big stick if you play your cards right. Sensitive methods will produce profits for you. Someone may admire you and this will boost your ego. Quite a lot can be achieved in private and you will come up smelling like roses. Take advice from the so-called back room to keep ahead of your competitors. Lessons of the past can stand you in good stead. Unorthodox methods should not be discounted. Be a bit adventurous with your personal funds if you feel you're on to a good thing. It does not suit you to vegetate and a little flutter could liven up the day. You may have to be the front person. It will do you no harm.

2. SATURDAY. Happy. Consolidate a gain before it slips away. Make a firm booking for a date or appointment. Funds can be increased considerably if you use a bit of common sense or foresight. Business should take priority in the morning. Later on however, you will know you have earned a break and can let your hair down. Someone older can have a good influence on you today. Don't judge everyone by appearances. Many a kind heart beats under a frosty outer cover. Joint interests are likely to be stimulated later in the day. This would be a good time to have a night out at a show or social gathering. Your partner seems to be full of beans and will probably alert you to your potential.

3. SUNDAY. Sensitive. A total lack of energy could keep you indoors all day. Two nights of very active and late entertainment may be a bit too much and you may be feeling a bit the worse for wear. It is a day, perhaps, when you could be taking stock of your assets. Pay attention to the boys and gals who cry poverty. If you feel like being sociable, keep well away from those so-called friends who are interested in you only as long as you pay the bills. At some point today you are likely to see through a con trick. A well-known personality of your neighborhood is likely to drop in for a chat. It is time you were getting to know the right people if you want to have a successful year. It could be a case of who you know, not what.

4. MONDAY. Frustrating. A tricky situation can have you in a spin. When in doubt, sign nothing. The small print on any contract involving money should be read carefully and even questioned. Avoid dealings with slick salesmen on the doorstep. Neither should you assume you are too clever, because there are many tricks of the trade that can still fool you. Someone in your circle of friends may be in trouble. Give practical help, but set your limits. Something dear to your heart may be disallowed or you may begin to lose heart. This is the time to stiffen your resolution, not to give in. Your day will come in due course. What is worth having is worth waiting for. But you could try to speed its arrival.

5. TUESDAY. Mixed. Remain on your guard when dealing with contracts. Something of a long-term nature should be thoroughly scrutinized before any decision is made one way or the other. Nevertheless, you may feel you are on firmer ground now. Someone will have romantic ideas about setting up home. You may be involved in brightening up your apartment before doing a bit of home entertaining. Private affairs mean a lot. Inside information can put you on to a winner with long odds or you could get an investment tip that pays off. Be careful about advice from people who have a lot to say. You must be careful to whom you talk or personal secrets will come to light. In-laws could get on your nerves if you see them too often.

6. WEDNESDAY. Demanding. Your sense of justice can be offended. It is better at this stage to be a live coward and not a dead hero or heroine. Things may seem to be stacked against you. If you have a difference of opinion with the law, try to moderate your language or attitude. Authority seems to be in no mood to be patient or tolerant. Penalties will grow rather than fade away if you persist. It may be very difficult to get rid of a persistent person who canvasses in your district. Don't put up with such pestering; just stand your ground. A parent may be having a hard time. Your charitable deeds may go unnoticed, but this should not bother you. Only a fool would give in, so be brave and carry on for a bit longer.

7. THURSDAY. Productive. Money can be well spent on brightening up the home. You have things to do and places to go. Friendly neighbors can cooperate or help. In-laws also seem to be in a positive and cheerful frame of mind. A journey should give pleasure as well as opportunity for better things ahead. Your partner has positive ideas. If there is no possibility of agreement, let experiment prove the point. It would be better to practice seeing and believing than just to stand there arguing. Share and

share alike could be the sensible order of the day. You could have
a pleasant surprise when a property or antique is valued. Now you
have to decide whether to realize an asset or hang on to it!

8. FRIDAY. Frustrating. Be careful how you tread at home. If
you live in lodgings, you could have a rough time. Try to make the
best of it if accommodations are hard to come by. But if you are
fed up with your rooms, look around till you find something
better. A lack of know-how could inhibit you. Exaggerated emotions are more upsetting than no feelings at all. You may find you
want to be on your own, away from emotional trauma. You really
need a lot of time to do your own thing and to think for yourself. If
you feel your security is being threatened, do something about it.
Dependence on others is not your thing just now. You need
breathing space and freedom to think and act for yourself.

9. SATURDAY. Erratic. Applaud your partner for positive
thinking. If you cannot make headway, at least you can admire
someone near you who does not let the grass grow underfoot. The
voice of authority may try to put you down. Use your wits and get
around official red tape. Local by-laws can be a problem. You
must use means other than the official channels to get things done.
Something big could be brewing in the locality. Keep clear of
influential people who could be involved. You could unwittingly
be tarred with a sticky brush. Joint action taken in open good faith
will salvage whatever has to be saved. A legal document can be
signed willingly. Good publicity is there for the asking.

10. SUNDAY. Changeable. It could be difficult to settle for
one course of action. The love of family may solve the problem.
Comfort can be a strong but gentle persuader. Travel plans are
likely to be shattered for you may lose interest. Should you have to
leave for foreign parts, there will have to be extra-special reasons.
An eccentric friend may choose to call today. Once you've got
over the surprise you will be glad of the interruption. A love match
in the family circle may be coming to light. There seems to be a
desire to promote this, so everyone could be on their best behavior
for the weekend. A break from college and studies will do you
good. You may gain a broader perspective at a distance.

11. MONDAY. Rewarding. Get organized early on finances. A
transfer of funds may be worthwhile. Reserves should not be
allowed to lie idle too long. Loving thoughts may move you to give
someone dear a gift. Conversely, you could be the lucky recipient.
High ideals are to be shared with those you rely upon most

lovingly. There is a soft side to your nature that is readily on tap today; and some folks may find difficulty in recognizing it. Charitable instincts can be easily aroused. Thoughts of the past can make you do something you will not regret. You have a long memory and will have learned from past experience. Today you are in a position to put ideas into practice.

12. TUESDAY. Productive. Be firm in all you do. Enthusiasm can rub off on a partner. Legalities can be used to advantage, especially in the interests of expansion. An opportunity to develop a family business should be accepted, with time allowed for further investigation of assets. Make the most of local contacts. This could be a day to come to satisfactory terms with a local advertiser or media outlet. Look to the future. Do not sell yourself cheaply. Maintain standards that will be seen as a hallmark of the future. If you are accused of taking life too seriously you will know that someone is taking notice. While this may be apparent to some, others will see that you also know a good thing when you see it.

13. WEDNESDAY. Successful. Relatives seem glad to have you around. Look after the little things and you won't go short on the bigger ones. Past prudence will pay off today as you see growth developing at the grass roots. Something could be annoying you. You could have a longing for something and not be satisfied till you get it. After that, of course, you'll probably wonder why you made such a song and dance about it! Correspondence is important. Keep your ear to the ground for snippets of news or information. If you are in the media professionally, this could be a day to remember. Advertise yourself. See that your observations are noted and be well prepared for any opportunity to give an opinion.

14. THURSDAY. Buoyant. Be self-assured. You can impress because you know this is a day when great things can happen. Something important is likely to take off. You will not want to hide your light, so should take full advantage of publicity which could put you on the spot. Love has a particular significance. This can mean marriage for some, an engagement with parental approval or the securing of your first home. Be happy to be happy, for on this depends your security. Private property deals should be worthwhile. You may take up a post of some importance in your locality and be glad traveling is cut out for a while. Conduct an interview or be interviewed with every confidence.

15. FRIDAY. Mixed. It may be difficult to please a partner. Business matters may have to be ironed out legally if you cannot avoid wrangling. Try to avoid upsetting your spouse or closest intimate over something that could be quite petty. When security is threatened, things get blown up out of proportion. Tempers can become frayed. Take your fair share of domestic chores if peace in the home means anything to you. You may be preoccupied with new ideas. Be patient with your loved ones who will not know what you have in mind unless you spill the beans. Be adventurous if you can see a way to make a profit. Being ahead will suit you. Go it alone if colleagues are too timid to have a go.

16. SATURDAY. Exciting.   Success is yours today. There could be the sound of wedding bells or of a key turning in a new lock. Family celebrations are definitely in order. A family reunion can bring back happy memories for some and great hopes for others. You always have a sense of history, but seldom get morbid about the past. Today you can tell the tales that enthrall the family circle and make everyone happy. You have a lot for which you can be rightly thankful. Yet you will know in your heart that you get nothing more than your entitlement. You can be happy and comfortable in secure surroundings. The fact that you are making someone else feel secure, as well, should give a lot of pleasure.

17. SUNDAY. Lucky.   Some folk will say you are lucky. You know that it's really a matter of good judgment. Things should go well today. You feel you can take a chance and it will come off. Your love life may get a welcome boost. An outing in the right company will do you a power of good. Partners are enthusiastic, so you are not going to be allowed to vegetate, even if you did want a quiet day. Children should prove a source of great pleasure and pride. A trip to see a sporting contest should please all the family. Participation would be even more to your liking. It is a good day for starting a vacation or making plans for one later in the year.

18. MONDAY. Tricky.   A skeleton may come out of a closet. Be careful to whom you express personal opinions. Make headway with an artistic interest, but do not expect your efforts to be appreciated by all. There will be some backbiting or surreptitious comments that are best ignored. Funds could run out when you have hopes of making a hit. Love life has its ups and downs. Remember you cannot win them all. It is up to you to trust to your intuition and not go on hearsay or idle comment. The start to the week may find you lacking enthusiasm. Forget the past weekend and live life at the moment. What's done cannot be undone, as Shakespeare is supposed to have observed.

19. TUESDAY. Sensitive. You need some encouragement at work. If there seems no opportunity for promotion or recognition, you will feel it is time to move on. The constructive encouragement of your boss or supervisor can keep your mind on the job in hand. Be prepared to look for a self-employed outlet. Home-based work can be more to your taste. An overseas opening may be less attractive now than a few days ago. Guard your health. Taking chances is really not wise at the moment. Medical advice will probably be to keep indoors and to take things more easily. Local problems can delay something important. Steer clear of miserable people who will make you dissatisfied with your lot.

20. WEDNESDAY. Mixed. Circumstances can change quite radically. When faced with the inevitable, as it may possibly appear, do your best to make changes that will work in your favor. Once you confront the necessity for making a decision squarely, you will find that other helpful things will also fall into place. Financial prospects can be boosted dramatically. Changes in technique or attitude can bring you rewards. You may meet someone at work who electrifies you. It could be love at first sight. Something else may go out of the window overnight, but this may hardly register in your present state of mind. A complete change of treatment could very possibly bring an immediate improvement in a health situation.

21. THURSDAY. Pleasant. Pay attention to what goes on around you. Listen rather than proclaim. Seniors may be tense or dissatisfied with current trends. It will not help matters to aggravate them. So, be careful what you say in mixed company. Be cautious also about signing contracts or legal documents. There is time at your disposal. Waste is not necessary. You can get good publicity if you are seen to be considerate and even tempered. Studies should go ahead smoothly and you can achieve success in examinations if you keep cool and don't try either slick moves or beating the clock. A journey early in the day may annoy you, but apparent delays will prove to have a reason.

22. FRIDAY. Difficult. A partner is likely to be full of initiative. Do nothing to retard such aspirations. Cooperate to make any joint ventures more certain of success. It's a case of joining them if you cannot beat them. There could be a legal wrangle to sort out. Direct attack seems the most sensible approach. Half-measures will not be acceptable. Even so, you may feel you are not in the driving seat, or that you are giving a lot of time to something that does not directly help you. This is something you will have to face up to in your own way. Diplomacy is not necessarily gentle, but must suit the prevailing temperature. A close relationship can survive or perish depending on how much it means to both people.

23. SATURDAY. Satisfactory. Be prepared to sell yourself. Without publicity, you could go unnoticed. Market trading can suit you, whether as a customer or trader. Get going early in the day or you will miss the best business. A message will probably bring good news. There could be an addition to the family. You may have hopes of an inheritance which could get a boost in the morning mail. Once the pressure of the day is eased, you may feel ready for a relaxing evening. Don't carry your business or family worries over into your social life. A loving relationship may seem to be growing on stony ground. Give it time and don't try to rush things. You may feel that your talents are not fully appreciated.

24. SUNDAY. Demanding. Dependents may be hard to understand. Joint decisions with your nearest and dearest will be difficult to put into practice. Don't push a partner too far or seek to make personal gain at the expense of others. Take time to relax; you need to meditate or reflect. A family event could throw plans out of the window. Be philosophic and expect to collect only what you put into any partnership. Income tax returns or correspondence can either weary you or have you a bit worried. Little can be done today, so do not worry needlessly. Immediate action is not possible, so you may find the weekend can be a bit of a bore. By considering others' needs, your personal problems can disappear.

25. MONDAY. Disconcerting. Your advice or presence could be in demand. Take everything with a pinch of salt. Don't be rushed or you could end up in a flat spin. Communication problems are likely to appear at some stage. This could be a hold-up of mail, trouble at an airport, failure of staff to turn up for work or some other frustrating incident that can try your patience. Use any apparently wasted time to reflect. An immediate decision is not necessary, but more profound opinion may be most essential. Studies can be protracted. If you are away from home and cannot notify family of your return, just relax till things get on the move again.

26. TUESDAY. Fortunate. Make an early decision to enjoy yourself. You need the right company which should be no problem. There can be wedding bells for some. Joint endeavors seem to be blessed today. Twin harness should get things going twice as fast as solo efforts. A journey is well starred. Business prospects improve if you are prepared to put yourself out and don't look for trouble. Legalities can be used to advantage. A language problem will be solved and agreement reached. Expand wherever you need. Creative talents can be used and publicized. You may feel that nothing is outside your scope, provided your partner is there to add weight and purpose. Love needs to be expressed in a positive way. If you have marriage in mind, do something about it.

27. WEDNESDAY. Productive. You probably need to make additional preparations. Something is not yet ready for lift-off. Bend to the task ahead and do not expect to make a lot of obvious progress. This is an excellent day for those who are studying for future betterment. Relaxed conditions should allow you to keep out of contact and devote your mind to higher things. A casual meeting with in-laws could lead to some doors being opened in the future. Listen to advice, but do not attempt to implement instructions at this stage. Too premature action will not speed the plow. Use fully the quiet and intelligent side of your nature. It is meant to be so directed, not left idle.

28. THURSDAY. Tricky. Take on responsibility. You may have to substitute for a superior. Do not be afraid of handling this task. Initially you may have doubts and things will not readily fall into line. In due course, you will find that things sort themselves out if you let well-established practices go forward. Little things will be sent to try you. If may be difficult to keep family informed of your schedule or whereabouts at times. Keep to the main task. A parent may have problems. Property matters can be haphazard and remain unresolved today. Do not try to take advantage of social position to settle an ownership matter. Officials can be uncooperative in the extreme. You should make profits, possibly more than expected.

MARCH

1. FRIDAY. Successful. Complete a business deal. Button up something important connected with the home. You could be entertaining someone rather special. This seems like a good time to go into some private or discreet consultation about the future of your business or career. Make inquiries well before any move is undertaken. It may be only a notion at the moment, but something big can be in the making. Even you may not understand what exactly is coming about. A family gathering seems likely, probably to commemorate a parental landmark. Newlyweds could hear good news about their first home. An antique dealer may call in to give a valuation you requested on a valuable antique you own.

2. SATURDAY. Useful. Be on friendly terms with everyone. It's no time to be too choosy or distant. Shopping around may prove more to your advantage if you look in the cosmopolitan areas. Those things that are taken for granted may be rather boring. A change could be good, provided you know what you are after and weigh any advice that is offered. Someone may be tempting you or leading you up the garden path. It's time you had an understanding so that you know who are your true friends. Avoid involvement that can obstruct your social plans. If you get the chance, take an offer from abroad. This could take you out of a dead-end scenario that just repeats itself.

3. SUNDAY. Rewarding. If you have capital in hand, you can expand a business venture. This line of thought can occupy your mind over the weekend. Sound advice and support can come from the head of the family. There seems to be someone near you with a strong sense of initiative and originality upon which you can depend if need be. Socializing is good for you and your mate. A new type of alarm may have to be fitted to the all the doors and windows. This can make you feel happier about leaving the home unoccupied. Friends are pleased to see you around. Recent problems over mortgage or house purchase may vanish quickly for some unexpected reason. Perhaps you have become a bit more educated on the subject of property and home ownership.

144

4. MONDAY. Confusing. Look after your resources. Chances should not be taken, though you may be tempted to show off. Private advice could be sought, but will be of little practical value at the moment. It may seem that precedent and formality control everything. This is not really the case, but it may encourage you to lash out or do something stupid. So be a bit more considerate of yourself and use your undoubted insight, rather than reacting to the actions or habits of others. It's a good day for acting. Follow a dramatic urge if you are so inclined. Photography may have special significance. Someone can give you comfort with gentle, kind words. Help someone who is not feeling well; be loving.

5. TUESDAY. Buoyant. Past recollections may have deep meaning. Translate your feelings into positive action to achieve excellent results. An important person may remember you. It could mark a turning point in your affairs. Property dealings should be especially successful. There could be a promotion waiting for you in the days ahead. Look after personal funds. Put some money away and you'll see it grow over the years. A surprise encounter can lead to an evening of happy reunion. It is time you tied up loose ends before making a special opening tomorrow. Such a lot of emotion can be released when you are happy and sure things are going well; you feel as if you're walking on air.

6. WEDNESDAY. Lucky. Settle down and relax. Preparations should be complete if you have a new venture in mind. Meditation can be a sensible occupation. It is something that will calm your nerves and allow your intuition to function freely. You seem likely to come to an important decision in the early part of the day. This may mean a change of course or attitude, which will be good for all concerned. Family involvement in your affairs seems the most natural thing in the world. Keen interest is being taken in your welfare and your hopes. A new development is nursing or caring can make an immediate impact on your life. You feel more in control and better able to be useful.

7. THURSDAY. Misleading. Personal progress could depend on others. Test the water before you dive in. Find out reactions before you commit yourself to any specific action. Influential people are a bit mixed up. Possibly they have split loyalties and are very wary about what they do or promise. So keep your eye on the main action and inquire or observe in order to hedge your bets. Gambling is not on. Do not make judgments based on appearance. Find out the true track record. A love affair can lose its momentum or significance in the course of the day. Your imagination may have been leading you to believe all sorts of things. When the wraps are off you see an entirely different picture.

8. FRIDAY. Difficult. Don't bother trying to explain complicated points to the ignorant. Make the most of those near and dear to you who face simple facts. Life can be so much more interesting if you cut out the cackle and get down to brass tacks. Marriage suits you. Involvement with children, or the decision to have a child, can make life all the more worthwhile. There could be a decision made about marriage if you are still unattached. Partnership can be strengthened by more direct action and a willingness to put more effort into the joint pool. Traveling problems can be frustrating. If a journey has to be made, have alternative means at your disposal, just in case of snags.

9. SATURDAY. Useful. Take time out to review your position. Start with finances and go through a schedule systematically. Weekend chores may take up some of your time, but are unlikely to occupy much of your thought or imagination. Weekend peace has seldom prevailed this year and the opportunity afforded now should be accepted with relief. Consider the outstanding possibilities of the year ahead. You are aware that expansion of travel, or success in gaining qualifications, are probably your most ardent hopes. Without the resources to support your efforts, you may lose out. It is up to you to conserve, or use your funds, with progress in mind. You can succeed if you make up your mind.

10. SUNDAY. Uncertain. Financial matters and practices are not your strong point today. Keep clear of monetary involvement. A broker or financial adviser can handle these matters with a lot more effect. There could be a surprise for you today. Do not jump too readily to conclusions. They may not be correct. Someone or something can touch a very sensitive nerve. You may be dazzled by a beauty or bemused by the charm of someone of the opposite sex. Have your dreams and enjoy them. Putting them into practice may be possible, but of this you cannot be sure. It may take a bit of time to realize a dream or a possibility. Be content at the moment to plan or speculate, but be ready to act.

11. MONDAY. Rewarding. Follow a hunch. Write or deliver a letter that you're sure will work wonders. Someone you admire may get in touch and renew a friendship. You live in hopes that this will blossom into a stronger tie. A parent may have sound and constructive views on a domestic matter. This is good reasoning. Take note and learn. Charitable intentions should be turned into positive action. It is a good day to make an impression on someone of importance, but see to it that your intentions are honorable or you could miss out. Weekend considerations about money may have determined your intentions today. Tie up loose ends and try to get into a more settled frame of mind.

12. TUESDAY. Challenging. You could be left to your own devices today. Routine tasks can keep you fully occupied. Sitting around with nothing to do would make you bored. So it is up to you as to whether you enjoy the day or let it dictate to you. Relatives should be contacted if you've recently been out of touch. Those minor matters that are the everyday run-of-the-mill background to life can more than ever be important. You are by nature an inquisitive person and cannot afford to let the grass grow under your feet. Though you may have high hopes of greater things, without the background interest of many less important matters, you will not be able to harness your energy.

13. WEDNESDAY. Exciting. Outmoded methods should be jettisoned. You have something to get out of your system. It may be time you installed up-to-date communications equipment. A love affair seems set to lead to greater things. Married folk may have a special interest in the performance of their children. The young seem to be ready for making a move toward the altar. It's all happening around you today, so don't be old-fashioned. There may be something you want to say and may think it is better left unsaid. Plans can be completed for a vacation. You could be going on a journey that will open up new horizons. Be optimistic about the future. Good news should come your way.

14. THURSDAY. Useful. You are again in a position to take stock of your assets and liabilities. Plans for a home move may be held up for an unknown reason. Just bide your time today and try to work out what is going on. This is a good day for collectors. With little effort on your part, you may be able to improve a collection. If positive and outgoing action is not needed on your part, it could mean that the action will come to you. So make full use of all the time at your disposal. This is a slack period prior to another initiative. There could be lots to get in order. The domestic front should take priority. You have to look to basics and security in order to prosper. A lick of paint is not enough.

15. FRIDAY. Frustrating. Your plans and intentions are not readily accepted. If you cannot gain cooperation, it may pay you to do it yourself. A change of heart by an erstwhile partner could throw you for a little while. This will not last. Tomorrow morning you have to take an important step forward. Last-minute preparations can be messed up if you are not resolute. You can be sure of financial support and have sufficient resources tucked away. Enthusiasm may be hard to engender in someone who should be less critical. An argument can clear the air, but it will not change a situation. A lot of energy may be used with old-fashioned domestic equipment. It's a good day to spend something and modernize.

16. SATURDAY. Enjoyable. It may seem that someone has seen the light. The dilemma of yesterday will have passed and is now history. Love life is once more on the right vibration. Things look good. A child may be having some sort of a celebration connected with recent success. Do not refuse a trip out of town if you have shopping in mind. There may be better bargains away from your usual haunts. In any case, it will be nice to have a change. Judgment should be excellent. Company suits your style. It's all happening again and you are glad to be getting around. You may want to confirm a link with someone in the neighborhood. You may have loving thoughts for the boy or girl next door.

17. SUNDAY. Misleading. Share your thoughts with the one you love. Leave others to wonder or speculate. There may be talk of infidelity or misbehavior. This is meant to annoy you and is being spread by jealous people. Attempts to get a personal project off the ground may be bogged down by financial strings or red tape. You have the right ideas, so be single-minded and you will eventually make your point. An engagement may be announced. It is still too early for a wedding, but that will allow time to get the funds together for a full-scale affair with all the trimmings. Don't let anyone put you off from what you know is right. Well-intentioned people do not know all the facts, you do.

18. MONDAY. Challenging. A firm commitment can be given today. You may make up your mind to work all-out to gain an objective. This could be the end of a situation that has been developing for some time. With the full facts known and understood it is time to turn over a new page and build on the prosperity of the past. A job may end and another commence. Expansion will depend on the amount of effort you put into your work. A dietary adjustment may be necessary. Perhaps you need to cut out something in order to get the right balance. There could be a party with your colleagues to celebrate a coming of age. Even if money problems are still with you, make the most of your chances.

19. TUESDAY. Lucky. At last you can see due reward for your work. If you are self-employed, you may seize an opportunity to sign a contract or make a deal. Modern methods are going to save time and thus increase your potential. Do not be afraid to get up to date while you have the capital at hand. A change of job could work wonders if you are getting bored. There's nothing like a change of scene to keep life going. Someone at work may have a strange effect on you. This could be developing into romance, perhaps, without your knowing just what is going on. A redundancy notice may turn out to be a happy break. Take the day as it comes and you will not make a lot of mistakes.

20. WEDNESDAY. Tricky. Keep your eyes on the young. They may be given more scope than is good for them and it could turn to license. Gentle persuasion coming from a head teacher will solve the problem or at least help. It could be a day of great beginnings. A love affair may be more than an emotional strain. You may be confused about money at the moment and this can have a negative effect on a loving relationship. Try to keep your emotions from affecting the more practical matters of the day. Avoid daydreaming or you could be in trouble. Have no dealings with salesmen at your doorstep. Be honest with yourself and you are less likely to deceive others, or to be deceived.

21. THURSDAY. Disconcerting. Your sense of humor may not be appreciated. Wry comment comes easily from you, but it is often misinterpreted by those who do not share your sense of reality. Be careful, when in mixed company, that you do not offend the opposite sex. Too much store may be set on an improving situation. You have to walk before you run. Placid people may infuriate you. Workers may seem to be idling when they are truly doing a job properly. Use common sense before you jump to conclusions or you could lose friends, colleagues and even key staff if you're a boss. It seems to be a matter of priorities. Come back to earth and rethink your methods. Travel may upset you.

22. FRIDAY. Difficult. You could be fed up with your job. A sharp reminder from a partner can get you out of the doldrums. Do not hang around waiting to be asked. Make an effort to get some joint project off the ground. Interfering in the affairs of others may satisfy you emotionally for a little while, but you can do as much damage as good in the long run. Diet needs careful handling. If meals are irregular, try to get better organized in the future. An older person may be having a rough time at your place of work. If you employ long-term staff, look after their interests as a priority this month, starting today. Job satisfaction means much to them also.

23. SATURDAY. Tricky. It's time to take stock. Check up on your outgoings and incomings. Surprise encounters can unsettle you if you are seeking peace and quiet. You have better hopes about a job. The question of salary could be a stumbling block. Don't jump out of the frying pan into the fire. A colleague could help you settle down to take a more rational view of things. In the end, you know any decision is very much your own pigeon. There could be trouble with electrical fixtures or gadgetry in the home. Avoid making an offer to help someone else with their problems in this field. You could press the wrong button and make matters worse. Stick to what you know and don't interfere.

24. SUNDAY. Pleasant. A future parent may give his blessing. It could be plain sailing from now in your romantic life. Start at once to make private arrangements. Information received today should be heartening. Keep this to yourself, or at least between you and your partner. Idle chatter can put a relationship in peril. If you have something to say that is meaningful, say it yourself. Go-betweens are likely to let you down or complicate matters. There may be a problem with your car. Surprise, surprise, a superior will offer you a lift! Continue your education. Take full advantage of an offer to study or be tutored by someone you respect. This could be the start of something really big.

25. MONDAY. Useful. Keep in the right circles. Influential help should be most useful at this moment. You will want to make a hit and should not be shy about it. Someone may act the dog in the manger. Remember your responsibilities, but weigh them up against the future possibilities. You'll come up with the right answer. Be positive and show the flag. If your backup is not up to standard, don't let this get you down. There will probably be a genuine reason for such a letdown. Be magnanimous and show you are above petty wrangling. Diet can be a bit off-line today. Try to have regular meals; if not, watch what you are eating. Foreign dishes can upset you if they are overdone.

26. TUESDAY. Mixed. Do not make any secret commitment. Make it your business to be seen around. You should be getting a lot from a close partnership that you have recently decided to promote or develop. Perhaps you should look to distant places for room to expand. Contact with cooperators overseas makes you feel a lot more comfortable and enthusiastic. There may be some-one trying to put a monkey wrench in the works behind the scenes. See that all your documentation is up to scratch if you have a flight schedule. Outmoded routines could hold you up. Have an agent or spokesman available if you are engaged in business elsewhere. You should be popular and keep on saying the right things.

27. WEDNESDAY. Inactive. Take things quietly at the office today. Show yourself where necessary, but say and do only what is necessary to retain your command. It is better to let others get on with work in hand while you take stock and note developments. There seems to be a more settled condition coming about which should leave you well satisfied at the end of the day. Someone where you work may be attracted to you. You are probably looking forward to the evening when you can get together under more relaxed conditions. Do your best today to look the part, whatever you are doing. It's not so much what you can do as what you appear to be that matters. Relax and enjoy your position.

28. THURSDAY. Successful. Now is the time to reap where you have sown. Be on your toes for financial gain. Originality should pay off. Someone may be admiring you from a distance and having some helpful influence on your affairs. Keep your ear to the ground for inside information that should be genuine today. Ro-mance may stand high in your order of priorities. Put on all the positive charm you can. Intuition and charisma are assets you cannot afford to waste. A business maneuver may surprise your competitors and put you way ahead. It is no time to be over-cautious when fortune favors the brave or he who is willing to be original. Install modern equipment to improve your efficiency.

29. FRIDAY. Rewarding. End the working week on a high note. Be confident that what you undertake will be popular and successful. Long-term aims are destined for recognition and true evaluation. Something you have worked long and hard for can materialize. Publicize yourself. Let everyone see and recognize you at your best. A stroke of apparent good luck could mean you have a much more comfortable time ahead. Financial worries may disappear and you could be on to a good thing. Romance can make life exciting, so enjoy living while the mood lasts. If you are looking for a settled life, today finds you in the mood to enjoy what is going on and decide that this is the life.

30. SATURDAY. Difficult. Friends may want you to break a promise. Pledges given should be honored, so you should have no reason to betray a trust. Someone in an eminent position seems set to balk at a social project you wish to promote. Miserable people may try hard, but you should stick to your guns when you know you're in the right. Avoid financial dealings today. There is likely to be some sort of slipup that could cost you money. Get your costs right before you set out on any major project. A romantic arrangement may fall through. You could arouse opposition of a parent. In the end you may find you are better without something that is not what it appears to be.

31. SUNDAY. Confusing. Be sociable, but do not neglect to have a partner when in mixed company. If you are ever out on a limb you will appreciate the timely support of a close ally. Enthusiasm can be generated by cooperation, so make yourself popular early in the day. You may have problems later on; so getting into the right circles or putting your views across may then be less helpful. A love affair may fold up. Tittle-tattle can ruin what appeared to be a going thing. It's best not to waste too much time on arguments. Be glad that you have other irons in the fire. A youngster may be more than a handful. Reflections late in the day may not help your state of mind. Snap out of it. You must look to the future and forget the tricky moments of the past.

APRIL

1. MONDAY. Fortunate. Feel good about being a confidant. Listen to someone who wants to share a secret. There should be an opportunity to make a discovery or think up something brilliant that puts a new slant on an old problem. Love life should blossom quite amazingly. The appearance of someone can turn you on. Do not just watch and wonder. Make an approach, and dreams could become possibilities. Financial matters seem to be improving and you will feel able to buy something special for someone special. A chance meeting with an old friend could mean the start of something worthwhile. Things are going well for you, so don't be shy. Make good use of your resources.

2. TUESDAY. Quiet. Quiet and solitude may suit your mood. It is best to keep things under your hat for the time being. Too much exposure of any sort could be harmful. Take time to get to the bottom of something that could have caused a hang-up. There is little point in withdrawing if it is only in self-pity. So be positive and don't let people and conditions get you down. There could be something you dearly want to do, but wish it to be kept a secret. It seems like an ideal day for success. Others, less intuitive than you, may find it hard to understand why you are moody. They may eventually realize that there are two distinct sides to your character. The sage must stop to brood at times.

3. WEDNESDAY. Disturbing. You feel the ball is in your court. Expect superiors or officials to be unaware of the fact. Make as much progress as possible without needing their help. A parent may have financial worries. There could be more going out than coming in. A school report on a child may be cause for worry or comment. If you have a youngster who is ill at ease with a teacher, try to do something to right the problem. Remember, no matter what the conditions, you are in a mood or position to take personal action. Feel confident that a neighbor can stand in for you in a crisis if it arises. Look for openings in study or the publishing world. Overseas contacts can lighten your day.

4. THURSDAY. Demanding. You should feel more at ease with a superior. Yesterday's problems can be seen in a much clearer light. Conditions where you work are likely to be difficult. There may be some pressure exerted to make you comply with outmoded practices. It might be hard for you to buck the establishment, but you will probably want to make some effort to bring sweetness and light to the situation. A dear friend may have to enter hospital for treatment. Show willingness to help and make things a bit more easy for those affected. You could be getting into a rut. Change your diet if you are either putting on too much weight or not increasing as you wish. Get things into focus.

5. FRIDAY. Tricky. All is not as it may seem. Put not your trust in princes or anyone else who can manipulate the purse strings. There is a definite need to get something straight in your finances. Partnership needs and resources can be confused with other personal assets. An argument over money is definitely in the cards. So keep a clear head and try hard to master your emotional reactions. You could have a set-to with your nearest and dearest over money, and really it's not worth fighting for. If you are short of ready cash, get out there and earn some. An attempt to find something out about a stranger's background could lead to trouble, so be careful how deep you dig for information.

6. SATURDAY. Confusing. This will be a day of stops and starts. Act on impulse if you have to, but be prepared for shocks. You are tempted to make changes without having too much evidence of the possible success or failure of your decisions. This could be unavoidable as you see it. Just be good enough to put family and friends in the picture if you can so that they may have some idea of what's going on. A doorstep salesperson can have something rather different to offer. If you're in doubt, don't buy. Electrical appliances could prove troublesome. If you know your ground from your livewire, it's not so bad. If you are ignorant of positive and negative, call in an expert. It is best to do nothing unless you are absolutely sure you know how.

7. SUNDAY. Enjoyable. If you're feeling good, enjoy the break. It may be nice to get out and enjoy the freedom that this day of rest offers. Someone will probably want to be with you to share your company and your time. It would be a good day for making practical plans for the future if you are young and in love. The world should seem a comfortable and friendly place. Enjoy natural pleasures. Feel glad that you can be treated as an equal and can reciprocate. Should you have some excess weight to take off, there's no time like the present. Relax and you'll have no problem. It's no day to be getting excited or be dashing around helter-skelter. A time for everything and everything in its time.

8. MONDAY. Disturbing. Think twice before answering a letter. Your time is valuable so you should not underestimate your powers or your worth. Traveling may be halted or you may be disinclined to move very far from the neighborhood. Something may be troubling you. Until you can clear your mind you are unlikely to make any progress. Put up with local delays; but do not let these reflect too much on your business or publicity away from your own doorstep. They could become detrimental to your business. In-laws may have to move and your partner may feel as if something has gone out of life. It is time to be patient and philosophic. Persevere with studies.

9. TUESDAY. Uncertain. Don't be a stick-in-the-mud! You may be fortunate in having influential friends who can remind you of your failings. It seems you are loath to change a regular practice. This may get you into trouble or slow your progress. So take the advice of a superior, an official or a tutor and make the most of your chances as they come. Love life will prosper if you make your feelings known. A parent seems to be on your wavelength. As long as you act your age, you'll be all right. But don't put too much faith in the old-fashioned approach. Studies can be boring, if not depressing, when carried out in isolation. You need a bit of life to restore your spirits. The boss may have holiday plans for you.

10. WEDNESDAY. Changeable.   The bed could be more attractive than the alarm. Rouse yourself or you could miss out on something. The attraction will be for lighter things than work. So try to get your priorities sorted out early in order to make the most of the daylight hours. Someone at your workplace can ruffle your feathers or just be a bore. Appearances could count for something, but you may find they don't answer all the problems. What you have to say, or the quickness of your mind, will have more meaning. If you have an interview you may find it hard to please, so keep alert and show your individuality by being quick-witted. Looks are not everything. Joint success will come with mutual energies pulling in the same direction. Make headway.

11. THURSDAY. Successful.   Domestic innovation is beneficial. Invite someone to visit you who is full of bright ideas. Electrical talents need to be cultivated or put to use. One of the family may be gifted in this way and you could be glad of this. A property deal or arrangement looks as if it will go through without a hitch after a lot of doubts in the past. Funds can be increased by extraordinary means. You may be surprised at your own ingenuity. A new hi-fi or video could be bought at a knock-down price. Keep your eyes and ears open for bargains that are unlikely to recur. Give someone you admire a surprise. A blind date could end up with extraordinary consequences, giving family a laugh.

12. FRIDAY. Challenging.   Play it cool or put on the charm. You may want to get something done around the home and have to use diplomacy to gain your ends. A craftsman or craftswoman could do something so much better than you, so why not get this organized? Love life is once again coming to a pleasant peak so it will be a shame to lose the chance to develop a relationship further. If you've met someone at work, or through a visit to a health club, you will want to find out more. Some folks may be setting about decorating or furnishing their first home. No matter how small or empty it seems now, you know you can make it into a snug nest. Good luck to you. You have the right idea.

13. SATURDAY. Sensitive.   Free time is all-important. You may have to listen to or submit to the demands of others who have a just claim on your time and presence. Impatience with the needs of others or the unavailability of cash or credit may do you no good. Competitive sport can get the gremlins out of your system. Blowing off steam should be confined to this sort of thing, rather than taking your frustration out on family or friends. You seem to find a patient relative who understands how you feel. A journey with a purpose early in the day can help you cope with discontented people later. Be positive and sociable. Don't let aggravating people get you down.

14. SUNDAY. Productive.   It's all happening today. You may have your mind on one thing only. Active thinking should put you in the top three with a lot going for you. There is possibly an engagement or decision to marry being worked up today. Time may seem short to those heavily involved, so a lot can happen in a very short span. You can make up your mind about using a special talent. Timing is all-important. Tactics can go out of the window once you get the bit between your teeth, so expect to stand on a few toes once you do get going. Nevertheless, the ball is definitely in your court and you must do what you think is best. That's how experience is developed. You can learn from your mistakes.

15. MONDAY. Mixed.   Workday routine will not turn you on. You may be late off the mark or held up by morning rush-hour traffic. Attending to the needs of someone old may hamper you. A journey you had hoped to make could seem as far away as ever, but you must not give up trying. Studies are going to be boring unless you have a change of subject. Original thinking or the chance to show off original work is all you ask for today. Be patient till there is an opportunity later in the day to get out of your overalls or uniform and be yourself. If you are looking for a job change, be prepared to chance your luck. Disheartening answers to inquiries will not always be given; there is a ray of hope.

16. TUESDAY. Misleading.   Double-harness is better than going it alone. There can be offers for partners or for your own partner, so be happy if you are missed out in some way. Put up with conditions that may turn you off. Something has to be sorted out and made to function before you feel satisfied. A considerable amount of cleaning up may fall to your lot. Get it done with resolution. The sooner it is over the better you'll like it. It may seem you are going to get away with something early in the day, but this may not materialize. Even so, make the most of your talents before noon and be prepared to share if you want to get ahead. Your mate needs to be admired.

17. WEDNESDAY. Profitable. A union can be arranged. This could be the one day of the calendar for you, or you could be a guest at a special occasion. It's time to count your blessings and be glad you have someone who understands you. A long-term agreement can be settled. Advertising should pay dividends. Someone who has previously treated you as a bit of a joke will now take a more considered view of your position and promise. Business expansion should be considered as a going thing. Look around for a good publicity agent or be prepared to travel around yourself to show the flag. Establishment of an overseas office seems a likely proposition. The bounds are not yet set, so make progress and build on a sound foundation.

18. THURSDAY. Challenging. A sporting event can be arranged. Children may figure in your schedule. Keep your options open and be prepared to improvise or entertain at short notice. Traveling in tandem is for your benefit as you'll probably feel in need of good company. A relationship can take on a more lasting or stable meaning. Past uncertainties can disappear and you should feel a lot happier. Give a partner some assurance. Together you can achieve much more when there is mutual confidence. A parting may be necessary, but there are no hard feelings: only a lot of mutual goodwill and understanding. You may be offered a joint editorship on a local paper. This could be a challenge for you.

19. FRIDAY. Disconcerting. You may rush in where angels fear to tread. Get something off your chest and be prepared to face the consequences that could result. Immediate action may be needed in a crisis. If none develops, be careful that your attitude does not cause one. Aggressive behavior is likely to come to light in your presence and this you can handle. Only when you are the unreasonable instigator of trouble will you lose out. So keep your ammunition till it is going to be needed. It may help you to dig into some deep secret, do a bit of investigating, and get to know more about others. Preserve funds. Joint resources can be poured down the drain on an impulse. So watch it and consult your partner.

20. SATURDAY. Disturbing. Be very careful if you're doing shopping for others. Don't get your money mixed with someone else's. Pickpockets may be busy in the most unexpected places, so trust no one very much. An apparent friend may try to deceive you. Pleasure plans may be ruined through careless arrangements. A trip can be called off at short notice. You may be in some doubt about the motivations of someone who seems to be giving something away for nothing. Do a bit of inquiring behind the scenes and you won't lose out. A private duty proves you are on the right track and that your heart is in the right place. Your own company can be all you need at some time in the day. Happy reflections.

21. SUNDAY. Mixed. Try to take things easy. Plans for a day out may have to be canceled. You may be feeling on top of the world, but could find that you cannot have it all your own way. Listen to what a practical superior or official has to say and don't push your luck against the establishment. Things will go well enough for you. You can be popular in the right company in the right place, but can't have it all ways. Trying to step into the boss's shoes would be most unwise at this stage. So be careful what you say, and abide by rules and convention till you are sure you can make positive changes. The health of someone may worry you if you are far away from home. It may be difficult to get medical attention, but you will cope. Have confidence in yourself.

22. MONDAY. Sensitive. Business contacts overseas should be first-class. Make the utmost use of communications. Entertainment value will be increased if you bring some outside talent into a competition. Theatrical talents should be advertised much more if you want to make progress at the speed you desire. Don't hide your light. You have a certain amount of convention and ritual to overcome if you want to liven things up. Be on your guard for those who are stirring things up in your private life. A jealous suitor or disappointed promoter could be putting you down behind the scenes. Never mind, make hay while the sun shines, but take note of what you know is going on. Don't be overcritical of yourself. Look for your assets and plug them.

23. TUESDAY. Excellent. A promotion seems likely. You may otherwise be informed that you are on a short waiting list. This is a day to be aware of your position and prospects. Make sure your good works are seen and your personality shines. Recent qualifications may mean you are now in charge and able to do more or less as you like. Take the willing advice of someone who has been there before you and knows all the angles. Then you will not go far wrong. A medical opinion gives you a lift. You can feel ten feet tall. Do something constructive for someone who has always stood by you through thick and thin. You may recognize a king among men who does not wish to seek the limelight.

24. WEDNESDAY. Productive. Marital bliss can be disturbed by business. Be careful who handles your home connections. There can be misunderstandings that could be easily avoided with a bit of forethought. Financial prospects are very good. Your influence or strategic position can lead to personal gain. Listen to the back-room advice. Possibilities of a merger should not be ruled out. If you are looking for expansion in this way, make a positive move to find out more about those who could be involved. The joint resources of a business partnership should be put to good use today. Capital lying dormant is quite useless in a thriving concern. A broker may talk to you and help you make up your mind.

25. THURSDAY. Demanding.   It's a day to be circumspect in all your doings. Trust your own judgment. Put only small trust in those who are considered to be wise or superior. Officials generally may be hard to get along with and difficult to understand. There may be some other difficulty or delay in getting a visa or arranging movement of goods overseas. Be patient. Getting on your high horse will solve nothing. A publisher may be unaware of the value of something you present. This you cannot help. It may take a bit of time to educate him in the folly of his ways. Studies can be seriously dislocated by the attitude of a professor or tutor. Time will sort things out, but the delay could be a setback.

26. FRIDAY. Tricky.   Diplomacy can get you places. Trying to throw your weight around will not get you an inch farther forward, probably the reverse. You may try a bit of material bribery and find this doesn't work, either. So be diplomatic. Realize who are your friends and stick to them. It's a good time to take your nearest and dearest out on the town. Don't dip into the joint kitty or you'll be in trouble. The question of money can be a sore subject. There could be some trouble over business funds. If this is your province, keep an eye open for juggling of the books or excessive expense accounts. Have a legal friend help you do a bit of investigating. It will probably pay you in the long run.

27. SATURDAY. Confusing.   Plans can go awry. Make your schedule for the day as foolproof as possible. Your boss may have ideas about fouling up your weekend. It could be a good time to act dumb or be missing when the telephone rings. There may be chores to perform that you are not going to like; even more so, if you are not allowed to handle things in your own way. Make an agreement with someone about a social affair. You have to give and take. There is no way in which you are going to get all you want. A close friend may have to go out of town or is involved in something you cannot share. This could lead to a discussion. Perhaps you can talk things over and agree.

28. SUNDAY. Disconcerting. You can have a lot of fun if you relax. Treat things lightly. Once you get involved with heavy stuff you are going to feel out of your depth. Self-important people are probably trying to browbeat you in some way. Once you get into a corner, it will be difficult to emerge unscathed. So look for gentle and lively company and avoid dull conversation. A sudden event could liven up proceedings, though you may not be directly involved. People with money to burn may impress you. Equally, you can appreciate words of wisdom from someone who is active in research or brokering. There could be a surprise developing concerning a legacy.

29. MONDAY. Mixed. Be reserved about what you know. It is too soon to make a public statement about something that concerns you personally. A little bird may whisper something in your ear and make you feel good. You could get very dogmatic about something. This may have its advantages but it could have negative repercussions if you are seen to be someone with only one ax to grind. Be generous and give time and consideration to those you know are in need or are lonely. Loneliness is something you can surely appreciate. Check up on your financial reserves. If you have debts to settle, do so. If there are debts to you still outstanding, again do something about them or forget them.

30. TUESDAY. Successful. It's all get up and go today. You should be quite confident that you are on the right track and in charge. Responsible actions will be appreciated in the right quarters. Make sure you publicize your assets and leave your liabilities till a later date. Optimistic action is needed now and you cannot afford to hang around waiting for something to turn up. Once you have made your first gain, consolidate and build from a secure base. An older relative will be glad to see you looking so well. It may be to your advantage to look for expansion. This could mean you do a fair amount of travelling or communicating today. See that none is wasted. Idle hours do not aid your situation.

MAY

1. WEDNESDAY. Lucky. You can make quite a hit. What you have to say is taken as gospel, so you can get your message across. Make an impact on the young who will be eager to hear your words of wisdom. There is good news from someone you love. You could be making headway, as well as someone's day a lot brighter. Be positive and speak your thoughts. Opportunities are excellent if you're in show biz. New engagements or renewal of a long-running gig is a possibility. You're less cynical today in your comments. It is possible you feel content and say the right things, especially when trying to amuse or please. A new development over a pet interest or hobby should please you.

2. THURSDAY. Tricky. Personal interests can conflict with others. It's not really the day for making a vow to a partner to be unselfish or considerate. Just play it cool and follow your own inclinations. Expect little or no cooperation, more probably a frosty reaction. You could have a legal tangle to sort out, or you may feel out of your depth because someone does not share your point of view. Try not to rock the boat any further. If left alone, it will probably come back on an even keel. A decision may have to be made and this could mean you have to be fair to both people concerned. In the end, you know that you have to take the initiative, but with a bit of tact you can win someone over. It's not easy.

3. FRIDAY. Demanding. Joint take-home pay can be a disappointment. Be prepared to draw on personal resources if there is a need. Look very closely at any financial so-called get-rich-quick bargain that may be offered today. Tempers can rise and fall like a yo-yo. It may be difficult to put your finger on something that is causing trouble, so be very careful about accusing anyone of not playing straight. It could be a good idea to check up on your insurance or investments. The request of a client may throw you for a while. If you are not clear as to what is happening, do some research and take your time before you make any statement. Keep off the Ouija board. Look out for crafty salesmen.

4. SATURDAY. Mixed. Play it by ear if you want a peaceable day. There can be a continuing disagreement over money or means. Your hopes of getting away for a few hours of recreation can be dashed. Children may be a nuisance and cost you a small fortune if they are allowed to twist your arm. It's best to be philosophic. You can play the eccentric or the romantic to advantage. That approach could get you out of a few scrapes or difficulties. Don't take things the wrong way. It's all very well to lead someone else a dance, but you should be aware that you can be gullible too and dazzled by someone or something. A quiet period with an old friend in private should restore any confidence you may have lost.

5. SUNDAY. Uncertain. Get yourself properly organized. If you have no particular yen to go anywhere or do anything, just relax and make the most of the break. Should you be obliged to undertake a duty, do it with a good heart. You cannot be in two places at the one time, so make the most of your present chances. A journey may be tempting, but the thought of the disturbance that can be caused may put you off. In-laws may decide not to visit. Settle down to read a good book or have a local discussion with those who understand a special subject and can express themselves. You could be a bit distant or snobbish today. Don't offend friends by being cool.

6. MONDAY. Difficult. Be on your best behavior as you start the week. It will be all too easy to upset a superior or a parent; or you may break the law on your way to work. Show respect for such people, though you may not feel it. A start on a new job or project could be problematic. Perhaps you have not got the right contacts yet or are being tested to see how you stand up to adverse conditions. So keep your cool. You will get your chance to take the initiative in due course; it is true that every dog has its day. This is not the best of days to have a medical checkup. You may not be the only one who has climbed out on the wrong side of the bed. It could well be that doctor's staff are below par.

7. TUESDAY. Excellent. Materially and emotionally you have a great day ahead. There may be a marriage or an engagement. A union will be strengthened and the seal set on a lasting venture. Sharing is a must and is certainly no hardship. Settle a journalistic contract. Affairs connected with beauty or art are well aspected. Superior people, or people who hold the purse strings can show appreciation of your tact and reliability in a practical way. You may be astounded at the valuation that is made. There is no question about being happy, either. Romance seems to surround you. This is no fleeting affair, nor a flight of fancy. If you have something special to offer, be sure it's to the right people.

8. WEDNESDAY. Easygoing.   You need a breather. Get your basic position properly into focus. The home can be more attractive than usual. Consider future plans for renewing or redecorating. Have a chat with an agent if you are short of ideas, but don't push yourself. Just let ideas come and go. Eventually something will stick. Family routine is something special to appreciate today. At other times, it may be old hat. There may be someone in your thoughts who is far from home. As you are a traveler yourself, either in mind or body, you can appreciate the value of a safe haven. So be considerate of all who might be in need of support or succor. Reflection and calm will do you good.

9. THURSDAY. Successful.   You are in a position to show understanding. Don't waste this opportunity to do a good turn. There seems to be considerable agreement about your ideas on brightening up the home. An offer of practical help should be accepted. Something is going on in the background that you feel will help. Influential people, possibly parents, may have a big decision to make. This could affect your security. You may be asked to arbitrate and can do so with assurance. There is no need for you to ape those who wield power. Be sure you can keep a confidence because you have the courage of your convictions. You could face a big test. Play it your way and all will be fine.

10. FRIDAY. Sensitive.   Don't sit about too long. Patience is not your strong point. There could be a lovers' tiff that is inclined to throw you for a while. You cannot please everyone, so be philosophic about it all. Studies can be pursued with enthusiasm. Ties of any description are going to be unacceptable today, so you had better not make a date or you could be upsetting someone later on. Publicity for a personal talent or creation should be sought or readily accepted, if offered. You cannot afford to hide your light at this stage. Children may be taking examinations and doing well. Persevere once you have made up your mind. A responsible word or action will impress.

11. SATURDAY. Difficult.   You could feel rather shatterd. The promises of yesterday may seem like yesterday's newspapers. Talents may now be rested if you are wise. There will be some who want you to go on with what you have been doing. This is asking too much. Keep your cool if there is a disagreement among close friends or family; even more so if finances are brought into the discussion. Should you imagine there could be a stumbling block to your progress, just give your mind time to think about possible alternatives. Side issues are really red herrings and should be largely discounted. Dependents may need your attention. Remember your priorities; you have a lot to put straight.

12. SUNDAY. Uncertain. You may be glad of company. The attention of someone very close to you is appreciated. There may seem to be a lot stacked against you, but this may be a sign of the times. Indeed, you are probably no worse off than anyone else, so stop feeling sorry for yourself. Strike a fair bargain about duties and keep the family content. Worries about health will not be resolved if you aren't prepared to be patient. You're not usually a good patient, so being confined in any way will make you unhappy. However, if you can't get out and about as you would like, there must be something else that will amuse you. You may resent interference from someone who says he knows all answers.

13. MONDAY. Rewarding. There is action again and you feel a lot better about life in general. A turning of the page or a decision made will mean things can never be quite the same. You may start work at a different place. Perhaps this is a completely new occupation. The prospect will at once thrill you and cause you doubts. Have confidence that you will make a hit. This could be a good day for those who want to start their own business. Be happy to take on responsibility and to stand on your own feet. There will be willing help from those who are involved with you or depend on your success. Nothing is done in isolation. Once you have made up your mind, you will have someone cheering you on. You may have to step into a superior's shoes for the day.

14. TUESDAY. Lucky. Moderate aims will have instant success. An employer or supplier may be enthusiastic about your potential. Let it be shown in material ways or it will do little good. You have a partner who is constant, yet adventurous. This should satisfy most needs. A joint approach at the moment can tie in the main considerations. Minor issues can be skipped as you get your guidelines laid down. There may be a legal settlement that pleases. Insist on good publicity for something that matters. Studies can be helped by conferring with others, either singly or in groups. One journey at least, is worth undertaking. You could be checking up on flights or exchange rates for a family vacation.

15. WEDNESDAY. Keep the peace and don't swim against the prevailing tide. It would be better to go along generally with what is offered rather than impose your own ideas on others. It may be that you are in a vacuum and have few of your own to offer at the moment. If this is the case, it is best if you relax and take notice of those who consider they have it all tied up. Time will tell. Partnership should be making steady and reliable progress. It may be a refreshing relief to have things done for you. There's no doubt that could get a bit boring eventually, but enjoy this quiet while you can. You may have to come to terms with a sticky situation very shortly. Get your thoughts into focus.

16. THURSDAY. Disturbing. Job changes could be to your advantage. Your partner may be negotiating better terms of employment. There could be some reason to consult your doctor and benefit from advice or an appointment. Be alert to changes that can improve the prospects or conditions of your daily routine. A major change could be with you or in the offing. You may be considering whether to emigrate or build on what you have at home. Advertising is something that can have its pros and cons. Make up your mind where you are best-served before making any firm contract. Examinations should be undertaken with confidence. Concentrate your mind on the basic essentials and you will find the wider philosophies will fit into place.

17. FRIDAY. Uncertain. Be prepared for errors. Inconsistencies can be difficult to trace to their source. So accept nothing at face value. Do some private, secret or discreet investigating before you give important issues the all-clear. Someone you meet today can attempt to lead you up the garden path. Don't be blinded by science. The arch-con man can look you straight in the eye and sell you trash. So it would be better to do without that than risk dropping a bundle. Funds may be getting low. It is better to spread it out thinly than to end up with nothing when you could be needing it badly. There are resources as yet untapped. Just try to recall where you have turned before when in a jam.

18. SATURDAY. Ordinary. Be positive when you know you are right. Investigations can prove your point. Consider what you are to do about your working conditions, then see your superior and expect action. This will be a frustrating day if you cannot direct energies to some definite purpose. Subordinates are of no use. Employing an agent is a waste of time. It is a case of either do the job yourself, if you want to get on, or see the chap at the top and state your case. There could be a slipup that affects your routine. An appointment may be forgotten. You may realize that your working knowledge of a subject is short of requirements. So be quiet when you feel uncertain.

19. SUNDAY. Misleading. Be optimistic. Get things done early in the day if you want to enjoy your time off. Quite a lot may be brewing out of sight. This is something you will eventually find out, but may be glad to ignore for a while anyway. Studies should be continued. Accept encouragement from someone who knows you can succeed. There will be considerable pressure on you at some time during the day. Past history can be raked up. It may be constructive, but only if you see it as something to avoid in the future. Look to the future and learn from the past. You have to get something out into the light in order to handle it in your own way. Otherwise, you feel helpless to make sense of it.

20. MONDAY. Difficult. A last-ditch attempt may be made to stop you. Expect some problems with customs or airport officials. The practicalities of a situation may be lost on a bureaucrat. It is time you took over a leading or influential position, but there may be some resentment at your promotion or nomination. Attempts to improve health prospects of a parent may meet with some discouragement today. Don't give up. Loose ends are likely to bother you. Taking over may be marred by the debris left behind by previous occupants. You have to adapt, so avoid getting fixed views and be philosophic about your current situation. It may take time, but it will work out for you.

21. TUESDAY. Mixed. The light touch can work wonders. Not all attempts at relating will prove successful. There could be a surprise waiting for you or someone you know who takes too much for granted. Business prospects are good. They will be even better if some originality and intuition come into play. Income can be boosted in a spectacular manner, given the right buttons to press. But there may be some temptation to let resources waste as easily as they are gained. This is where you and someone close to you may disagree. They say that money is the root of all evil. It depends on how you use it. You may show interest in an unexpected twosome which comes as a surprise.

22. WEDNESDAY. Demanding. You may feel you are missing out on something. The need to stick to routine may infuriate you. Studies can be interrupted by people with nothing to do. Talking for the sake of talking will really get you down. A function can be disturbed and throw a whole day's production out of gear.

In your position of trust you will not want to be misjudged on the failure of others. Cheating in examinations may be suggested, but you're not about to. Action needs to be stimulated among those who deal with the needs or belongings of others. Exercise your authority to get a broker into action. Your intuition may tell you that something is about to break in the business world.

23. THURSDAY. Misleading. Romantic ideas can mislead you. Don't build up hopes on something you have not yet sounded out. Substantial progress can be made in business if you stick to a tried-and-true procedure. It could be time to conserve the company resources. Perhaps you should consider gathering in all you can and also about developing in another direction. There's no point in being negative. Faint heart never won fair lady, but first of all you must know who is genuinely fair and who is the unscrupulous one. You could get a surprise late in the day. Social arrangements may need to be altered. Friends are a strength during the day, but evening company is not up to snuff.

24. FRIDAY. Happy. You may be a bit ahead of your time. Intuition may tell you that a relationship can be renewed. You can naturally have some doubts if there is no outward and visible sign of such a development. Trust in your judgment, however, and be optimistic. A quiet period is approaching. You will appreciate doing things that demand confidence. Time with loved ones is going to be time well spent. Though few will know, you are going to be visited by a special group of friends who mean a great deal to you. Look for the good in others and try to cope with their shortcomings. Insight can mean a lot. It is what you are that counts, not what you might appear to be.

25. SATURDAY. Confusing. Keep a low profile until you are sure of your whereabouts. You may be ignorant of what is going on, or the people you meet may not be helpful. Do not get upset if you seem to be lagging behind. There will be a sound reason why you may appear to be dull. It could be a defensive ploy that you are only too glad to fall back on. Getting into the limelight will not appeal. Take a serious look at your basic information before making any decision that could affect your future. It may be necessary to go back to the drawing board and get things correct. Nevertheless, you will know you have the love and support of someone who is quite dear to you.

26. SUNDAY. Pleasant. An obsession can be challenged. You are made to face up to facts. Allow someone who has their feet firmly on the ground to express an opinion; listen instead of closing your mind. There may be developments afoot regarding increased income. Keep your own counsel at the moment, but pay attention to what is being said around you. A job may be promised you for tomorrow. The affection of your nearest and dearest is something you appreciate very deeply at this moment. Do not take personal slights too much to heart. If you have anything charitable to do, do it today. The better the day the better the deed, and obstructions can be overcome. Be loving and true; you'll find peace of mind.

27. MONDAY. Challenging. Ideals can become practicalities. Get someone with imagination to come down to earth and translate for you. It will work. You should have unbounded energy and high hopes. This is the way to start the week. A period ahead of you now should lead you to success so don't wait to be asked. Go out and advertise your assets and above all your personality. The goodwill of in-laws can act as a boost to your intentions. A journey can take you off on your own to foreign parts and adventure that you would not miss for the world. In a way, you are a bit of an evangelist. What you set out to do must be accomplished. The manner in which you set about a task can inspire others.

28. TUESDAY. Successful. Someone in authority may beat you to the draw. Accept such action and the end result, though you may have done it in a different way. You may disagree with a senior partner. A third person can settle the issue without resort to legalities or throwing the book at you. You seem to have your feet on the bottom rung and eyes on the top. This is the best way to build for the future. Maintain standards and improve your knowhow. Studies are bound to result in improving your present position. All depends on you and the way you handle your opportunities. It may seem a bit tough at first, or the time span may seem long, but never mind. You can make it and in style.

29. WEDNESDAY. Mixed. Pressure may be brought to bear on workers. Do not take too much aggravation from staff who air unnecessary grievances. A straight talk can clear up a lot of problems. Health could be upset if you don't have something attended to. It's no good bemoaning your condition if you are not prepared to see your doctor. You have hopes of getting out of a present situation where your life is not your own. This can be accomplished by one of two means. Try to gain the confidence and cooperation of your partner. Or, get someone's blessing to go off on your own and find out what lies over the crest of the hill. That seems to be a fair offer and one you will find hard to resist.

30. THURSDAY. Inactive. Look after what is properly yours. It may be a case of survival of the fittest. A senior partner could be in a good mood and allow you more latitude. Direct your energies and interests toward those basic essentials you value most. As you normally have little inclination to hoard or hang on to things, a slight change of tempo could do you good. Make a break from your usual routine and seek peace and quiet. Try to consider just exactly what you are worth in material terms and, more to the point, in terms of values you can exchange. The year is bringing possibilities of progress in a social way, so you have to ponder what sort of foundation is best for your needs. It is not a day to waste in idle contemplation.

31. FRIDAY. Misleading. Avoid getting uptight about earnings or resources. There is plenty of time in life to concentrate on other things. You can do someone a favor with the best intentions. Make it understood that what you do with your own possessions is your business. A rather exceptional friend may give you bright ideas. Do not toy with ones that are unlikely to make sense. Practicalities are not all dull and routine. You are bound to have a brainwave or hear of something out of the ordinary that can change your way of life, if it is used constructively. Otherwise, you can be up and down, and not know where your next penny is coming from. That is no way to go on if you want to get to the top.

JUNE

1. SATURDAY. Disturbing. Someone is taking quite an interest in your affairs. This could be an introductory phase in a relationship. If you are a bit wary, there is probably good reason. So consider what lies in this for you before you commit yourself. Hasty decisions can backfire. Don't set off on a journey unprepared. A challenge can be accepted. There could be a sensible, intelligent reaction or a straightforward, practical decision to take someone on. Either way, you get the adrenaline flowing and sparks can fly. Before you venture into the big and competitive world of publicity, have a thought for what you are leaving behind. Initiative is called for and has to be well judged to be effective.

2. SUNDAY. Sensitive. Optimism rules. Pride can triumph over prudence for a while, anyway. Don't be content with a miserly share of the action, but remember your responsibilities also. You may be looking for big things and have difficulty in coming to terms with reality. Allow intuition to guide you because this is always your best yardstick. There may be a toss-up whether to travel or stay around home. Only you can make the decision. A senior partner seems to be agreeing with you. There is some mileage in this relationship. Parental influence on a marriage situation can be helpful and stabilizing. If you feel a bit inarticulate, use this constructively and choose your words with care. It's true especially when dealing with foreigners or in-laws.

3. MONDAY. Erratic. Work at making someone happy. You will want to see nice things and produce something that is attractive. A pleasant day with your colleagues or co-workers is probable. There may be a harmonious atmosphere prevailing. If you are an employer, this is a good time to communicate with staff and achieve their cooperation. An approach can be made to entice you from your present situation. You will know whether the proposal is fair or not. Get your facts right. Inquiries made today will not stir up a hornet's nest. Diplomacy works. Not all investigative types are to be trusted. There may be something rattling in the cupboard and it may be bones of a long-forgotten problem.

4. TUESDAY. Easygoing. Unknown territory could be entered. You have a need to be secure and to know where you stand. Some time should be given to quiet consideration of the future. Even more than that, think about the basic platform on which you will build for progress. A peaceful day at home will fill your bill at the moment. If you seem to be unneeded, don't consider this a loss. Just get down to straightening out whatever needs to be, and get ready for the next move which will be quite soon. A move may have been considered recently. You are now much nearer a decision. Property matters could be important. These little things that mean home can give comfort. You may be sentimental.

5. WEDNESDAY. Uncertain. It is possible you are in the doghouse. You will not be allowed to dictate terms to superiors. Just play it down if you have to see the boss. The book may be thrown at you, legally. Consider your security before tampering with problems that are not truly yours. Domestic harmony can be disturbed by an interfering parent. Before making a property deal, get all the facts. You should have someone available who lets you in on a few secrets that will ensure you avoid mistakes. Finances appear to be no problem. It may be stubbornness on the part of an official that puts a monkey wrench in the works. Just play it cool again and don't give up.

6. THURSDAY. Difficult. You may wonder whether you are coming or going. Competitive feelings are aroused, while natural conservatism counsels consideration. An instant decision could land you in hot water or a failure to take action could cause you to lose face or a contract. In a way, you could be back to square one and left to make choices based on intuition. Know the situation and do what you think is right. Take the advice of a professional publicity type with a pinch of salt. At the same time, do not lack initiative. A lot is going for you today. You stand to gain, possibly in romance, and possibly in other ways. These would allow you to show your talent and gain popularity. So don't be too inhibited.

7. FRIDAY. Mixed. Positive decisions will be welcomed. Co-operate and be successful. You can be won over or win someone important over to your side if you are bold and willing to stand up for what you know is genuine. An engagement to show off a special talent can be agreed upon. You could be offered star billing. Financial matters may be worrying you, but you should look for the main advantage and stop getting bogged down by incidentals. Have confidence. Odd types will wield little influence over you if you just go ahead with freedom. A parent's blessing may be freely given and you feel on top of the world. Holidays can start. Traveling to distant parts is to your liking.

8. SATURDAY. Exciting. A lot seems to be happening in your married life. If you are single, you will be enjoying personal involvement with someone who shares your interests. Traveling is in the air or in the cards! Something important is likely to be agreed upon and a firm date set for an event; or a long-term contract will be signed. Expansion is in vogue. There may be an addition to the family or a mutual decision to make that will become a fact later on. Feel confident that what you do today is going to lead to greater things. Be adventurous and cooperate with those who show initiative and have a desire to get on in the world. Your partner will mean a lot to you this day.

9. SUNDAY. Sensitive. Practical application will bring material returns. You may be open to criticism for botching a job. If it's done as a genuine free-will offering you may be a bit disappointed; but at least you will have had a go. Optimism must rise above a feeling of failure. If you are of service that is the main thing. You may have to work against your will in your normal occupation and that could be a different matter. Take no liberties with your diet today. A snack may see you through, but you would be better off with a regular meal schedule. Someone may drop in and give you some technical advice. This should save you no end of time and labor in the future.

10. MONDAY. Excellent. Get going while hopes run high. Solo efforts may not be as effective as joint operations. So get someone who knows and appreciates your style to pile aboard and speed the plow or the journey. A relationship has certain assets that should be developed at once. You may be expanding businesswise or on the move to meet someone on legal business. The prospects are excellent. A lot of ground and a lot of detail can be covered to the satisfaction of all concerned. Married life should be going great guns. A vacation with your nearest and dearest can be fitted in with business travel. You can thus save money on travel expenses and perhaps part of your accommodation costs.

11. TUESDAY. Challenging. There are two minds with but a single thought as you are in harmony with your mate. Legal consultation will sort out a problem and lead to a new initiative. Be positive that you want to pursue a broader scope for yourself and therefore expand. Take advantage of an offer or an interest in a partnership that has clear possibilities. Publicity should be encouraged. You can have a direct impact or will find that publicity professionals are more effective than usual. Do not underestimate the effect a partner will have on your future. Share and share alike. Let each show initiative and make speed at double the normal expectation. This could be a breakthrough for you in a year of opportunity.

12. WEDNESDAY. Joint decisions could be the most important of the year. It is time to reach an agreement and turn over a new leaf, if not start a new chapter of life. You may form a company, enter a partnership or start a consulting firm today. The need for an opposite number is paramount, whether as a partner or as a client. So put you best foot forward and appreciate that from now on you have to put yourself out on behalf of others while making the most of your personal gifts. Look ahead to great things. A legal issue can be settled or a new matter taken on. It is a day of beginnings and none of them are trivial. You could attend a wedding later in the day or perhaps the reception.

13. THURSDAY. Confusing. Investment can be a risky business today. Take the advice of a broker rather than push your luck. A consultation with your bank manager may not be a bad idea, but it could bring you down to earth with a bang. This is all to the good if you are to maintain standards and not cruise off into the clouds or beyond. Handling the financial affairs of others could be a bit dicey. A will or a legacy can be the cause of misunderstanding. You are in danger of leaving an investigation unfinished and being hauled over the coals for carelessness. Flashes of inspiration will not get you out of all the problems today, so do your homework before you attempt a task. A merger could hit snags.

14. FRIDAY. Disconcerting. It could be a day of great possibilities. Fortune may favor the brave, so you are not going to relish sitting about and missing the action. Judgment is needed since you are likely to respond instantly to opportunity. Intuition is again your strongest armor. No one else can live your life and the urge to live it to the full will be very strong. So while the more conservative may counsel caution, you are probably in no mood to listen. Nevertheless, your actions will bring their due reward. A journey at short notice may lead to success or failure. There is no knowing. The realist in you will determine the answer. That's life!

15. SATURDAY. Uncertain. There is strong pressure to put all your eggs in one basket. Underlying doubts can mean something or nothing. It depends on your immediate situation and the possibilities of the moment whether you accept any restrictions or just go merrily on your way. Romance could be at a peak. Responsibilities will be felt, but may be brushed aside, at least for a time. Life is for living. Popularity is to be enjoyed. Earlier hopes of expansion may seem to be realized, but the fruit of the harvest is not yet available. Do not lose enthusiasm. Neither should you ignore the odd word of caution that will bring you back to basics every so often.

16. SUNDAY. Enjoyable. Positive cooperation means such a lot. Make the most of your mate's company. Feel free to do things together. It is a great day for living it up, with no holds barred. Get out for the fresh air and sunshine and make the most of every opportunity to enjoy your freedom. The full value of a close relationship can be appreciated when two minds work as one and each respects the feelings of the other. In some ways, you may feel quite philosophic. There could be good news for a student who is full of hope for the future. Examination results may have been pleasing. The world may seem to be your oyster. Share the spoils if your joint efforts are being appreciated by those who really care.

17. MONDAY. Challenging.   A step in the right direction may bring excitement. Responsibility should be undertaken as a direct challenge to your professional expertise. Be your own person. Show that you have ideas of your own which are valid in practical terms. Business life can be stimulating, as well as personally rewarding. You may have a proposal to make to someone rather special. Be sure to make a point of your material possibilities. An honest appreciation can cut both ways and you have nothing to hide. Improvise or experiment while you have the opportunity and the room to maneuver. The best will be brought to light if you act naturally and can be seen in that light.

18. TUESDAY. Disturbing.   It may be time to take things a bit more easily. Relaxing in some holiday resort will suit you to the ground. Someone can make you feel that your moment of love has come. Be generous and you will be admired. Make the most of the earlier part of the day and don't be afraid of exposure if you want to be appreciated. The right sort of publicity could do you good. Later on there may be legalities that could trip you up. A senior partner may resent your progress. A challenge to your authority may unsettle you. See that you have a finer point of an agreement tied up. Do not abuse the letter of the law or seek to upset officials. They are seeking to uphold what is clearly laid down.

19. WEDNESDAY. Rewarding.   Do not undersell yourself. Be aware of the value of human dignity. In the business world there is a need for conservation and a constructive use of resources. Well-filled order books will depend on reliable production and a stable price for products. You seem to have a lot of friends who are to be trusted. This will obviously depend on your social image. So a sense of public responsibility, thought for your fellow beings and a positive determination to influence the current scene will mean a lot to you. Neighborly contacts may not be particularly exciting, but they will give you a sense of being in on the ground floor. You may settle a contract or make a binding agreement that has long-term possibilities. Be firm but friendly.

20. THURSDAY. Mixed.   Social life can be exciting at the moment. You may have great plans and willing supporters. Your image should be excellent, so if you want to achieve something for your community, there is no lack of potential. Finances could be worrying you. This may mean you are inclined to run before you

walk, or that you haven't done your personal calculations properly, or it could even mean that you are getting in a flap about
nothing. Unorthodox methods are not going to pay off as well as
those developed during a period of experiment and trial and error.
Your love life should be working wonders for you, yet there may
be distractions. Stick to what is tangible and forget the rest.

21. FRIDAY. Frustrating.   Appreciate the words of wisdom of
your banker or broker. A new stage of development can be
entered. For a while you may feel out of your depth, but this will
pass. Just allow yourself to relax and appreciate that you have to
learn a great deal, but that you have good advisers and backup. It
may be a quiet or private world you are entering, but contact with
those who know your innermost secrets will be maintained. There
may be some ill-feeling in the neighborhood. At times, you may be
depressed or feel you are being ostracized. This is probably not the
case, so give some time to reflection and you will understand
better what is going on. Gaining publicity is not likely to help.

22. SATURDAY. Sensitive.   You may be getting steamed up
about a love affair. Feeling sorry for yourself is not the answer. If
you feel guilty, you should come clean; and if you are being made
to look small, the answer lies with you. You have possible gains or
blessings in another direction. As one door closes another opens.
Be glad that you have what others may lack. There is no need to
make a fuss about the fact; just be glad. You could be hatching up
something. Considerable backroom intelligence may be needed
and you are going to resent prior publicity. Restrain yourself if you
feel you are being exploited. The gentle touch is much more
appropriate. You can win by charisma. This could be a slow
business, so look before you leap.

23. SUNDAY. Demanding.   A decision may be called for. You
have to come to terms with yourself before pronouncing for others. A close relationship reaches the point of determination one
way or the other. At one time, you will be full of enthusiasm and
positivity and at others you will wish to retreat. Anything important that is going to affect your future must be of this nature. So
once again, trust your intuition. Weigh up the pros and cons, as
you have probably been doing for the past few weeks and you will
come to your point of no return, when all will be solved. If a
publisher is putting pressure on you, give it some thought before
acting. Studies may have left you worn out. Take a breather.

24. MONDAY. Misleading. The best-laid plan may go astray. Talks on money matters can break down. Don't get in a tizzy or try to pick up the pieces too hurriedly. There will be time to reflect, and you are capable of making a firm decision when the time is right. You may feel you are being held back or that you're being held personally responsible for more than your fair share. Leave conjecture to the forecasters. Concentrate on first things. A love affair can still be causing a certain amount of heart searching. Something from the past may be holding you back. Don't be so concerned about your public image as others may see it. Their viewpoint could be the opposite of what you imagine. Be yourself.

25. TUESDAY. Tricky. The ball is right in your court. Decisions made should be positive. See that you have done your homework properly or some slipup can cost you a lot of money. Expert advice may not be up to expectations, so you could be better off trusting your intuition. Agents are out. However, fortune can again favor the brave, provided the brave do not become foolhardy. You recognize the possibility of expansion and immediate progress, so may be called upon to choose your moment. A relationship should now be on better terms and this should make life a lot more easy for you. Know that others are cheering you on. This alone should give you heart.

26. WEDNESDAY. Misleading. Do not be misled by slick salesmen. Your resources need to be maintained, not flushed down the drain. Someone may be playing on your emotions. Family commitment can be getting you down, more so if you feel you are not getting proper support or understanding from your partner. An approach to your banker may not be very productive, but at least you will be put in the picture. This is better than accepting the misleading views of clerks or lesser minions. Something may go awry with a deal. If engaged in any merger or in contracts with large organizations, be very careful that you read the small print. Someone may have the wrong end of the stick.

27. THURSDAY. Mixed. You can turn a blind eye to something that is sensible, but not strictly legal. Private agreements or negotiations can solve problems that overt action would not. Recognize the need to be constantly on your toes and keyed up. This could be wearing if you take it too literally. You would be better off letting natural functions, intuition and insight control your reactions. Financial affairs could be unpredictable. What you are advised may be unprintable! So you are really in charge of your own destiny if you but realized it. Influence may be accepted or rejected. A glamorous person can distract you for a little while. This will be light entertainment for which you can be thankful.

28. FRIDAY. Inactive. Clear your desk as early as possible. You may be on the move and glad to be away from all the action. Something needs to be agreed, one way or the other, in the early hours. This could mean you are late getting to bed, so not interested in today's affairs to any great extent. A lull in the weekly routine can leave you with a long weekend if you play your cards right. But you will not be banking on that. Balancing the books can fully occupy your waking hours in more ways than one, or may be the last thing you want to do. When you find yourself in a vacuum, it is possibly just as well to relax and wait for something to happen. The lull will probably be too short.

29. SATURDAY. Disturbing. Stick to routine. There could be a backlog of musts to clear up. Get cracking and don't watch the clock or you will lose heart. Traveling and idle chitchat should be cut to the minimum. Someone may try to interfere with your weekend plans and this could either get your back up or make you unhappy. Just stick to what you had planned and don't be swayed one way or the other. A neighbor may be depending on you for help. You, in your turn, can be a good neighbor, even if it hurts. Maintain standards. Stand on your own feet and avoid involvement till you have free time to enjoy what you see and do. Shopping could mean a heavy load. No one offers help then.

30. SUNDAY. Confusing. Possibly everyone is unsociable. Could it be that the fault lies with you? Hard work can be made of everything if you feel negative. There may be a strong temptation to get out and see the world. The competition could be heavy. A challenge may be accepted or rejected. It depends upon whether you are trying to impress someone special or just feeling resentful and let down. If you want to be popular you will have to make some sort of showing. Some things you will have to keep to yourself. Rumors or scandal may affect you, but this is no reason to go out of circulation. Give a thought for someone who cannot get around freely, and do something positive.

JULY

1. MONDAY. Routine. Charity begins at home. If you have any doubts about priorities, just remember this golden rule. It could be a quiet day, but on the other hand there can be basic matters that need attention. So that would not leave you a lot of time on your hands. Consider anything to do with personal security. Perhaps it could be appropriate to revise home safety devices if you expect to go off on vacation shortly. Priorities are important. Domestic matters of any kind could need some consideration. The family may be visiting soon. Someone may remark that you need to get your house in order and it will score a hit.

2. TUESDAY. Rewarding. Make visitors welcome. You can treat everyone on equal terms, the sign of a good host or hostess. Private engagements seem to be sought, or you are in demand for your personal views and advice. Keep up with the news. There may be an opportunity to do someone important a favor or to accept such. Get to the bottom of anything that may have been puzzling you, in a diplomatic way. Yesterday's preoccupations may have eased your mind somewhat and you feel you can understand most things, given the room. An unusual request can lead to an improvement in your financial position. There may be things you want to do to get out of a rut. Be adventurous and imaginative today and you'll make some folk take notice.

3. WEDNESDAY. Happy. Finalize any negotiations or arrangements. If you are buying or selling property, take advantage of an agent who is on the ball. Dependents may be becoming more self-sufficient. This is something you may welcome. But it may also make you realize that you need less hassle in order to do the things that turn you on. So you will be pleased to have willing assistance and glad to get your house in better order. A visitor is likely to bring you good news. An auction may attract you, especially if you have a taste for old things or connections with the past. You could unearth a minor treasure if you probe around a bit. Helping someone with a financial problem can give you a boost.

4. THURSDAY. Demanding. Be very careful as to how you go about your business. Beware of where and how long you park; the law may show no mercy, despite its being Independence Day. Some disagreement may be encountered with a parent. Appreciate that superiors have problems. One is likely to fly off the handle and take it out on you. So have your answers prepared. It could be difficult to relax because of tension around you. An important display, or an opportunity to show off your talent, can be put at risk if you get too uptight. Tension can keep you right on your toes and able to make a hit. It all depends on the way you want to put yourself across. Don't be too upset if you fail to get an immediate, positive response. A child can be a little too mischievous.

5. FRIDAY. Successful. Get cracking. Make up for lost time and opportunity. There is a need to do something about your public image; so make use of publicity if the opportunity arises. A long trip may be taken and thoroughly enjoyed. You have a mission that cannot be delayed in its execution. Students have an opportunity to make direct headway. Love life should pick up quickly after a short lull. There could be a proposal, possibly on the spur of the moment. Once you feel you have someone who cares, you are naturally inclined to wait for no other opinion. You are intuitive enough to know what you want and what you like. The young will cooperate. Judgment should be good.

6. SATURDAY. Demanding. Necessities can govern your actions. If you have to work when you would rather be playing, that's just too bad. Try to make the most of whatever opportunity you get. Keep your comments under control or you may feel like biting your tongue. Local relationships can be anything but congenial. Leave neighbors to sort out their own problems. Don't interfere, and give short shrift to anyone who meddles in your business. It will be better to clear the air than store feelings up inside. Someone you know may be ill. Put your best foot forward to help. If you just sit around and don't make an effort you're going to feel very frustrated.

7. SUNDAY. Confusing. You will have to be philosophic. There will be business or some financial worries you will want to resolve. Imagination can run riot when you cannot get down to practicalities. You would be better off reading a good book than trying to sort out the family finances. There may be a threat of losing your job. Wait till that's a fact before getting in a cold sweat. If the worst comes to worst, you have the initiative and good luck this year to adjust. Someone may adopt a disguise of importance and lead you astray. Do not take anyone you don't know well at face value. Too many cooks spoil the broth and you can do without false prophets. Keep your cool and rely on your own judgment.

8. MONDAY. Exciting. Take your time knowing that you're on the right track. Cooperation is the name of the game. A partner may please you. There is every hope of consolidating a position you have just gained and thus feeling a lot more secure. It may be necessary to take a partner into your confidence on a matter of local interest. Do your homework properly and attend to each detail. There should be no slipup. If you delegate, or are yourself a delegate, be sure of facts and the limits to which you can negotiate or agree. Legalities will work for you, provided you make no attempt to abuse a privilege. Studies can be speeded up by a cooperative effort. If you have a driving test soon, get someone to fire technical and legal questions at you this evening.

9. TUESDAY. Happy. It will be a happy day for settling legal points. Feel free to expand, knowing that there is a great future in doing so. Your partner may have something special to tell you today. If there is to be the patter of tiny feet, you will feel on top of the world. A long journey could lie ahead or be embarked upon. This should blow away the cobwebs and put a new slant on things. It is still a good time to enjoy cooperation for what you can get out of it. An examination may still be of importance and this continues to be a good time for preparation or comparing notes. Professional advice will not go amiss. Be glad to give or take. Be optimistic.

10. WEDNESDAY. Profitable. Your luck should be holding out. Someone is getting very attached to you, even though you may be apart. Influential people in your private life could be making things far more easy for you in their own quiet way. You may be let in on a secret. There is considerable enthusiasm for what you are doing or the way you are doing it. Put your best foot forward and take those who support your efforts along with you. The lesson of true partnership will have been made very clear over the week. Make sure it is fully implemented today. You could get financial backing without too much fuss, but keep this to yourself.

11. THURSDAY. Erratic. Well-intentioned plans may be opposed. It may seem impossible to get any agreement on basic policies or principles. You should go it alone where you feel it wise and be very careful with whom you share your secrets. Inside information can put you wise to conniving or downright treachery that may be used against you. This may have an effect, but perhaps you are best left to make up your own mind and ignore the more lurid possibilities. Bankers may be on your side when you are in need, or they may possibly close the shutters. It will be a clear decision, so treat all events as possibilities and be honest in your dealings. You are not really alone.

12. FRIDAY. Disconcerting. Climatic conditions can get you down. Being out of your depth or away from your usual stamping ground may land you in trouble. If you are out on a limb, be prepared to stand up for your rights or take the consequences. It may be necessary to leave an older member of the family or a close friend behind while you go off on a business journey. Rather than worry, make arrangements for a neighbor to look in to see how things are going. Do not take yourself too seriously. You must have a break from routine, no matter what the circumstances. Otherwise, you could crack up. Foreigners may misunderstand you, or you could be at a loss with them. It is difficult to interpret.

13. SATURDAY. Manageable. You have far to go. Get all the details clear. Air terminal problems could be minimal if you have made reasonable preparation. If you have been somewhat careless, you can be sure there will be a hitch that is time-wasting. Don't expect security staff to let you go through everything scot-free unless you show a bit of courtesy and awareness. A lot depends on the way you handle yourself. Your image will be tarnished if you act in a heavy-handed way when there is no cause. A devious person can break barriers, but this practice is not recommended. Give credit to someone who is studying. A little bit of morale boosting will work wonders. In-laws may be very kind.

14. SUNDAY. Mixed. You seem to be in the public eye. Make a good entrance since this is half the battle. It is not the day for staying indoors, so take a break and get into the limelight. Show biz-folk can hit the headlines. Publicity or advertising will come without effort. You could meet someone who is going to end up as an adviser or agent. Make full use of your charm where you want it to register the most. It is highly possible you are going to be selective. Some may want to fiddle while Rome burns. You haven't got time for such luxuries, knowing that you have to make your mark today. Flattery will be attempted to win your favor. Don't be misled. You should be the one to call the tune.

15. MONDAY. Useful. Dealings behind closed doors can be successful. Nevertheless, you should be careful what you sign or agree to with those who are from abroad or who are nitpickers

about definitions. A moral crisis can be reached. Something will
have to be interpreted in the light of principles and not practice. A
satisfactory arrangement can be made on your personal salary for
responsibilities now being carried out. The long-term situation
may yet be undecided. Don't rush things. All will be sorted out in
the end. Matters could be developing toward an arrangement
about a merger. Have a word late in the day with someone influential on that score. You may suffer from travel sickness today.

16. TUESDAY. Disconcerting. Be content with your progress
to date. Push your luck and you could be back to square one. A
skeleton may be dragged out of a closet, so it is best you are not
around when that occurs. Be sociable, but choose your friends
carefully. Older and more stable company is appreciated. Resources you have nurtured for years should not be pulled out of
their cubby hole to satisfy a whim. A publisher may try to extract
something from you that is not yet ready for publication. Be on
your guard against careless talk or misrepresentation, whether by
you or about you. Stick to routine and you will be all right. Take
on too much and you could be up the creek minus a paddle.

17. WEDNESDAY. Changeable. You may feel that even your
best friends don't want you. It's rather like the feeling of being
snubbed. If that's how it seems, just don't bother. Anyway, it
could be just your imagination! Finances may not stretch to social
ambitions. You can either feel sorry for yourself or be philosophical. If it's worth having, no doubt you will do something about it.
If not, then why get hot and bothered? There may be an opening
you will appreciate, out of town or off your beaten track. It's time
to be adventurous and put out feelers, at least, if not take positive
steps. Someone from a foreign land may strike up a friendship.
Some of the things said may confuse you, but you'll catch on.

18. THURSDAY. Mixed. Social aims may be confounded by a
banker or official. Don't let this change your mind, but you may
have to bide your time till the climate is clearer. New evidence that
has official backing could scuttle plans for a little while. You have
other fish to fry, so should redirect your energies and not take a
reversal too badly. Business intervention can give you private
comfort. After-hours dealing can start something going that will
lead to a different approach. An active business colleague seems
keen to get you back into the public eye. Listen and make preparations, but don't start anything off till you are ready. Otherwise,
you could lose it all.

19. FRIDAY. Useful. Put your finger in the pie, but do so quietly. Improve your position without being too obvious. Private deals are the best and you will have a willing ally in a place where it is all going on. Romance is in the air early in the day, so make your plans when you have the chance. Counter-attractions or distractions could intervene and slow you up. Intuitive action may lead to financial gain. It could be that you can invest well in something electrical or time-saving. A quick transfer of funds can meet a need. You may have a specialist friend who gives good advice. Do someone a good turn while you're in the mood. Tomorrow could be too late. So then a friend will turn to someone else.

20. SATURDAY. Disturbing. Be careful about what you are doing. Get out of a rut that stops you from thinking straight. There is a chance that you are misunderstood, that you act dumb or just can't be bothered to understand what someone is saying to you. This is no way to go on. It may be time to dig in your toes; but there should be a good reason other than self-defense or stubbornness. It may seem that you cannot change a set routine. Perhaps you don't want to. There is a need to make up your own mind without getting pulled this way and that. Take time to think things out in a positive way and don't be blackmailed into doing what goes against reason. Dreams may be upsetting. Maybe you have a friend who can find a positive interpretation.

21. SUNDAY. Mixed. Personal initiative may bring personal problems. Your love life can be the object of some public discussion. Or you may want to get something you have kept secret until now out into the open. Don't be devious in your dealings. It may be hard to keep your cool, but this could bring things to a head more quickly. If you have prepared yourself beforehand you should be able to counter any negative reaction to your proposals. Quite naturally, you will want to get on with your own life. Relationships may be strained, especially if your nearest and dearest has to be away from home at the weekend. A good book can soothe your nerves, perhaps.

22. MONDAY. Inactive. Good judgment counts for a lot. You could be out of town on a mission, so some folks may think you are out of circulation. That will suit you. Later on you will reap what you have sown. It is an excellent day for getting down to studies and for taking examinations. The go-ahead for a production or a publicity scheme can be agreed upon. Some could say this is a lucky day for you. You will probably know a little better and assume that you have timed things well and will thus get your due deserts. However, you won't argue too much about the meaning of words, unless you are posed with that on a question paper! Go your own sweet way at your own pace; all will fall into place.

23. TUESDAY. Lucky. Make good use of your car. For that matter, any sort of transport will be an asset. Good news is on the way or has arrived by now. Contact with someone a long way from you can be restored and improved. Someone may be going home or you may be off on a mission you are going to welcome. Develop an interest in the media. Publicize where you can. Seek professional advice on a personal matter and follow instructions. You feel you have taken off after a long wait. There will be a change of goals later in the day, so tie up all loose ends before you close a chapter. In-laws make life easy for you and you are glad you keep in touch. It's nice to be wanted.

24. WEDNESDAY. Sensitive. Control a natural desire to make a fortune in a day. Business activities will ensure financial reward. If you get the bit between your teeth you may undo what success you have achieved. It's all up to you whether you act in a conventional manner or try something out of the ordinary. You may pull something off, but on the other hand, the moment of truth could be a calamity. So if you have to do something special or extraordinary, try to make it pleasurable and not painful. You should feel very pleased about a relationship that is developing nicely. Your career prospects, too, seem to be going great guns. Indeed, you seem to be satisfying a number of aims and ambitions.

25. THURSDAY. Slow. You may hear of a union. It could mark an important point in someone's life. Your grapevine seems to be working well. Look after material things. A business matter can now be closed and something new is taking off. This may or may not have an impact on your affairs, but at least you should keep yourself in the picture. Early birds catch the worm this morning. Your little friends may whisper something in your ear that you can put to good use. An investment could prove worthwhile, but keep the source of your information under wraps. You are not generally prepared to venture beyond the immediate material needs of the day. It could be engrossing.

26. FRIDAY. Confusing. There is a decision to be made. Without doubt, you have to stand up and be counted. The law or authority in some form may take a dim view of your attitude. Be careful when driving, for instance. Be sure you have alternative transport available in case of emergency. You must not be caught wanting if your services are needed out of town or even overseas. Parting from a parent can pull at your heart strings. Check on excise regulations if exporting for the first time. You can face delays that could affect your income and future. So be prepared for all sorts of situations. Do not take anything or anyone for granted. Shoulder your responsibilities.

27. SATURDAY. Distressing. There will be little hope of having the weekend free. Pressure from people who want to stay anonymous can put you off your stroke. A journey may turn out to be a mistake and you would have been better off at home. Local disturbances or dissatisfaction can make life somewhat miserable for part of the day. There is probably far too much to do and you'll feel like running off and forgetting all about it. By letting your hair down, you can partly succeed, but your conscience may prick you. It would be best to get on with what you know is unavoidable and make your own fun as it strikes you. Careless folk may upset you. That is really their loss.

28. SUNDAY. Difficult. Do not rely on others. Careless talk or forgetfulness is likely to upset your schedule. Family involvement can be a bit too much and you would feel better left to your own devices. A message can come at an unfortunate time such as when you are in the attic or taking a bath. A dash to the telephone may be too late and you will wonder all day who called. There may be a career or reputation matter to discuss. Try to get things into perspective without missing any detail. In the end you may leave it till tomorrow, particularly if too many people try to influence your judgment. You may feel sadly out of touch with what is going on around you. That is just as well; it is probably quite trivial.

29. MONDAY. Mixed. Counter-bids for a piece of property can surprise you. Be prepared to take unorthodox steps to get what you want. A piece of valuable bric-a-brac may be dropped. If you are on the ball, there could be some way of restoring it. Spend your money sensibly and that does not mean to hang about waiting for a bargain. The early bird is going to catch the worm, though that may not appear to be the case at times. Love life can be rough. Either that or someone in the family is having second thoughts about an engagement. Your reputation may be challenged. A bit of modern-day security technology could save your apartment from a housebreaker. But that could remind you to lock up before you go off to business.

30. TUESDAY. Lucky. There is not such a need to be quick off the mark. Time spent in consideration or preparation will not be wasted. An old and respected member of the family circle may visit for a little while. The photograph albums will probably be brought to light and reminiscences take over the day. Private arrangements for a future get-together should be considered or set in motion. Concentrate your mind today. You seem to be wrapped up in past history or wanting to get in touch with distant relatives. Do some discreet counseling with an agent or dealer if you are in the property market. Keep your ear to the ground for a good sale or special offer. You hear of a bargain from an unusual source.

31. WEDNESDAY. Rewarding. Positive thinking gets you places. A child may appear to grow up quite amazingly fast and take on responsibilities. You have good reports of an examination or of studies that concern you or a youngster. An official, possibly a man of letters, has a special role to play in your day. Creative talents should be exploited to the full. Your love life is doing fine. Perhaps you should have a word with a parent. Permission should be sought to form an organization that provides entertainment. You will feel you must make some impact, either at the local level or through a wider area. No door is closed, so make hay while the sun shines. Some favorable publicity could work wonders.

AUGUST

1. THURSDAY. Manageable. Take your opportunities when you can. Judgment should be good, but avoid gambling either with money or love. Positive progress can be made socially or in ways that will produce results in your career. Talents should be fully exploited as you decide, not as some would suggest. Do beware of those who are trying to take advantage of your generosity. Naiveté is all too easily spotted by the wily customers you can meet today. Romance should be kept on an even keel by having respect for well-tried values. Something may be very tempting, but there can be a lot of superficial dressing that isn't really truly reflective of the inner core. You may need to dress the window yourself.

2. FRIDAY. Erratic. Don't take life so seriously. You may just be fed up with your job. If that is the case, why not look around for another? But see that you do not lose out on conditions or salary. There may be a promotion in the pipeline and you are longing to get into a different place to enjoy the change. Problems with a car or bicycle may mean you have to get up early and walk to your destination. That won't turn you on, for a start. Talk over possible changes of working conditions with staff. If you do not keep them in the picture, you could have lowered production or resignations to deal with. There is every reason to expect changes that are good for reputation.

3. SATURDAY. Sensitive. Tread carefully with your boss or the law. You may be judged as usurping authority, whereas this is your last intention. Exercise authority only when it is your right and then only where it means you can improve a situation. Do not make an issue of it. There is an excellent opportunity to make money if you go about it in the right way. Some may resent this success and try to influence others against you. It will not work, but you must be on your guard. There are those who will apply the letter of the law, though not the spirit. No good will come from crying over spilt milk. Just keep your weather eye open for any disagreeable types. Traveling is not in the cards.

4. SUNDAY. Enjoyable. A marriage may be arranged. The better the day, the better the deed. Cordial relationships with neighbors means that you and your mate can be free to have a day out without worry about your home. This may give you a chance to patch up something that has been rankling for a little while. You could have a lot of quite serious talking to do without being bored in any way. A weekend conference may take up your time. Plans for expansion of a business or project should be discussed and all viewpoints considered. The legalities of a position can be settled in principle so that action can be taken on resumption of normal trading tomorrow. A special letter or invitation should be written.

5. MONDAY. Uncertain. Your partner may be a little touchy. Hasty actions can lead to misused potential. A career can be put in jeopardy through uncooperative attitudes. Be sure this does not apply to you. Get something cleared up at business before making any attempt to expand. Too many cooks may spoil the broth which can apply to work-related affairs. The wise advice of a senior partner or a consultant should be heeded. Legal complications will be coming your way if you do not act more discreetly. If you are the target of attack, seek advice and you will feel a lot more at ease. Take things one at a time. You must first qualify before you can earn a better position. Be patient and use your head.

6. TUESDAY. Inactive. Early relief from problems can make you feel a lot more happy at the start of the day. You are probably in need of peace and quiet after yesterday. Provided you can get your partner to agree, this could be an ideal day to both take a backseat and do a bit of looking around. A joint shopping expedition may be just the thing to get you away from everyday pressures, yet also do something constructive. There is something you may want to look into. Perhaps it affects your dependents, or you are doing someone a favor by looking after their financial problems. Recent legal wrangles may have left you a bit deflated. You will get over it, never fear. Start by forgetting all about them.

7. WEDNESDAY. Useful. You have a choice of directions. A head-on approach could meet with unexpected opposition. If you value your reputation, you can take a stand for what appears to be an expeditious solution. Your choice should prove well-founded. Misleading rumors can give you the wrong slant. That is all the more reason why you have to do your homework before slipping into top gear. You ought to be able to get the right information if you are discreet. If you try to buy your way into something, you could be dealing with the wrong people. Extortion is in the cards in one form or another. Personal resources may be put at risk if you do anything of a dishonest nature.

8. THURSDAY. Sensitive. Be optimistic and practical. Nothing is going to drop into your lap unless it is to be used. Extremes should be considered. This will mean you have a choice but the problem will be to make that choice correctly. Provided you are positive and look to the future, very little will go wrong. If you doubt your abilities, or listen too much to those who secretly envy you, it is possible you could stagnate or even miss your chance. So keep your eyes and ears open for the occasional opportunity to shine. Studies can keep you confined. Take advantage of such seclusion to get down to constructive work. It is tomorrow, not today, that will show clearly the proof of the pudding.

9. FRIDAY. Mixed. A position in teaching or publicity may be offered you. It is time you made a name for yourself, so come to terms with the situation. Past history may be cited to put you off making a major decision. Take note of precedent, but do not let negative trends stop you from making progress. You are now in a position to tie up loose ends and wipe a slate completely clean. It is impossible to be in two places at once or to appear as open to some, yet secretive to others. Undercurrents may be understood, but they should not be allowed to decide your future at this stage. Take a step forward and get out of the past if it impedes.

10. SATURDAY. Confusing. There could be a showdown. You may be drawn in to referee a long-standing disagreement. See that you maintain your decorum and don't take sides. A negative view of things is going to be of little value. Officials may be deciding issues on unreliable or outdated information. If you cannot intervene or lend a helping hand, it may be as well to wait until a more settled time when prejudice is not so obvious. Publishing something important can prove difficult. Professionals are possibly right, but not very optimistic about the future. They could be relying too heavily on precedent, with their heads in the sand. Look for people with vision and optimism for advice.

11. SUNDAY. Productive. The quickness of the hand deceives the eye. Be right on your toes to get the best out of your chances. Artistic interests can turn you on. Someone will have to be won over by you or you will explode. Be engaging. Don't give up trying to hold someone's attention. The green-eyed monster could come into the picture if you cannot get what you're after. But on the whole, you are able to attract and hold. Surprise tactics are most useful. Flattery, too, should not be discounted as a legitimate weapon. Financial interests will be well-served by keeping an open mind and a good agent who knows a bargain when it's there. You are not looking after business today, just your reputation.

12. MONDAY. Rewarding. Restore someone to a place of importance. Your handling of a delicate operation can put you at the top of someone's popularity poll. There is no need to brood over possible solutions or decisions. Relax and allow your intuition to do the donkey work. Insight or the common touch gives you a lead over business rivals. Added to that, you should be able to get on the inside lane if you keep your grapevine in good working order. A charitable deed or an interest in charitable works will give you a happy outlet for either energies or personal influence. Let your light shine in the darkest corners to be most effective. But don't spoil it by broadcasting it far and wide.

13. TUESDAY. Tricky. The social round is not for you. You will probably have a go and find you are left out in the cold by some, or that your usual circle of friends is currently nonexistent. It may be prices that keep things quiet. Or you may be getting a bit fed up with company that really is not your sort. Money can be wasted or hoarded. If you haven't got it you cannot spend it and if you get it easily you will be inclined to waste it. It can all be a bit perplexing. This could be a trying day from a business standpoint. Expense accounts may be questioned. If you have any large contracts to handle, look to the financial setup before making a commitment. Slick people are after your hard-earned money.

14. WEDNESDAY. Challenging. There are hopes and prospects after all. You may need the good cheer of someone important to liven you up. Be prepared to take over a leading role and make good publicity for yourself. A project can get official sponsorship and be sure of lift-off. You may be offered an overseas post with great prospects for the future. A celebration seems to be called for. There is a definite possibility that you could have new in-laws very soon. It will suit your style to mix with the right people. It will not be for any particular reason other than they are good company. It may come as a pleasant revelation and confirm something you have always felt, but could never quite define.

15. THURSDAY. Fortunate. Discretion is the better part of valor. Do good in a quiet way. You have a reputation to look after, but there should be no ulterior motive in anything charitable you attempt today. An appearance in public can help some who are unable to enjoy the sunshine. Be very gentle with a loved one who may be feeling like a goldfish now, then at other times all in the dark. It's a case of making the best of both worlds for everyone's benefit. You are conscious of the value of behind-the-scenes people who seem to get very little out of their public reputations. Do something to put matters more in line with reality. You can be popular in your own quiet way.

16. FRIDAY. Useful. False modesty will not work. If you mean to do something, get it done. Inner drive may be needed to achieve your ends. You may appear to be obstinate, but wait to see what the end results will be. Taking too much criticism from those who do all the talking and not enough of the action will undoubtedly be unwarranted. Poor publicity can result from wrong thinking. It is far better to get tangible results than to rely on the media to do your work for you. On the quiet, you may be quite encouraged by the reaction to your suggestions offered to top brass. There may be a promotion at the end of the line. It will have been well-earned. You remember something from the past.

17. SATURDAY. Pleasant. Generous offers should be accepted in the spirit in which they are made. Something may be getting under your skin, possibly at business. Be patient with those who have to make a show in order to make ends meet. Personal inclinations are likely to clash with those of a close friend or lover. That is all part of the game. An opportunity overseas is something that you must consider positively. This could be a red-letter day for you. Personal initiative can be rewarded, though it may seem that you are being rushed in some way. A parent seems to be heading for the sun, either on vacation or to a new home. You have to make the most of higher education or the professional services of someone who is tops.

18. SUNDAY. Easygoing. Your day is your own. Don't be lost for ideas, but do not expect others to come rushing at your call. People you know may be out of the country or on vacation. Take things as they come if you feel so inclined; if you have plans, just get going with them. The personal approach is the best. Perhaps you are too wrapped up in yourself to notice what's going on around you. This is not a bad thing, because above all, you have to depend on your intuition and own judgment to make life worthwhile. This occasionally leads to misunderstandings by those who never bother to get to the bottom of your nature. Perhaps you have a feeling that all will go well in the future.

19. MONDAY. Uncertain. Do not be rushed into a business deal. Your reputation could be at stake. Take advice from someone who knows the ropes and stick to your principles. You may still be considering an offer. Today may be the last when things will be going smoothly enough for you to be objective. Changes at head office could upset your routine. Don't take this too personally. Perhaps it is time you made a move and developed talents. Qualifications have to mean something important at this point in your career. Look on the bright side and take note of what you are being offered on very generous terms. It's a great day for the outdoors, once you get work out of the way. Don't rush.

20. TUESDAY. Confusing. Expert advice could be very handy. There may be a strong inclination building up within you to make a break and become more independent. Perhaps this is right and perhaps it is wrong. No one will be able to understand fully what is going on but you. So be very conscious of your responsibilities. In particular, do nothing with resources that cannot be stopped if found to be in error. Get-rich-quick plans should be investigated more fully. You know that your financial position this year can be erratic, to say the least. So when you are being tempted, it will pay you to think again. After all, you may feel you can do as you like with your assets. On your own head be it, and good luck!

21. WEDNESDAY. Excellent. Money matters can still be sensitive. There is more chance of helpful inside information that may keep you on the right track. Do not toy with anyone's affections, nor should you be oversensitive about your own. Deep feelings and desires can move mountains. An official wants to meet you or has something special to tell you. An official letter could bring good news. You may be in the good books now with a teacher or educational theorist who holds a prominent position. An introduction could encourage you to greater efforts with hopes of promotion. It's a case of do as I say and you are half-way there. Give some time to a good cause. Raise funds. Use your charm and gentle manners to persuade.

22. THURSDAY. Mixed. Your movements can be restricted. If your car has given up the ghost, this may remind you to keep up with regular servicing. Routine may be getting you down. The sight of well-to-do people sunning themselves can make you resentful. This is a sheer waste of time as you will soon readily agree. When someone with influence makes you an offer, look at it squarely. You may be pleased or may wonder why. Nice people do not bear grudges and you may either charm someone or be charmed. It's up to you to be positive and enjoy what is offered. Someone from overseas can be attracted to you and this should lift you out of your boredom or self-imposed misery. Find time for love.

23. FRIDAY. Inactive. Take time out to catch up with mail. Mental interests and pursuits are most pressing. This can mean you would rather be on your own than in company. Neighborhood involvement is in. Outside attractions may leave you cold, as there may be better fish to fry in your own locality. It could be wise to cultivate local talent or visit local places of attraction. You may be missing out on something important if you don't keep in touch with the passing scene right here on your doorstep. Colleagues may drop in on you, but you don't want to be pressed or involved in things that are for those with ideas of grandeur. Stick to your own kind of pleasures.

24. SATURDAY. Uncertain. There is plenty of choice before you. Confusion may reign if you cannot make up your mind where to go on vacation. All sorts of people may be trying to get in touch with you on something that seems quite simple in your eyes. Make a list of priorities. You could have to learn a great deal in a short time. See that you get first things first. There is a temptation to go all-out, but this may lead to a shortfall that you cannot retrieve. A relationship may be under strain due to the absence of one partner. A breakdown in communications will complicate matters more. This may seem to be stretching things too far. You will have to curb your enthusiasm and take things as they come.

25. SUNDAY. Uncertain. Study track records before making important decisions. You are in a position to weigh up the technical possibilities of different systems. Domestic problems need your attention. You should not be afraid to take your own, independent initiative if you feel something has to be renewed, renovated or completely replaced. The early hours could find you walking the floor trying to make up your mind about the future. Just relax and get your priorities sorted out. Business can be pressing. You cannot be in two places at once, so should be content with one occupation and appreciate that charity begins at home. Make changes in the home where they are necessary.

26. MONDAY. Rewarding. A great deal of love could be coming your way. Be generous in showing your affection. In other words, be yourself. A business deal can be settled with an overseas client or branch office. This could mark the end of something that has attracted a lot of attention. Look ahead now to starting something rather different. Another trade or practice understood means more than just another feather in your cap. It could lead to a better job in the future. Use your position to do some sorting out of private affairs. There may be something that affects the family which is better given a gentle airing than staying hidden in secrecy. Someone may blow their top late tonight or in the early hours.

27. TUESDAY. Successful. Make hay while the sun shines for you. A promise you made should be kept. Perhaps you want to think about settling down. You have a talent that is in demand, so don't be shy. See, however, that you get your just reward for any performance you may give. A courtship with someone far away could be going great guns. Traveling just for fun is right up your street at the moment. You'll probably be the envy of friends who have not been as progressive as yourself. It is possibly a matter of taste as well as good fortune. You bear no grudges and are glad to be your own person. Feel free when you are on the move. Be glad that someone stands by you when you settle. It is nice to know you have an ally at your side.

28. WEDNESDAY. Disconcerting. Artistic talents may not be appreciated. Love life can be in a muddle. You may dazzle someone without knowing the effect you make. Or you may be madly in love with someone you know is unattainable. Living in a dream can wear you down more quickly than hard manual work. So get out of it and act your age. Something you want to produce or promote can be out of the question at the moment, just for shortage of the money it would require. Do not attempt gambling to solve a money worry. There is only one outcome there and you know it will not be an improvement. Enjoy your day by doing things you know you can handle. Bear no one a grudge.

29. THURSDAY. Uncertain. It is all happening in your love life today. Admirers abound. You can have your hands full trying to answer your fan mail. Don't let the grass grow under your feet. Make dates now if you want to get your weekend straightened out. It may be the end of a break from work, and night duty could be looming up on the horizon. Make every effort to get a promoter or publicity agent to move into action on your behalf. News should be good. Be optimistic and you could take off. If you are in show biz, you may feel this is the last chance you will have before a deadline. The young enthrall you with their easy wit and understanding. It is a pleasure to observe and learn.

30. FRIDAY. Challenging. Take more interest in what you consume. Just for a change, become interested in what goes into your system and you will be astonished, if not amazed. Some dietary instruction may have to be given and received. If you have to see a doctor or specialist, be sure to ask questions if you are in the dark. Work can be more rewarding. Possibly there is something new or different about your surroundings. Take a tip from one who knows about ways to earn a living, or the tricks of the trade that can supplement your normal income. You should be able to earn something on the side quite honestly. Get yourself toned up if you are out of condition. You may be torn between strenuous action and idleness.

31. SATURDAY. Mixed. Concentrate on making a name for yourself. Practical measures count more than publicity or studies today. Sporting ventures or the use of muscle can put you in the limelight. Leave studies alone for the weekend. They will begin to pall when you see others out enjoying the fresh air. It may be too late to make a trip out of town. Your dearest love may be hard to find when you have free time. Take no chances with a job-vacancy offer. Get with it as fast as you can and check up. You need to be sure of things and not have to rely on promises. In-laws can be out when you visit. In future, you'll make an appointment. It is not in your best interests to be casual.

SEPTEMBER

1. SUNDAY. Disturbing. Outside pressures may upset your weekend. Cooperation at any level is difficult to achieve. Career prospects, or lack of them, can be bothering you and making life for all around you a bit of a misery. Your partner can be justified in bringing you back to reality, or leaving you to your own devices. Interference in a marriage by someone who should know better could cause more complications than you need. Do not worry yourself over possible legal problems when there is nothing constructive you can do at this moment. Better to let things hang fire till you are in a better position to instill confidence into those who depend on your guidance. Try not to be a martyr.

2. MONDAY. Rewarding. Things will suddenly click into place on this Labor Day. There could be a change of management in business or a completely revised approach in the months ahead, bringing in new blood and new ideas. Promotion is possible with an increase in salary far above expectations. Share your joys, because much may have hinged on a partnership and cooperative efforts. Something positive and helpful may come from contacts with friends who are overseas. Your love life may take a turn for the better. There could be an engagement or declaration naming the day. The big chief seems to be enthusiastic about your prospects, so you could be starting off on something important.

3. TUESDAY. Sensitive. Control your emotions if you can. Extraordinary pressure may be placed on your patience. Other people's problems may become more of a liability than you care to tolerate. Finance matters may have to be reviewed on the spur of the moment, if you are approached for a loan. Do nothing without consulting your partner. If he or she is not involved, you may at least get a second opinion on the best way to handle matters. Banking facilities are available, if needed. Your superior may be sounding you out about a business matter. Keep up to date with your information just in case something or someone needs an immediate reaction. Keep your eyes and ears open for changes.

4. WEDNESDAY. Rewarding. You should feel more settled and confident. Having done your homework you should be more in control of events. Private discussions or arrangements can keep you out of trouble. Do not let your left hand know exactly what the right hand is doing. Just keep your options open so that you have a trump or two up your sleeve. Someone you treat as an equal will approve of being kept in the picture. This could be a good evening for a tête-à-tête. Something to your advantage can come to light and add to your store of knowledge. Research pays off, though there may be no general appreciation of the fact. Do someone in need a favor. You won't regret it, and the person you help will not forget it.

5. THURSDAY. Challenging. Make progress when you get the chance. Have no second thoughts on a course of action, once you have made up your mind. Develop business interests in unexplored areas. The desire to range far and wide should be accepted and something purposeful done to bring about results. You will be looking for immediate results if you get going. Friends can be particularly enthusiastic in what you are up to. Promote yourself while the going is good. Self-advertisement can be effective. Make a journey, if called upon to do so, at short notice. Opportunity can make a brief appearance. You have to be on the ball to take advantage. Social contacts aid you in your search for knowledge.

6. FRIDAY. Satisfactory. A hectic day lies ahead. There could be complications or many opportunities. It depends largely on your attitude as to whether positive gains are made or you take a step backward. Too much concentration on the past, or tradition, or old-fashioned ideas, can slow you down. Positive thinking will keep you ahead of the field. It is a day to boost morale. Someone may speak of love and you see into the future through rose colored glasses. This need not be a dream. At the moment, you have the right contacts and can make the right moves. So make the most of your chances and don't hang around too long waiting for the next big break. For all you know, there may never be another.

7. SATURDAY. Exciting. You can see the woods despite the trees. It may be a relief to be in the driver's seat and responsible for your own actions. Act independently when you feel you have a clear road ahead. There is considerable expertise at hand if you need advice or reassurance. Influential help is close by and quite understanding of the current situation. You may feel you are fast approaching a major point of change in your life. This could affect your career and, in a way, make you conscious of your possibilities. Make changes where you think they are necessary. You are not to be pushed around, but can give a direct lead to those who, like you, are eager for new developments.

8. SUNDAY. Challenging.   Realize your full potential. This will be a day for great things, given the right environment. Expect to be in the public eye and do nothing that may discredit you. There is another chapter opening up that you must learn to develop, with the future in mind. Subtlety may be a key factor in the day's affairs. You can be fascinated or can fascinate others. All, let it be said, with good intent and no ulterior motive. Get to know someone special in a private and personal way. You should not let glamour or praise tarnish or undermine your good intentions. Flattery will seem shallow, while true affection and understanding can be appreciated. You know exactly where you are going.

9. MONDAY. Mixed.   This will be another day to implement your ideas. Start off as you mean to continue. Do not let the grass grow under your feet. An energetic friend can either urge you on or lend support to your initiative. Two heads are better than one. Consolidate gains. Install a means of communication somewhere to your advantage. There may be a move to settle something connected with your social life. A life membership may be accepted on the spur of the moment. Obviously you are inclined to put your eggs in one basket. There may be someone around you who is unreliable or erratic. Be careful how you go about handling equipment you do not yet understand. Hang on to money!

10. TUESDAY. Useful.   Enjoy some good company. You may be in love and not too interested in practicalities. Social involvement gives you an extra boost. You could be in party mood and out of touch with more down-to-earth affairs. Money can flow like water when you are letting your hair down. Business finances can be boosted by fair trading and an enlarging market. Yet you need to keep an eye on unnecessary waste of resources through bad management. Excessive overheads can reduce gains to near losses if some control is not strengthened. Entertaining at company expense can be quite heavy. It may be worth the cost or it may not.

11. WEDNESDAY. Productive.   Be quietly firm with yourself and those with whom you deal. A period of noncommunication could bring a point home to someone who is becoming a thorn in the flesh. A neighbor may be in trouble and you are in a position to help. Practical measures are called for. There is no point in being depressed and doing nothing about it, so make a move to pitch in

with your contribution. Information received in private or from a
private source can let you into a secret. Use such good news to
advantage. It will help you cope with other things that may be
getting you down. Someone with influence will have a quiet word
in your ear. You have the same ideas and should try to keep
control of events insofar as is possible.

12. THURSDAY. Sensitive. Unorthodox methods can prove a
success. Do nothing by halves. Press home an advantage, though
you may not be giving that impression to the casual observer. A
long-felt want can be satisfied. You are conscious of background
and family upbringing that has kept you single-minded over the
years. Give someone you respect a boost by proving that a near
impossibility can, in fact, be made possible. There is a lot of quiet
satisfaction around you. Some may think you are biting off more
than you can chew. It is up to you to prove the contrary. Someone
in need is likely to benefit from your perseverance or persuasion,
so don't give up.

13. FRIDAY. Erratic. Your position could be challenged. There
could also be some attempt to undermine your efforts. Do not take
too much notice of people who say or promise a lot, but seldom
perform. Sour grapes seems to be a favorite diet for some, though
you may find it hard to understand why this should be so. It is time
you made a move. The last hours before this initiative can be filled
with doubts and hopes as you come to terms with a new and
developing set of circumstances. Be of good heart. You can master
anything that comes along. You should have full confidence in
yourself and in those who share your dreams and schemes. A
reliable piece of technology can be installed to record messages.

14. SATURDAY. Changeable. Business affairs will be irk-
some. So make the most of social opportunities. Irritable people
who are far too concerned about getting on will impede or distract
you. There may be some canvassing for your support and this will
not appeal to your sense of propriety. An ardent friend seems
ready to take up the cudgels on your behalf. Feel free to make
yourself understood among friends. Personal initiative is needed.
Throw off those trifling ties that so often mess up the freedom of
your weekend. Make a bold decision to get out and do something
you have put off for too long. If public opinion is against you, or
appears to be bent on nitpicking, leave it to settle down.

15. SUNDAY. Mixed. Make your good intentions clear. Someone will return your love in full measure. Parental disfavor should

not be allowed to outweigh your hopes. But do not seek to usurp power or to antagonize where there is no ill intention against you, as yet. Be careful how you put yourself over. Responsibility will come to you soon enough without your getting out of step and raising problems. Take a trip for pleasure. Get well away from work or business or you will not be fit to live with. There could be good news from a loved one overseas that can keep your spirits up when things get you down. Reputations can be won and lost today. Be considerate.

16. MONDAY. Disconcerting. Risky ventures can be attractive. Good judgment is needed to keep you from being a fool. It may be that you ignore wise advice from friends or take ill advice from the same source. At some time you will be tempted to do something quite out of line with your normal behavior. Be glad if this eccentricity shows up in others that you meet. Because in that way, you an appreciate that there, but for the grace of that person, go I. Learn by mistakes. Cash-flow problems at business can make you impatient and cause you to overreact. Be careful with your own funds. If you want to make something work for public benefit, be more conservative in your approach. It is a day for surprises.

17. TUESDAY. Satisfactory. Continue to guard your resources. Take good advice from a business executive with his finger on the pulse of financial affairs. There could be an opening in your career field that you will be wise to consider. Be prepared to change or adjust according to demands. Too positive action can upset the applecart, yet you are aware that something has to be done and done quickly. Intuition should guide you better than conscious decisions. It is possible you are fascinated by someone or some event. Romance can take on different guises. You could be adventurous, yet dreamy. It is not a day, therefore, to be overly practical. Just stick to routine and you will be O.K.

18. WEDNESDAY. Productive. Accept any assistance that comes from the top graciously. This would be a good day for developing your business and taking on more responsibility or a greater work load. The result will show in your bank account. Promotion is likely. Recognition for effort in one way or another must be to your advantage. Once you are sure you have got something going, make it firm. Give up nothing that has been hard-earned. Application will get you places whereas too casual an approach will cause you to lose income and security. Do not mind adverse comment for a while. It will show that your methods are appreciated. Stay silent till you are quite sure of your facts.

19. THURSDAY. Rewarding. Press on with what you have to do. Talking may be important, but there must be action as well. A great deal of negotiating or arranging can be attempted. Time is of the essence and you will not attempt to mince words. Analysis is important. To get all the facts, you have to listen and explain what you are after. Willing cooperation should come from enthusiasts like yourself who see things clearly and have a mission. A new communications system may be at your disposal. Keep up to date with local developments. Positive advertising, instruction, keeping up with the times, all of these are the things that you should be doing today. Don't just talk, do something constructive.

20. FRIDAY. Disconcerting. Someone you love may go out of your life for a while. You could be homesick or in need of affection. Do not feel sorry for yourself. If there is something lacking in your life, either accept the fact or do something about a remedy. Dependence on another may rile you, so be yourself. A skeleton dragged from a cupboard will upset plans. You may have to turn your attention to someone in need. If this seems to be a drawback, you should be honest enough to accept the challenge or turn your back. Conscience can work overtime. There is no point in doing wrong. So come clean and clear the air and your conscience, if necessary. You'll feel better and you will enjoy peace of mind.

21. SATURDAY. Erratic. High hopes can spur you to outdo yourself. Avoid putting domestic harmony at risk. An all-out assault on weekend domestic chores can clear things up in no time. So work with good intentions and really go to town. Revelations can prove useful. Inquiries made tactfully at a public information center could bring an answer to a problem. Do not underrate or overestimate your potential. It may be sensible to arrive at a compromise over something quite important. Before pleasing everyone else, consider how your actions are going to affect you. There may be some encouragement, perhaps even bribery, to get you out of a property. Do not rush into a decision.

22. SUNDAY. Tricky. Resist the temptation to get involved too deeply with a friend. You could be on the wrong track. Some sort of arrangement can come to naught. This will be a face-saver, so don't get upset if you have to wait or recant. Keep your ear to the ground for genuine information. Be considerate of those who prefer their own counsel and carry on quietly. You should be able to gain an advantage by guile. This does not mean you are deceitful, but you may recognize that deceit is being practiced against you. But you know instinctively how to handle it. Turn the tables, but be gentle where necessary. Feelings may be sensitive, but you will know what you are doing. Protect your own character.

23. MONDAY. Manageable.   Face up bravely to a challenge. Resolve a decision and take the consequences. You may be asked to take on a major role or to go out on your own to make a living. This could be the parting of the ways in some respects, yet a completely new look at life in another. It is not a simple matter, so treat it with due respect. A partner or member of your family may decide to make a change. This is a natural development that should be accepted. Creative talents might have to be exploited now. You may feel you have to become involved with the public or give up altogether. Considerate relatives or friends will support you, if that becomes necessary. But you are best at doing things in your own way, for a start. Just don't feel lonely.

24. TUESDAY. Misleading.   Don't be sidetracked. Face up squarely to your own problems. If you are loaded with the woes and shortcomings of friends or colleagues, you could be taking on too much. Seek identity so that no one can doubt who you are. It is absolutely essential that you show off your talent. It's a case of all or nothing, so there could be upsets and disagreements. But at least you will get out of a rut. Shortage of money could inhibit you. There is no shortage of talent and that's what counts. Do not be misled or put off by materialistic people who are envious and have nothing themselves to offer. Romance can be at a crossroads. Be sincere and you will be all right.

25. WEDNESDAY. Mixed.   A change of heart could put you back in favor. Make the most of your love life. A journey should be attempted or you can welcome someone who is glad to have come back to see you. Pleasure comes in different ways. You find ways and means of making good use of your spare time without any prompting. Get dressed up and make yourself feel good. Catch someone's eye; that is important. It will do something for your ego and could also be good publicity. Avoid late duties if you can. After the hero of the year's show comes the cleanup squad. You could be burdened with something you would feel better without. If you have to submit, do it as willingly as possible.

26. THURSDAY. Challenging.   Get out of that rut. You could have a break today if hours were long yesterday. If you are self-employed, this is a good time to consider cutting out wastage and introducing new schedules or more up-to-date methods. To be competitive, you must be ahead of your competitors. Health can be rejuvenated. Dieting may be connected with this improvement. For some, the effect of electrical treatment could be significant. A working holiday could suit your purpose. Traveling on the firm's time may seem to you a sensible reward for extra hours worked in the past. Advice or techniques imported from abroad will be seen to work well. Export and survive, you may say.

27. FRIDAY. Demanding. It will be hard to get things in balance. If you feel everyone and everything are against you, that could well be so. It is an attitude of mind and one out of which you should snap right now! It will be difficult to make a good impression. If you are the boss, look after your staff in a practical way. Gilding the lily is a waste of time. They want to see results. If you are a lone worker, business may be hard to come by. Don't give up the ghost. If anything, cut costs and be more competitive. Any remedy for failure is going to be rough. It is better to be independent and stick to your principles than to accept defeat. But take care of health. Keep up your strength.

28. SATURDAY. Sensitive. Be positive. Don't push your luck, though. Cooperate willingly with those who are cooperative. A certain amount of resentment can be engendered against your good intentions. This is something that will be noted, but also seen as poor taste or sour grapes. A friendly atmosphere surrounds you when you are being purposeful. Involve a partner who is as enthusiastic as are you. A wedding can go off nicely. There may be a hitch at the honeymoon departure stage. But this is probably due to bad management and it will be taken in good spirit. Don't be casual about legal matters. Wear your seat belt and look out for local by-laws.

29. SUNDAY. Excellent. It will be a day to feel free and easy. Enjoy whatever turns you on. Sharing is the source of all good things and you will be miserable if you are on your own. The social scene should attract. You know how to get things out of your system when in good company. A communal atmosphere will be good for all. Make plans for a holiday, or better still, get with it and enjoy one. Let your mate make the decisions when you need to relax, but don't put up with just anything. But it is not very likely that you will be let down by anyone who cares for you. It could all be made for you today. Remember to show your gratitude to the one who matters most in your scheme of things.

30. MONDAY. Disturbing. There are squalls ahead. Top people do not fit into your plans at all comfortably. Getting money in advance from a banker can be like getting blood from a stone. Rethink your case if you must. Give yourself a bit of breathing space before you try again. An agreement seems likely to break down. Talks of involvement by larger business organizations will amount to very little. It is probably as well to look after your own affairs and not ask or seek wider cover at this stage. Do not lose faith in yourself because you cannot make everything click at once. Persevere and you will prevail in the end. Other people's problems cannot be resolved without some activity on their part.

OCTOBER

1. TUESDAY. Erratic. Stick to that which you know and un-derstand. Sudden decisions can get you in hot water. You may have a lot to catch up on, which is no good reason for hurrying. So, play it by ear in your usual manner and don't be influenced by friends or foes. Social involvement may pall. Too enthusiastic folks will be inclined to wear you out. Do things that are within your budget and avoid purchasing on credit things that are strictly nonessential. A minor flutter can make you feel reckless and could release some pent-up feelings. Within limits, this could be good for you. It is a whole lot better than blowing your top and losing a friend, for instance.

2. WEDNESDAY. Tricky. Something can be buttoned up. It may take the intervention of someone with considerable influence to swing the balance in your favor. So be glad you have someone who is cooperative in the right place. Overoptimism can lead to an immediate problem. Do not take anything for granted. Older folk may want you to stick to well tried-and-true methods when you are looking for a new line. Publishing can be full of drawbacks. Your intention to keep things light may meet with opposition from those who are far too serious for your liking. Take it with a pinch of salt and bide your time. Stay at home if you find traveling costs are exorbitant. Why bang your head against a wall?

3. THURSDAY. Disturbing. Disruption of business practice can put you in a spin. Call in a professional adviser on the double if you are unable to cope. Instant action may be necessary. Past history may be raked up and make you wish you had not mentioned something. In this sort of situation, the more you leave unsaid, the better. Be on your guard for the casually dropped hint that is meant to hurt. Resist the urge to hit back when you are in the public eye. What you need is good publicity and that may be better handled by an understanding and enthusiastic friend. Responsible people, especially in the business or social world, can be hard to pin down. It would be best for you to steer clear of them if you want a quiet life.

4. FRIDAY. Excellent. Be sure that someone loves you. Wear your heart on your sleeve if you feel so inclined, because it is not a day when you want to hide things. The gentle touch will win contracts and hearts. Anything connected with art or grace is well starred today. Examinations can be undertaken and passed without effort. It's really all in the mind, so an easy conscience means you are half-way there before you start. Good news comes from someone a long way off. There could be a reunion, just right for the end of the working week. You should be optimistic. Start off as you mean to go on and expect to come up smelling roses, no matter what you attempt. Business should be booming. You could really now be getting to see the light at the end of the tunnel.

5. SATURDAY. Misleading. You will find today is a rather mixed bag. Do not allow friends to interfere with your affairs. While you are engrossed in business there could be some dirty work at the crossroads. Financial interests should be safeguarded. On no account should you seek to mix personal with business interests. While you can directly benefit from career or business involvement, you are in no position to cope with financial affairs on a major scale. So know your limitations. Friends can be out of touch with reality. Do not commit yourself too far ahead socially. You could have something coming up that is going to take priority. Neither should you depend too much on a casual relationship.

6. SUNDAY. Rewarding. Settle down to a good day. Take it easy with company that makes you feel at ease. If you stick to those of your own generation, you need not worry about appearances or keeping up with the Joneses. Some may think you are taking it a bit too easy. You have something you want to do and so you will tend to concentrate on just that. So never mind what others may think; you will take it the way that suits you best. An old friend may make an appearance. This day you can confirm something that has been anticipated for a time. Hopes can be realized and the future made more secure. It should be a great day for lovers who are not in a position to take a wider view of life.

7. MONDAY. Confusing. You are likely to be in league with someone larger than life. If you are led astray it will be your own fault. Take a good look at someone who should be setting you an example, as you could be tempted to start off on the wrong foot. Money problems will be solved in your own way if you take time. Others, no matter how well-intentioned, can make matters worse. Again, you are aware that getting into debt is no way to live your life. Dependence on someone is not really smart. Someone close to you may need support or even pity. So try to be practical if you want to make a hit. The weather can interfere with a social project that must take off today. A sponsor may change his mind.

8. TUESDAY. Mixed. The ball is in your court. Positive decisions will be called for, so don't be too ready to count the cost. Without doubt you can make mistakes. It is up to you to decide whether the losses will exceed the gains or vice versa. Depend on no one for guidance, though you may appreciate a push from trustworthy friends. Business deals, or the administration of a business deal, can call for immediate action and a quick assessment of likely results. Your intuition may be working overtime. Poor publicity may retard the lift-off of something dear to your heart. Make the most of a poor situation and take matters into your own hands. Old-fashioned methods can go out of the window under pressure of progress.

9. WEDNESDAY. Happy. Slow down. Slip smoothly into the gear that suits your mood. At some point, you are going to see the light and get a lot of joy from the experience. You could be in demand without having to extol yourself. After recent events, this could be a pleasant change. What is done behind closed doors can turn you on or make you very happy with the way things are going. It may be romance or it may just be the desire for a change that makes you appreciate attention. In return, you are now in a position to understand and help someone who will benefit from your services or your love. Feel happier about your resources. There will always be enough when it is needed.

10. THURSDAY. Demanding. Give nothing away. It can be your turn to play dumb, or just take notice and say nothing. Copy the example set by the three wise monkeys and you will not go far wrong. It may benefit you to do some digging into the past. You could have an unexpected visitor who brings back memories. There will be a step forward in a little while and this could be a breathing space before the taking-off stage. If some people wish to pry into your solitude or your private affairs, send them off with a

stern warning. A time and place for all things should be the order
of the day. So take your time. Think back to the way you think
your ancestors may have coped. Take courage and be prepared.

11. FRIDAY. Difficult. Jump to it. Time may seem to be running out when you are really only starting. So look out for becoming impatient and putting your foot in it with the people who
matter. A career opportunity may seem to pass from your grasp.
Do not fuss about it. If you are meant to benefit, there will be
another chance to grab the brass ring. Too much may be asked of
you by people at the sharp end who should know better. Keep
control of whatever you undertake. Be expeditious, but do not be
rushed by those who are not, in the end, prepared to take the
blame. Your reputation may well be at risk. Be your own boss and
justify whatever you do. That way, you will be safe.

12. SATURDAY. Exciting. Grasp opportunities with both
hands. The good word of someone in the know can improve your
prospects. It is an excellent time for starting off a personal project,
self-employment or any other outlet that will bear your hallmark.
Sponsorship for worthwhile developments or interests should be
sought and will be gained. You seem to know the right sort of
people who have a mind to put their money where their good
intentions lie. Friends may ask you to take on a leading role at the
club or in some aspect of public and social life. You should feel
honored and also well able to become an asset. Be the center of
attraction with your partner at a social affair in the evening.

13. SUNDAY. Challenging. The pace probably heats up. Involvement in pleasant, yet exciting, interests should keep you
going in top gear all day. There is something special you may want
to complete before tomorrow, so you should enlist the willing help
of friends. They are as keen as you to see the end result. Negotiations may start in a friendly way on a social matter. Introduce
yourself to those who appear to be genuine. Pastimes with a
purpose are in order. Should you feel there is excess energy to be
expended, make sure you get into company that is not just talking
and sitting around. It is a great opportunity for chatting up someone and getting a friendship off the ground. You never know how
far this could develop.

14. MONDAY. Misleading. A hasty word can cause complications. Be quick to see things, but avoid hasty action. In some ways,
you could be quick off the mark and, at the same time, a bit unsure
of yourself. Dreams can interfere with action. All in all, it will be a

good day to be original, but you will not know how you will be received till you have a shot. So play it by ear and hope for the best if you are still a bit in the dark. Romance can come when least expected. Do not mix business with pleasure, so be prepared to change your tune, or to change horses in midstream when the occasion suits you. Others can play on your weaknesses, of course. Don't be too trusting.

15. TUESDAY. Satisfactory. Don't let doubts put you off. Nothing ventured, etc. It may be time to stop and think, but be sure you do not start to feel sorry for yourself. Too much concentration on the past will slow down your progress. Official action may seem to be working against you rather than to your advantage. It may be necessary to question the right of authorities to interfere in your affairs. Expect no special service from a bank manager. Nor should you think a business deal will go through on someone's casual approval. You may be asked to explain something important to the top brass. Be sure you have the facts at your fingertips. Be fair and you will be popular in the end.

16. WEDNESDAY. Tricky. Someone can be keeping you in the dark. Don't move till you can see some light. Careless words will cause problems, so you should watch your step. Be alert and on the lookout for others who are going to drop you off in the car. A cantankerous neighbor may take up some of your time. Make a positive attempt to be useful. Think of the future and let bygones be bygones wherever possible. Look out for shortchanging if you are shopping. The chat may be worth more than the purchase. Mischievous gossip can be safely ignored if you are trying to round up some helpful information. Drive with more care than usual. Keep your mind on the job in hand; never let it wander.

17. THURSDAY. Challenging. Quit backpedaling. Forget about past failures and think about future prospects. It may be essential to attend to matters that have been allowed to lapse. Get on and make up for lost time, but do not bemoan your luck. Should there be a skeleton in your closet, get it out and be done with it. Storing up ill-will, or having doubts about your ability, can produce nothing except more problems. You may be looking for something in the local paper and find it has not been published. Find out why. It's not the best of times to advertise, but you may feel that something has to be tried. If it's money down the drain, that's just too bad. Nothing ventured, nothing gained!

18. FRIDAY. Enjoyable. Accept a position of importance. Be prepared to stand in for someone important as a spokesperson or public demonstrator. Your word should be your bond in an agreement of honor. A psychic person may have some influence on you. At last you could realize that you have a talent which should be developed. Maternal influence may have quite a striking impact on your private behavior. You may want to do something that could be considered daring, but know you have to keep it in the family. There could be a change of accommodation that suits you nicely. Move and only then make it known. Private life should be livening up. You have little spare time. This will probably please you.

19. SATURDAY. Useful. There is good news for a member of the family. A parting may be necessary, but it is not pleasant. Give someone a good send-off and don't be too sentimental. There is a challenge to face from someone who thinks you are in the wrong place. Make your views clear. Some people you encounter will be sensitive and others will have skins like a rhinoceros. Treat each case on its own merits. Shopping can be rewarding or you may take in a lot of business. Money will be used well. Trust your judgment. A tipster or good judge of character can give you information that helps with a deal. Some home improvements can be considered. Priorities may be hard to decide.

20. SUNDAY. Happy. The action may center around home. If you are having a family get-together, see that all are informed well in advance so that business does not interfere. Celebrate the popularity of someone close. The family album is likely to get an airing again. Digging may be practiced in a number of ways. Some may prefer the garden to resurrecting past memories. It is a day to be relaxed and not too concerned about the passage of time. It may be nice to see someone who is growing old gracefully and does not seem his or her age. Wisdom comes from an uncle or a friend who has a word on the quiet. Make a public appearance, just to save tongues from wagging.

21. MONDAY. Productive. A hunch can work. There is an equal chance that you could jump out of the frying pan and into the fire. So you have to know what you are about in order to make a hit. Build on what is reliable. Good publicity will help. Local contacts seem to pay off. Try something new you have to show off with a local audience. Too sudden an exposure to the wider range of media could upset the applecart. You have something to offer that is way ahead of conventional taste. Private introductions will help you break the ice whereas direct contact could ruin things.

Know yourself and you are made. Guard your resources, whether financial or emotional. Be considerate. Gambles may not pay off.

22. TUESDAY. Easygoing. Get yourself ready for the day when your talent will be appreciated. Throw off the miseries if you feel that little seems to be taking shape. You have the scope to attempt anything you please. So look to your love life. Stimulate that which gives you pleasure. It would be ideal for a holiday if only to break up the monotony of the week. Children can take a special place in your affections. Career interests seem to be taking their proper place in your plan of things. You may feel you have this department of life under control and now have time on your hands, as it were, to think of diversions. So why not enjoy the day and take life as it comes for a nice change?

23. WEDNESDAY. Difficult. Do nothing by halves. Opposition can bring out the best or the worst in you, once you have dug your toes in. You may have to decide whether or not to receive hospital attention. Just get yourself straightened out so that relatives and friends know what is happening. A job in a hospital or other place of caring may be offered. If you are dissatisfied with present conditions, do not make hasty judgments about a move. You should get an opportunity today that can make the future seem brighter. So avoid any commitment that will be difficult to break. A superior may want you to do more than your fair share. Do not push those who work under you. Mutual trust is essential.

24. THURSDAY. Sensitive. There are still problems to sort out. Those with fixed views are going to be hard to persuade. Show your love for someone you admire. Be thoroughly practical, though not mercenary. Love of itself is not enough, so you should make up your mind to back your words with actions. It is a great day for romance. There can be indications that the special day may soon be chosen. All seems to be going well in a business venture that is now reaping rewards. Provided you can deal with criticism and old-fashioned attitudes, you are well on the way to a triumph you may not have expected. Remember that this is a year of opportunity, so do not minimize your potential.

25. FRIDAY. Successful. The gentle touch will work wonders. Knowing where you stand in someone's affections can make you doubly sure of your own. Investigate the possibility of a long-term publicity campaign. A partnership will benefit from careful introduction via the media. Be subtle if you are dealing with business people other than those in your own circle. Charm can produce unknown assets. Older counsel can be taken to advantage. The merging of old with new is to be applauded. Constructive discussions can clear up legalities without fuss. Persevere in your endeavors. A relationship is strengthened when you keep to a steady course. Indecision can lead to a parting.

26. SATURDAY. Disconcerting.   It is impossible to split yourself in two. So make up your mind about priorities and stop any squabbles. Sitting on the fence is going to please no one in the end. A loved one may want to be out and about when you would rather stay indoors. You should not mind your partner seeking the limelight or doing business if the situation demands. Injudicious actions by one partner or the other can make a marriage rather shaky. This is the sort of situation on which you can strengthen or weaken the common purpose. Be patient if you are involved. If you are an onlooker, keep your own counsel until you are asked for advice. And don't be surprised if you never are.

27. SUNDAY. Excellent.   Use your influence to help someone in need. Understand what you are after and seek support or sponsorship from the most reliable place. Private involvement in the affairs of others can lead to a bonus you will appreciate. Recognition can come from unexpected places. A public role should be undertaken with humility. You should be seen as one who understands, has sympathy and also the know-how to accomplish great deeds. Do not be modest, but just be aware of your own potential and the needs of your fellow humans. If asked to find out something for a notable, go about it with intent. You could be on to something really big.

28. MONDAY. Tricky.   Emotions may sway your judgment. If you are in love, today could be a heart-breaker. Try to keep your feet on the ground even if your mind is on cloud nine. Financial upsets can soon bring you down to earth, but you will want to avoid this sort of crisis. So be careful how you handle money or other assets. This applies more so if they belong to others. An attraction for a career may be stimulated by a chance meeting with someone. Do not take everything at face value, but you can show appreciation to someone who is kind on your first day in a new office. Your love life can be undergoing a change. If you have too many irons in the fire, get rid of a few.

29. TUESDAY. Mixed.   Loving embers can be persuaded to glow. It could be an old flame or a new discovery. Perhaps you can never be quite sure. Make the most of secret hours with someone.

An introduction may lead to a new discovery, so never lose hope. Use tact if you want to get inside information. Your powers of persuasion can be doubted or challenged. It is up to you to prove your worth. Publishing or advertising could be hard work. It may be difficult to come to an understanding with the people concerned, or to plan an adequate campaign. Wait till you are quite sure of your ground. Studies can be delayed or upset. Examination results may be held up in the mail. This could cause much anxiety.

30. WEDNESDAY. Difficult.   Hidden problems can have you upset. It would be better to wait till the cause is clear than get in a flat spin about something that may never happen. Overactive glands are going to cause you more problems than an inactive transport system. If you must blow your top, make it a constructive explosion that will startle someone up out of their lethargy. Suspicions can perhaps be confirmed. If so, take positive action to sort out your problem. Seek the aid of someone with professional know-how to clear up an export-import query. A third person will solve a problem that you cannot resolve on your own. Inside information is the key to a private poser. Don't be afriad to ask.

31. THURSDAY. Misleading.   Avoid unnecessary traveling. Your services may be better used nearer to home. Charity is said to begin there, though you may not be feeling too charitable toward anyone. Some deception is possible. Schedules may have to be altered to meet changing conditions. Dealing with foreign clients may have to be suspended for some reason. Exchange difficulties are a possibility. At a more personal level, you may be feeling insecure. Someone may question your intelligence or knowledge and you get into a fluster. Do not take yourself too seriously. A little learning is a dangerous thing. So if you want to air your knowledge, be sure you have the measure of your audience. Otherwise you could look like a fool.

NOVEMBER

1. FRIDAY. Challenging. Exert all your influence to make your mark. Reputation can be all-important at this stage. Make a hit with someone just to prove you are a person of substance. Keep your word; show that you have a sense of justice and proportion. Much depends on inner self-confidence. So do not be concerned very much with outward show. Success and acclaim come when you are seen to have that confidence which only comes from knowing exactly what you are about. Take advantage of any support offered by those behind the scenes. A campaign can only be waged effectively if you have backup. Given a free run, you should be in luck. Make the most of all your opportunities.

2. SATURDAY. Buoyant. Being the center of attraction will suit you. You may be taking on new responsibilities, hitting the headlines and thoroughly enjoying the experience. For some, this can mark a union to last a lifetime. Look kindly on all around you. Try to find peace or satisfaction in all you do. It seems you had a great send-off by a parent or someone with influence in the right quarters. A new business venture should make an immediate impact. Start as you mean to go on. Make your goods attractive and be positive in your manner. Love plays a great part in your day, whether connected with your emotional life or the way you earn a living. A private service or contract has great meaning.

3. SUNDAY. Pleasant. Stick to a planned social day. You will need to maintain a degree of composure when required, but may have to understand the feelings of friends who are disturbed. Do not let your goodwill be abused by practical jokers or ill-mannered folk. A break may be encouraged. Look for constructive encouragement in a friend who has influence. On your own, you may be tempted to fly off the handle or do something that is not quite in the right tone. A third party can work to your advantage, so don't be too independent. If you are getting too heavily involved with a friend of the opposite sex, it might be well to have a chaperone. Otherwise, arrange for a parent to be at home.

4. MONDAY. Lucky. Personal interests should be satisfied. Look after number one when you have to state your case. Too much emphasis cannot be placed on getting something sorted out to your advantage. Responsibility can be accepted and authority exercised through you. The spoken word should be sufficient to make your viewpoint understood and accepted. But you may have occasion to make an appearance just to prove a point. Good neighbors make life more easy for you. An interview should have a satisfactory outcome. Long-term advertising can be considered, but see that you really get down to the nitty-gritty. Waste no time today. You can be starting on something that will last a long time.

5. TUESDAY. Mixed. Put up with some delays. Look to the future because you should know that there is going to be a surge forward soon. It may seem that conservatism is eating away at your prospects. Do not look at the situation in a negative way. If you cannot get your message across to some, you have to rethink. Personal gain has to be achieved on a popularity basis. It follows you have to persuade all shades of opinion to your way of thinking. Subtlety may work with some and not with others. Information may be hard to come by at first, but the day will see improvements. Do not bear a grudge against someone who sticks to the rules. They may feel it pays off to do so.

6. WEDNESDAY. Productive. Important matters will be resolved. Even if nothing is declared publicly, this is a day of decision. Concentrate on whatever has to be completed. Make your position quite clear to close friends and family. Old scores can be rubbed out and fade into the past; the future is now all-important. A family get-together or a meeting of directors will settle an issue once and for all. You could be given a major role to play and you should be glad to have a lot of hidden or discreet power at your elbow. A fund-raising project should be wound up since it has been a great success. You may want to transfer money between accounts, now you are clearer in your mind about your intentions.

7. THURSDAY. Successful. Confirm a prior arrangement, it may save disappointment. It is now time to take action on promises. Stabilize your position. It is time you recognized the support you have among your neighbors or everyday acquaintances. A personal declaration made late in the day can mean you are really off on the track of success. You have the strong support of an official behind the scenes who is treating all with a deal of delicacy. Show understanding yourself for a parent or influential local personage who is prepared to take a backseat while you make the news. Waste no time on idle speech-making. Get to the core of the issue as directly as you can. Undertake a useful journey.

8. FRIDAY. Demanding. Safeguard your reputation. Forging ahead too quickly can give you a get-rich-quick reputation. This should not be tolerated, so see that it is disproved. Officials can be single-minded. Do not try to pull the wool over any eyes, just in case you are brought to a halt with a bang. Instant action by a superior can bring you to a full stop quickly, just when you think you have it made. Carelessness is likely to creep into your habits. As yet, you have to practice some prudence. So don't jump to conclusions or try out schemes that are immature. You would not like to be told you are still wet behind the ears, would you? So be a bit considerate of self and others.

9. SATURDAY. Inactive. Once again, it is back to the weekend chores. Should you be feeling a bit shattered, physically or morally, take a breather. Let all the pressure wash over you, while you stick to those things that are personal and private. There may be something you want to tidy up before next week, and a spell on your own is all you ask. Details are important to you, but probably of no interest to anyone else in your circle of acquaintances. Some preparation may be in order before an evening farewell. At some time during the day you have to come to terms with your social commitments and the price you have to pay for your entertainment.

10. SUNDAY. Productive. An old friend can rekindle a spark. Relationships take a turn for the better when you find time to be kind to those around you. You may want to do something out of the ordinary, just to show that you feel great. Make sure you give that special person a pleasant surprise. Good news should encourage you to go ahead with plans. You may propose or accept a proposal. Somehow you have to take opportunity as it arises, so whatever is in your mind should be put to the test. You may be aware that business expansion can mean a much accelerated need to make resources available. This can also mean you gain in proportion to your output. Look to the future.

11. MONDAY. Exciting. Practical progress is yours for the asking. Positive decisions can lead to important gains. Use your initiative and intuition wisely. Investment plans should be formulated promptly, taking due note of inside information. Without this sort of background, you will be inadequate. So don't let your enthusiasm, which has been building up over the last few days, get out of hand. You can perform a stroke of genius if you keep your feet on the ground while your head is in the clouds. Do not assume you know it all. Just be sure you keep in line with procedures and official practice and you could be on a winner. But there are also things at home you need to do.

12. TUESDAY. Disconcerting. Flippancy can frustrate your chances. Be circumspect, especially when in desirable company. Someone very dear to you is expecting a sensible answer to an important matter. Do not put your foot in it by jumping to conclusions. At last you may begin to feel comfortable in your present surroundings. It may be that you are being accepted for what you are rather than for what was earlier assumed. A journey may break continuity of constructive negotiations. If you have to carry out a business contract, do not rely too heavily upon experts or agents. You have a good grip of what is what and are well able to direct the whole affair. Avoid driving if you can.

13. WEDNESDAY. Tricky. Heavy pressure from an unknown source can be worrying. If you feel you are being harassed, do some quiet ferreting out to disclose the culprit. This could pose you problems, as you are likely to be under scrutiny from those with power. Seek the unconditional aid of officials if you have problems that must be disclosed eventually. Getting in at once to nip something in the bud is very much in your favor. It is better that you recognize possible failings and look for an immediate solution. Attention to charitable works can take up nearly all of your waking time. You are not unnoticed. Good news can mark good deeds. Advertising begins to pay off.

14. THURSDAY. Frustrating. Keep well clear of intrigue. You will never be able to judge the undercurrent today. So mind your own business and do nothing out of turn. Driving may be hazardous, even more so if you push your luck. Officials may tend to carry out rough justice to save time. It may seem there is little room or time for courtesies or good manners. Neighbors may be either uncommunicative or have their problems, or both. Make it your business to find out; but do not be surprised if you are given a short, sharp rebuff. Confidentiality can be violated. Be careful that you are not the guilty person. It follows you should be careful to whom you impart private information.

15. FRIDAY. Difficult. Emotions can be suppressed. Resist the temptation to bottle things up for any reason. It is much better for you to get something off your chest, though this will no doubt upset someone. Recriminations will get no sensible response. If someone has it in for you, that is their problem. Stick to your course and be prepared to change only when others see the light. Have faith in your inner capacity without getting uptight about it. Too much concentration on your purity of feeling can blind you to reason. Things may not be as they seem. It will take some time to relax and accept them as they are. Security begins to mean something.

16. SATURDAY. Sensitive. Little things can complicate matters. Steer clear of contracts, arrangements or commitments on paper. A property deal will almost certainly hit snags, no matter how clear the issue may seem to you. Make private inquiries and try to short-circuit the minor details, if they can be sorted out at a later date. Make positive moves to install security equipment in the home, or in a lodging, if you are only a short-term resident. There is a possibility of carelessness that can be countered by being direct. So make your position clear, putting faith in what you know is practical and leaving the talking to those who have nothing better to do. Privacy is important.

17. SUNDAY. Rewarding. The welfare of a parent can supersede all other interests. This is an early task you can perform with a feeling of love. Having got that sorted out, you are free to make the best of your own affairs. Security may seem to be the keynote. An established relationship should now be emerging in your love life. It seems like a good day to talk things over or get prepared for the great event. Children may be unusually well behaved when you are concentrating on developing a talent. You may be reminded that you are a chip off the old block. Persevere with whatever you take up today. Only good will come from it. You are no longer playing games or taking chances, but are making the most of your life.

18. MONDAY. Misleading. The course of true love never did run smooth. Take consolation from that fact. Perhaps you can talk your way out of a problem with a partner. Or there may be some logical reason why things do not go as smoothly as you would like. Taking chances will not improve your prospects. It may be necessary to go off on business or to spend more time than you like on a company deal. Finances, in general, seem to be an irritation to your happiness at the moment. So, whether personal or business, avoid having to consider financial situations. Appearances can perplex you. Given a certain amount of credulity, you can accept some things. But there may be too much at certain times, even for your clear sight and reasonable attitude, to swallow.

19. TUESDAY. Difficult. The unexpected can throw you. A love affair can lose its intrigue. Being too straightforward does not help courtship or even having a bit of fun. Mercenary people are going to get under your skin. A different cashier or accountant may get the usual business routine into a mess. Friends seem to be pushing too far and expecting too much. You need to find out who your true friends are. Forgetting your problems by getting mired in work may not solve your problem. If you can let off steam in this way, all very well. But be careful you don't upset your colleagues in the process. You could jump out of the frying pan into the fire. If carrying heavy things, don't drop them on your toes.

20. WEDNESDAY. Fortunate. It's about time you made some progress. Hard work is rewarded today. The main snags should be sorted out to your satisfaction. Cash-flow problems are cured. You have no problems with workers. If work and business are your main interests today, you are riding high. If other things are important, you should be feeling fit enough to cope with anything and enjoy the action. Hopes can be realized in a tangible way. So if it's money you're after, you could make a killing. If it's exercise, there is plenty of space for you to perform. You can be in the public eye and eager to make a showing. If all you want is a quiet life, you seem to have the ball in your court and can choose your own company. What more could you ask?

21. THURSDAY. Uncertain. Straighten out something important. Clear the air of uncertainty. It may mean you leave your job or that you get rid of some of your work force. Leave no one in doubt as to your intentions. Force may be imposed on you, by the law or an official. Face this squarely and take your medicine if it is deserved. But make your position clear, and do not accept accusations or innuendo about which you have no knowledge. There may be some deception being practiced against you, leaving a bad taste in your mouth. Wait a while. Face whatever you have to early in the day. Later on, you will appreciate the value of legal aid or cooperation and feel much happier. You have a reliable partner.

22. FRIDAY. Changeable. Accept help or assistance from a true friend. At the same time, do not tempt providence by being careless with someone else's feelings or reputation, or even your own. Play it by ear, making good use of any legal advantage. Business activities can be wasted. A partner seems likely to go it alone and mess up all that has been achieved in double harness. You, in your turn, should try to do something constructive and not make a bad situation worse. Loving relationships mean more now than at any other time this month. It could be a great day for a couple. Entertaining can be on the menu. A lot of happiness surrounds you. You can spread your mood among your friends.

23. SATURDAY. Difficult. Prepare or plan anything that is important. Things can go off in a poor state of readiness and get you into hot water. A disagreement with an agent can set you back for a while. Do not delve too deeply into the affairs of another or you could stir up trouble. Keep your partner informed of your intentions, if not your whereabouts. Quick moving can cut out usual lines of communication, but there is no reason to make that absolute. It may be hard to get a separation arranged to suit all the people involved. Take time if there seems no hope of a sensible solution. There must be more given to the essential consideration. Sleep on it. Perhaps your opposite number may get an inspiration and all things can be resolved.

24. SUNDAY. Useful. It will be a day of hopes, disappoint-ments and more hopes. Play it by ear. Push nothing you are not sure of. A public appearance will go down well and you should be popular for a period. Doubts about your own ability should be faced. Take stock of your assets, then you will see that you are not as inadequate as some may think or say. Independent reactions are to be avoided. Keep your intentions to yourself until you have control can the play. Your partner may be worried about funds. Explain how you can make gains, even though the kitty may be low at the moment. Conditions change from moment to moment. A superior will give you authority to act on your own behalf, late in the day. That will be one problem cleared up.

25. MONDAY. Lucky. Stick to your guns. Once you have made up your mind, carry on with the good work. Much time can be saved if a little goodwill is shown. Cut corners without missing out the details. In a private way, you should be able to handle more business than if you were to go through the usual channels. Dependents will benefit from your foresight. You should be able to unravel at least one mystery or find out facts that will be helpful in the future. An out-of-court settlement can be agreed upon and implemented. There is no time like the present for sorting out joint problems, especially if money or effects are involved. You may benefit from a legacy unexpectedly.

26. TUESDAY. Easygoing. A change of tempo allows you to relax. Not that you will waste the time at your disposal. A journey may be necessary or you may have to get down to some essential studies. Early indications suggest you may be in line for recognition. An official may pull a few strings for you. This may be quite unknown to you, so carry on with what you have to do. Keep in touch with in-laws if you find time. Make contact with overseas bases or look into exchange matters. In some way, you are in the process of engineering changes through a gradual approach. Preparation is therefore important. Call in a professional if you need advice. It could be very beneficial.

27. WEDNESDAY. Sensitive. Avoid the risk of making heavy going. Use diplomacy rather than the hard sell. Obstinate people should not be allowed to get under your skin. An export/import problem will not be resolved by surreptitious methods. Do not be bullied into doing something that is not aboveboard. Negotiate a foreign contract with delicacy. Look to the long-term benefit. Be prepared to give someone the benefit of the doubt if you know the intentions are honorable. Spread your wings and your influence. There is little you cannot envisage. So you should keep your options wide open and deal only with those who take you as you are, an honest broker, without doubt.

28. THURSDAY. Mixed. Justify your reputation. If you are host to family and relatives this Thanksgiving, accept offers of help. This could be either food or money, both welcome. Efforts and preparation can culminate in success. This should not be allowed to cloud your positive intentions. Keep a sense of independence always within you. Do not be pushed around. Equally, do not seek to take over a superior's mantle till you are truly capable. Opportunity today means you are on the way to success. It could be fleeting or permanent. The future is yours and you should be happy to make the most of it. There could be a financial breakthrough.

29. FRIDAY. Sensitive. Don't spoil the stew for a shortage of meat. Minor details may be important, even though a nuisance. Annoying people may try to engage you in conversation when you are busy. Do not make a public spectacle of yourself. See that you do not trivialize; and keep your composure. A personal desire may conflict with your best business interests. This could be an interesting quandary. Use your intuition and wits to solve your own problem. A word out of place can put you in a tight spot. Heed a quiet word or nudge from someone who sees all, but keeps out of the limelight. If you forget your lines, be glad of a prompter. Ad libbing can create even more problems. You could wind up behind the eightball.

30. SATURDAY. Happy. This would be a good day to celebrate a birthday. You seem to be in the catbird seat, all set to celebrate the occasion. Some jollification would be in order. In a sense, you are looking for the action and ready to act your proper part. A person of some importance could give you the encouragement you need as you start off on your own, or if you set out on a personal mission. Good friends tend to be a bit boisterous. It could be that you want to let your hair down. So you will welcome the chance to greet everyone, old and young alike, in the manner that suits you best. In the company of friends you feel there is no need to act a part. It looks as if you are going to enjoy this evening.

DECEMBER

1. SUNDAY. Tricky. Good intentions can be misinterpreted. Take things, more or less, as they come. Expectations can be way above realizations. You may feel washed out after an evening out. If that's the case, go easy on your involvements with friends or those who share your interests. A disappointment may come regarding some high-minded venture you are promoting. This is not the end of the road. Dependence on others can be a weak link in your armor. Perhaps you should be more independent? Avoid getting involved in ventures that are not genuine. It may be all too easy to take someone at face value and make a boner. Look out for the cheat and try to avoid cheating others.

2. MONDAY. Disconcerting. A good friend may put you up for the night. The day is not going to be easy, so you are probably glad you saved a long journey. Traveling will get you down. Stick only to agreed-upon schedules or arrangements. If necessary, be a stick-in-the-mud and just depend on well-tried methods. You can brood unnecessarily over something that really needs to be aired. If company bores you, get out of it. Responsibilities may lie heavy if you are not able to accept the need to keep a low profile for a while. At this point you cannot expect to make progress. Too much depends on preparation and your scrutiny of hidden or private factors. Give support to someone who may be in need.

3. TUESDAY. Challenging.   Play your cards discreetly. Luck is with you if you keep a low profile and study what you are doing. Likewise, you should take note of all that goes on around you without making your position known. This could be an excellent day for stabilizing a personal position. A long-term contract can be agreed upon. You could take on your first permanent contract or job for a long time. It is a day to combine enthusiasm with security and ensure you waste neither time nor money. Business opportunities abound if you keep your eyes open. Funds can be boosted with surprising ease if you watch the usual indicators and play it by ear. Business funds may be well directed and set for next year.

4. WEDNESDAY. Rewarding.   Concentrate on essentials. This could be the last full day you have to sort out Christmas schedules and arrangements. Take all as it comes. Be positive when something important has to be resolved. Stand for no time wasting. There may be a break to slip away from company to meditate. This is an excellent idea and can restore your vitality. Come to grips with a problem or situation that has to be resolved. Depend on your own judgment, so let intuition work freely. Perhaps you have a need to do something special of a charitable nature. Someone you know may be having an operation in a hospital. It's a good day for removals of any sort.

5. THURSDAY. Mixed.   Pay your dues. Don't kid yourself that you can get off scot-free. The end of the day can see you in a position of strength if you don't muff your chances before then. Reputation can receive a boost, but this could be a face-saving exercise with little of substance to back it up. Realize there is no such thing as luck; it is all a matter of judgment and you always get what you deserve. The ball is going to be right in your court by late in the day. This is an opportunity on which you cannot afford to miss out. Immediate action may be called for at some time. You are starting something off with purpose. If it is your birthday today, you have a very exciting year ahead.

6. FRIDAY. Disconcerting.   Make arrangements early in the day. Do not depend on officials or others who have influence to know the answers. It may surprise you to see how chances are taken by those who should be conservative. A parent may want to live it up a bit and may make you feel out of place. It is a good day to decide that it is better not to join them if you cannot win. Just give it time and hope for the best. Carelessness can be noticeable. If you are running your own business, beware of what is still unfinished, and overgenerous people who are living on expense accounts. Progress will come through calculated measures and sound judgment, not one-off exercises that have no substance.

7. SATURDAY. Fortunate. Comfort means a lot. Do not be smug or complacent, but make the most of what you have. Private resources come in handy in a pinch. You should benefit from a kind act by someone who keeps a caring eye on you. Heed the signs of fatigue or overindulgence and take things easy. A shopping expedition can solve a lot of Christmas present problems. Show love in a practical way, making as little fuss as possible. It's a private sort of day when you should be sharing. Be quietly confident that you are doing the right thing at the moment. But keep your ear to the ground and keep yourself up to date with current practices. Love life looks good from all standpoints.

8. SUNDAY. Confusing. There is money at your disposal. Consider well before you put it into circulation. Making a show or seeking the bubble reputation can be very tempting. It should be the long-term position that seeks your support or advocacy. So do not be misled by false gods. It can very well be an easy-come, easy-go sort of day. If by any chance you are spending money, there is every possibility it will be spent unwisely. If you are trying your best to impress someone you admire with material things, you could well bomb out. Set your sights above the purely material and you will have a much more enjoyable day. Someone you meet can absolutely dazzle you. Don't be blinded, however.

9. MONDAY. Difficult. Conserve your energy early in the day. You may need all your resilience later on. A love affair can seem to go sour. Be patient. If you know it will never make the grade, just accept the situation. If someone is hurt without cause, you must judge your moment to make amends. Indiscreet talking can cause no end of business problems. Loose ends must be tied up today, even though this will be not be an easy matter. Fiddling around, trying to make an impression, can lead to personal complications. If others try to make life difficult for you, work hard to avoid getting involved. Someone around you is likely to get hurt, so don't be too naive. But keep your guard up at all times!

10. TUESDAY. Productive. Come to grips with facts. Take nothing as gospel. Handle business or pleasure efficiently. Speed off the mark will help you get through a day that will have its emotional complications. Have a straight talk with someone you love and try to clear up a misunderstanding. Try to find out exactly where you stand. An alert mind is definitely an asset. Local folk seem to be cooperative in the main. There may be some underlying grudge upsetting a few. This is probably something you can counter by keeping a cheerful and optimistic attitude on show. Traveling has its ups and downs. Avoid taking someone of the opposite when traveling. Do not pick up any hitchhikers.

11. WEDNESDAY. Successful. Stick to well-tried schemes. Confidences should be kept, no matter what. It's a good day to promote yourself or your image. If you are interviewing, or being interviewed, you will have the opportunity to profit from the encounter. Your position can be improved by someone with authority stepping into the breach on your behalf. Relatives take on more responsibility for family matters and you feel you are now better respected. Maintain close links with someone who may represent an ideal you hope to achieve. This would be an excellent day to blow your own trumpet in a responsible way. Advertising should attract that which you want. Make the most of your talents.

12. THURSDAY. Easygoing. A family get-together may mark the beginning of another year in your life. Take things easy and enjoy the break. It may seem that a lot of water has flowed under the bridge since last December. The year ahead will have an entirely different range of experiences waiting for you. At times like this, you can reflect on the past and look forward to prospects of the future. A new leaf is being turned, even though nothing may seem to be happening. Look after your personal security. This can be a psychological matter, but it is also a good day to be practical about such things. If alarm systems need checking, now is the time. Don't wait till lives depend on it.

13. FRIDAY. Frustrating. You could be stretched to the limit. Be philosophic if you feel you cannot control events. Do not encourage waste or excess in any form. What looks as though it were a great proposition can be quite useless to you. Too much business is going to spoil home life. On the other hand, you may be inclined to give the office a miss today and not do yourself a lot of good. Hunches may or may not pay off. Be imaginative if you have to buy family presents. Do not stray far from your usual shopping haunts to get a bargain. Take the guidance of so-called experts with a pinch of salt. On the whole, you will have to play it by ear. If your intuition is up to scratch you should not fare badly.

14. SATURDAY. Slow. Make it a personal and private day. No doubt you have a lot to do on this weekend. It is now just over a week to the Christmas celebrations. Do not take on duties or any authority that you cannot cope with. Officialdom may not be very helpful today, though things will improve as the day goes on. You may need to call on private resources, transfer some money, or call on someone on the outside for support. A property matter can be dealt with in a discreet manner. You may want to see someone from the past before the year comes to an end. Do not put off till tomorrow what you can and should do today. There can be a disarming air of complacency which does not suit you.

15. SUNDAY. Sensitive. Control your feelings. A romance can be a success or failure, according to your reactions. Don't fly off the handle if you think a mistake has been made. Give encouragement to those who show promise. The young, in particular, need to be given a boost or shown a good example which they can follow. Versatility can be put to good use. Financial problems may seem to cause romantic upset or disillusion. If a relationship is worthwhile, this would be the last thing to matter. So get your priorities right and take note. A personal initiative can mean you have a chance to show off. See that you give a good performance, but remember, your life won't hang in the balance.

16. MONDAY. Happy. Take advantage of an offer. A sponsor may propose something to get you going. This could be the chance you need to show your worth. The ball is in your court, so pull out all the stops. A marriage may be arranged if you approach a parent for permission. Officials seem likely to support something that is going to give pleasure to many. Love life may be having its ups and downs, today providing the up factor, so make the most of it. A sudden change can make you feel better off financially, or perhaps you just feel wanted. That counts for a lot. Independent action by two can lead to a union. The left hand may be not be coordinated with the right, without your realizing the fact.

17. TUESDAY. Tricky. Slow down into low gear. Take on whatever is asked and absorb the strain gradually. There may be a communications hitch. Getting about under your own steam seems to be the order of the day. You may be thinking slowly or involved with dull people who will drive you up the wall. Conditions at work can be oppressive. If you are looking for decent output, you will have to get the whip out for some. As of now, the carrot does not seem to attract much attention. Look after your health. Colds should be prevented rather than cured. No matter what some may say, you should be a bit more conservative than usual. Extra duties can mean you have little time for entertainment or pleasure.

18. WEDNESDAY. Uncertain. Decisions can be made. A working relationship can either end or prosper. Fundamentals will be discussed and a no-nonsense solution arrived at. New staffing may be considered. There can be a weeding out, as well. You may be strongly attracted to someone who is in the limelight. Look at this situation squarely. Keep your hopes within sensible bounds. Someone behind the scenes may be putting in a good word for you at a crucial moment. Give yourself a bit of rope to gain from this intervention. Arrangements may be in hand for changes of routine or duty, to be implemented in the New Year. If you feel out of it, get someone to find out what is going on. Think of your future.

19. THURSDAY. Exciting. Love and loyalty go hand in hand. Whether you are married or unattached, this could be a day to remember. You may spend a lot of money and will get a kick out of the proceedings. The giving or buying of gifts can be matched by receiving. A lot is to be gained by cooperation. Old ties can be strengthened and new agreements ratified. There is a need to expand. As you seem to be in a position to listen and understand, see that all is done efficiently and aboveboard. The evening should be up to highest expectations. You are likely to be in love and only too pleased to have someone all to yourself, for a time at least. The unspoken word means a lot. A glance will suffice.

20. FRIDAY. Demanding. It will be a touchy day in your relationships. Defending the rights of others can land you in trouble. This may not bother you when you know your cause is just. But it might stir up a hornet's nest of opposition to you and your place in society. If you have to put your reputation at stake, see that you are in the right. A legal consideration can give you the correct approach. Keep your cool and let others blow their tops. Your nearest and dearest may be under a lot of pressure. Lend a helping hand. Do not waste joint talents, because the future can depend on mutual strength being used in tandem. Be careful what you say, and how you react when riled.

21. SATURDAY. Disconcerting. Self-assertion can be a problem. Cooperate because this is essential. But do not lose your identity. A partnership may have its first great test. So now is the time to take stock of all that is important in your life. Arrangements for the coming Christmas break can be hard to complete. A parent may have a problem that is difficult to sort out at the moment. Some rearrangement of accommodation may be necessary. You cannot solve all problems today, but you should be able to make major decisions and clear the decks. Don't get independent. Remember that two heads are better than one. An official may try to stop your progress. Stop and listen, at least.

22. SUNDAY. Useful. Be happy to be in the limelight. You may have something special to say, or influence to exert. Love life can be especially satisfying. Privacy is welcome here, though you may not be so modest when acting in a social capacity. New hopes can be inspired by someone who knows you very well from the past. Your position or security may be threatened. This could be purely imagination on your part. Or you may, perhaps, have an insight to developments that are hidden at the moment. Have no fear of upsets. If you are honest and do not make a fuss, you will find all is O.K. Joint professional success can be aided today if you meet the right people. Much often depends on sheer chance.

23. MONDAY. Mixed. Much may have to be accomplished. This is a short working week, so a lot can be attempted in a little time. Traveling can be a waste of time. If you can manage, get someone else to do the running about while you get on with more responsible tasks. Overseas travel can possibly be cut out altogether. Mail from distant places is likely to be delayed. Stay away from home if you feel this will expedite progress. There could be a vacuum in a course of studies. Revision of earlier teaching may help, but you are probably not in the mood to get down to serious work so near the holiday period. It may be necessary to get rid of old ideas, or someone on whom you have long depended.

24. TUESDAY. Confusing. Someone from the past is again on the scene. This should bring back happy, if not passionate, memories. Changing your style can be difficult, so you may feel ill at ease when you know you cannot change or turn the clock back. Personal initiative can get you out of a potential jam. Skeletons that emerge from a cupboard can be fairly accepted if you choose to play it straight down the line. Do not lose courage. Much has to be rearranged to accommodate guests or make old friends comfortable. Be prepared to put your best foot forward in order to have a clear conscience. You will be glad of your bed tonight. Be considerate of those you love, even if you have to revise plans.

25. WEDNESDAY. MERRY CHRISTMAS! You should be in top form today. Arrangements will now be seen to work. Practicalities prove a point you have made over the past few days.

Be available for anyone who shares your feelings of goodwill. There may be some time to reflect on your progress and future hopes. If so, you are probably quite pleased with yourself and this will rub off on those you meet or entertain. It could be a financially smooth day. Generosity seems to be the keyword. The common touch applies also, and you may find yourself mixing with all sorts of people. Backgrounds and beliefs are of no consequence in this festive season. Have a great day and make sure others do, too.

26. THURSDAY. Manageable. Action could be what you want. Don't be impatient or aggressive if you cannot get your own way, or if your friends are not in a boisterous mood. It should be a fortunate day. Perhaps you impress someone with your manner. For some reason, you should be feeling well satisfied with yourself. Financial conditions are possibly better than you expected at this stage of the month. An outing to find early sales could be interesting, though you may be a bit too liberal with your check book. Do not attempt to mix personal interests with business. If some want to talk shop, walk away rather than get into an argument. You are probably bound to have an exchange with someone, though.

27. FRIDAY. Erratic. Know who your true friends really are. You may be saying farewell to old friends who are returning home. It is a time to confirm long-standing relationships with relatives or colleagues. You will know what has stood the test of time. Some difference of opinion with your bank manager, or an official who is rather antisocial, can cause a certain amount of distress. There is time to put things right, so take note and wait till people are more amenable. A top job concerning a club or association may not appeal to you. You may want to drop out of an organization because you dislike its constitution or complete absence of goals.

28. SATURDAY. Difficult. A spending spree is probably not recommended. Your judgment can be anything but good. Friends have ideas of their own and are not very cooperative. Personal initiative is more in your line, anyway, so why be burdened with company you don't want? There can be crossed wires somewhere that will mess up your day. Do not attempt to push your luck, play on your popularity or talk to people you don't know well. Communications are suspect, or people will not understand what you are putting across. Once more, be careful of mixing business with personal interests. The choice between the two is your own and you cannot ride two horses at once. Watch your purse or wallet.

29. SUNDAY. Inactive. The pressure or excitement of the past week can catch up with you. Take all as it comes. Do nothing unless you want to and bother no one with your plans or ideas. This is a good time to get under cover and possibly prepare for the New Year. The few days' respite between holidays can come in handy. You may want to take up meditation or yoga. Such an interest needs to be considered well before a decision is reached or action taken. Someone may need your sensitive care. Be charitable in some way; time well spent is time at rest. Private matters are of prime importance. Only those who are very close will be allowed into your confidence or possibly your presence.

30. MONDAY. Fortunate. Be discreet in promoting your own interests. There is no need to be shy; probably diplomatic is the best way to suggest you go about your business. Expansion or opportunity can be expected. You should stand to gain personally in a material way. Good feeling is exchanged and you seem to be on the right track for convincing all levels of management that you know your stuff. Your bank manager should now be in a better frame of mind and more cooperative. A bit of inside information can put you on to a good investment. It is not a day to stand still and wait. You have to take opportunity when it is offered.

31. TUESDAY. Happy. The year is coming rapidly to its close. You may be glad to see the new year, yet rather sentimental about the old. It is a common situation for many. But as you seem to be a philosopher, you may give it more consideration than most. Be positive in your thoughts. Obviously, you must build on the past and you will have learned considerably in the last twelve months. Someone very near and dear to you will share your sentiments, as well as the last few hours of the passing 1991! It will be a fitting close to the year, one that will bring much joy. And tomorrow, you will be in full fighting trim, when it will be all yours to use. So thanks to the old, and here's to good luck and prosperity in the new year, 1992!

OCTOBER

1. MONDAY. Positive. A meeting with your lawyer or accountant could be to your advantage. If expert advice on a property matter is needed, do not delay. Traveling should bring happiness. Look for a business opportunity overseas. Someone important could be coming a long way to see you. It will be a day to remember. Remain on friendly terms with influential people in the community. Social contacts are important if you intend to make progress. An examination or interview could be successful; you will be in a mood to celebrate with your friends. Make arrangements regarding a passport while you have a chance.

2. TUESDAY. Mixed. Too many cooks will spoil the broth. Do no more than your fair share. Keep out from under the feet of people who are in a hurry. A legal difference will not be settled today. There are too many little things to sort out and not the patience, expertise or time to do the job properly. Your partner will probably have a lot to do and little time for idle chitchat. Do a little research or try to get some inside information. A financial deal can be settled provided you are diplomatic and do not publicize all you know. Being secretive could upset a partner who is probably aware that something is going on and would like details.

3. WEDNESDAY. Tricky. An unnecessary journey will annoy you. Avoid a confrontation that will only be nonproductive. Make arrangements to take in all possibilities. Your love life may be going through a sticky patch. Friends will have their own likes, which will probably not coincide with yours. Mixed company may be preferable to a hen or a stag party, for you will at least be able to air opinions and keep things alive. Avoid spending money on useless items you know will not please a friend or relative. Take specialized advice, even though it may seem to be unusual. You could be dealing with some odd people today.

4. THURSDAY. Disquieting. You will be best off well away from your usual stamping ground. There could be a problem with the authorities or someone in an official position. Do not aggravate the situation. Accept the fact that you may not feel up to scratch. Money may be hard to come by, or the rate of exchange could turn against you. Somewhere far away could be ideal if you are looking for a financial coup. You can save with one hand and expand with the other. Look for opportunity, but also be aware of your limitations. The fact that you may be watched can inhibit you. Stand firmly on your convictions and live for the future.

5. FRIDAY. Challenging. Concentrate on what you have to complete. The end result is what counts. Some uncertainty about payment can make you upset and probably a bit antisocial. There are ways and means of getting your just reward for personal efforts. Do not get in a rut. Be prepared to try another angle. An employer could be misguided or perhaps deceitful. Do not accept everything you are told as being gospel. Have something up your sleeve in anticipation of a letdown. There could be talk of embezzlement or someone going bankrupt. Should this affect you, be ready to make changes. A lover can be acting rather oddly.

6. SATURDAY. Useful. Be prepared to put yourself out for someone in need. You should have bulging closets and cupboards and thus be able to cope with all demands. Appreciate the fact that someone wants to comfort and protect you. Be ready to return the compliment. A legal expert may have something good to report. If you are seeking advice, go to the top; you will be well received. A business success is probable. You could be given a partnership or granted a favor. Look for those who wish to cooperate, and be prepared to show your worth. Things that are substantial will always be better than those that are unknown.

7. SUNDAY. Genial. It's a day to be sociable. Others are in a mood to branch out. You could be helping them with advice or comfort. Discussions with close friends can be revealing as well as fruitful. Someone could tell you all about what is really going on in your locality. This should help you relax. It can be a relief to share a confidence or simply a bit of good news with someone you see rarely. If some people seem to be looking after your business as well as their own, their interest will have its benefits. You can arrange a stand-in if you want to go off somewhere. A social chat with a business acquaintance can be productive.

8. MONDAY. Sensitive. A friend could be quite unpredictable. Do not allow anyone to interfere in your financial arrangements. Teamwork is the key to success. Positive drive will bring immediate results. A partnership can be fully tested today. That which is unreliable will break or reveal weaknesses. But true values should show clearly, and you could be the winner. Someone very close to your heart will appreciate your generosity if you are not possessive. It is a day to get things out of your system. Those who think along the same lines as you will realize you are going places. A contract could be in the offing.

9. TUESDAY. Positive. You may feel you have succeeded. Something close to your heart could be within your grasp or just a whisker away. A journey to see someone special will have you on cloud nine. Or you may be waiting to greet a loved one who is coming back home after an extended visit. Friends can be extra helpful when you are short of something. Social involvement will probably take you farther afield than you expect. Enjoy this new experience. Examination results or studies should be encouraging. Your love life should be opening up new hopes for the future. Make plans or begin preparing for a later event.

10. WEDNESDAY. Misleading. Be very careful how you treat others. Whatever you say or do can be misunderstood. Unwelcome facts may be discovered when you make personal inquiries. Do not expect help or congratulations for your efforts on behalf of someone. There could be problems over a will or property sharing. Look after family interests to the best of your ability. No end of problems will materialize today. This could be good for you, since you are likely to be on your own and can appreciate your liabilities as well as your assets. Best to let things calm down before making any significant new move.

11. THURSDAY. Optimistic. Look on the bright side. Positive thoughts can lead to positive action. You will not be caught short if you keep up to date regarding what is going on around you. Traveling promises to be good for you. Start negotiations for business development. You will want to find out a great deal. Be free in exchanging views and you will have a confidence returned. A visit to meet a friend can open up new possibilities. You may have come to a decision in the early hours. Once that is cleared, you will want to get out to enjoy the fresh air or a change of scenery.

12. FRIDAY. Mediocre. Look for cooperative people. Officials are not apt to be in that category, but you will find good company nevertheless. Your bank may be tightening regulations. Avoid borrowing and lending. Accept instructions from a superior, even though you may feel they are wrong. Look for an opening elsewhere. Business can better be conducted with the lower echelon than the top. You could be fined for an offense. Marriage may be arranged on the spur of the moment. Your partner should be ready and willing to go off on a trip. Do not stand still and let the grass grow under your feet.

13. SATURDAY. Enjoyable. Let your nearest and dearest have plenty of leeway. You may be going on a journey or seeing off your partner. Not the day to be restricted in any way. You will share best by being openhanded and ready to grant others their complete freedom. A discussion or agreement may be arranged with a business personality. Look for expansion in overseas markets. Export/import restrictions can be lifted. You can advise or accept advice. The seal of authority will be placed on something that is important to you. Finalize preparations for a step forward. A producer or publisher is prepared to take positive action.

14. SUNDAY. Unforgettable. Do something original or out of the ordinary. Extraordinary people can entertain or attract you. Something you do in public is apt to be commented upon favorably. You could be the center of attraction for at least a little while. Be alert to what is going on around you, but do not make this too obvious. You have to be alive to all possibilities and in a position to show magnanimity. No doubt you will enjoy being on a pedestal. A change of occupation or career could be in the offing. It may seem you have been here before and that it is time you did something about it. Strengthen your resources.

15. MONDAY. Starred. Build up your resources. Your credibility may depend on the way you keep up the pace. Life at the top can be wearing, but you should have the tenacity to cope with anything. Some aggravation may come from the sidelines. Leave this to others who may be better able than you to accommodate. Information from a private source, or hard work by those in the background will keep you up with developments. A secret meeting should make you feel you are wanted. You are in a position to provide for the future and should let someone special know this fact. Look to the long term.

16. TUESDAY. Jolting. There could be talk of love. An engagement could be arranged. Accept an invitation to a friend's wedding or anniversary celebration. The unusual could throw you today. Perhaps you expect everything to flow smoothly after hearing good news, but this will not be so. You must expect to put up with changes. An unexpected visit from friends can leave you short of supplies. You will be able to improvise quite adequately, and give them a surprise also. Expenses may be higher than you anticipate. Pay up and be cheerful when you must, but make a mental note that this must not recur.

17. WEDNESDAY. Mixed. Early activities can be productive. There could be something going on that slightly mystifies you. Avoid making any transaction involving your own finances. Look after business matters as a priority. Consider ways to develop an overseas outlet. A journey could give you an opportunity to make a name for yourself. Active cooperation will add company funds. Be direct in your dealings. Someone may try to distract your attention from the main goal. Do not take glamour too seriously. Window dressing will not bring results comparable to positive action in double harness. Your partner has a clear intention.

18. THURSDAY. Profitable. You may be putting all of your eggs in one basket. It could be a day you will remember for a long time. Something of importance will start today. There is a social atmosphere. You could be in love and well aware of what you are doing. Be glad you have plenty to share. Friends may mean more than you care to disclose. A union of families, or the signing of a contract, can lead to new understanding with someone you admire. Social involvement could put you on talking terms with a local dignitary. You may be given a reward or other recognition for your social endeavors. Make the most of your chances.

19. FRIDAY. Changeable. Keep a low profile. Traveling or too much involvement in the public spotlight can be bad for your image. Take advice from a specialist who you know will keep mum about personal details. An official or professional person from overseas may be unable to explain exactly what you want. Official clearance could be difficult to achieve. There may be some misunderstanding about currency or exchange rates. Go to the local source to get an honest answer. Corners can be cut. New office equipment should produce results in record time. You have the opportunity to sit back and keep tabs on what is going on.

20. SATURDAY. Fortunate. Concentrate on essentials. Inside information or intuitive knowledge is better than all the textbooks. Contact with a friend or relative from a distance can give you a boost. Be gentle and do not say too much. You will gain more by listening than talking. An old debt can be settled and a chapter closed. There can be a certain amount of feeling for what once was, but it is wisest to let bygones be bygones and bury the past. Considerable joy will be felt for a job well done. You have been aware of your limitations recently. A cloud can disappear as you recognize what you can achieve.

21. SUNDAY. Exciting. Do your own thing. It is a time to come into your own and make an entry. Important issues may be under discussion in your club or at a public level. You may feel you have something to contribute. Be prepared to share a platform or to take charge of a gathering. You may be aware that changes in business circles are imminent. A word in the right direction can set the ball in motion. Friends will be extremely cooperative once they know you have a special contact. Be aware of your responsibilities and do not abuse a position you may hold or may be likely to hold. The talking has to stop sometime; practicalities will then count.

22. MONDAY. Guarded. Be aware of your own needs. Also be sure that you can judge for yourself. A difference of opinion between you and a close ally or opponent can make you sharpen your claws. Keep on your toes and seek to widen your scope rather than draw back. Marriage can be under pressure. Your partner must be allowed more room; you will be made very well aware of the fact. Travel if you want to make the most of new opportunity. A solo journey may upset someone who thinks they should tag along. Your time is valuable. You will be much more efficient if allowed to make your own decisions.

23. TUESDAY. Sociable. You seem to be in demand. Social attractions should not be resisted. Nor should you try too hard to put off someone charming who wants to get to know you better. Be positive, as suits your Sagittarius style. Encourage a lighthearted approach wherever you go. A great deal of good can be done if you exercise a light touch. Someone you meet at a party may open your eyes. Take personal action to settle a business deal in record time. With all facts and with the right people in place at the right time, you should find it hard to make a mistake. Someone of importance may take you under his wing.

24. WEDNESDAY. Intense. Be responsible for your own actions. The fact that conditions can confuse you at times is no excuse for a mistake. Independent action is called for now. A new approach may have to be attempted but it could be riskier than you think. Keep your feet on the ground if practical or financial matters need attention. There is scope for romance if kept separate from practical considerations. You are not yet in a position to make both fit into your plans. An attempt to escape from responsibility may not be successful. Accept what must come and make the most of it. An odd person can intrigue you.

25. THURSDAY. Changeable. An old-fashioned cure can save the day. Something is likely to develop that draws you back to basics. New situations will seem like something you recall from the past. A dream may help you cope with a problem that arises. Hang on to your money. Private funds may be needed in an emergency. A long-term settlement can be completed. You should feel happier that a worry is taken care of and you have reserves to meet all likely events. You should accrue rather than distribute your resources, but you will know they can be well used by those in greater need than yourself.

26. FRIDAY. Mixed. People are apt to get the wrong impression; this cannot be avoided. If you have business to do, look for a reliable agent or broker who will do what is necessary in private. Misunderstandings are apt to apply all around. You may think there is a plot afoot to undermine your credibility. Relatives will not seem very cooperative even when you attempt to see things their way. Official intervention in a dispute will not achieve anything. There are people behind the scenes causing general disruption. An awaited letter will still be delayed. You can make private inquiries, but avoid doing so via official channels.

27. SATURDAY. Erratic. A partner can help you out of a jam. The urge to go it alone may be strong. You will find you are tempted to bite off much more than you can chew. Traveling has problems. Local needs must be served, yet you may erroneously think prospects are better on the other side of the road. Stick to what you know. Do not indulge in wild ideas above your station. Precedent should be noted. You may be obliged to conform, so get used to the situation. Seek the views of a third party who knows more about you than you think. Your needs will be supplied if you go about it in the right way. Do not plunge ahead like a bull.

28. SUNDAY. Easygoing. Home sweet home should attract you. A late journey may keep you out of circulation for most of the day. There can be some tidying up to do before you are satisfied that you can take a break. Letter writing and bill paying should be brought up to date. Arrangements for the coming month can be made and schedules posted. You will have little time on your hands, although neighbors and family members may think you have left home. There can be helpful contact with locals or relatives. This will have to be on a confidential level, or simply to find out the latest news and what needs to be given priority.

29. MONDAY. Changeable. Renew old ties. Check up on your bank account, especially if you are in a new environment. Private meetings seem to be the order of the day. You may meet someone very special early in the day. Chatty folk will occupy your time later on. Family matters should be attended to without delay. Screen out all other influences and remain strictly private until you have everything buttoned up. A deal can be settled peacefully;; once you bring in legalities there could be trouble. The law does not understand sentiment or emotions. If you have intense feelings for someone special, see that they are aware of your intentions.

30. TUESDAY. Satisfactory. Old wounds can be healed. You may be reminded of the past in a way that touches your heart. A guardian or parent may be lovingly prepared to forget past misdeeds. A loved one will come back into your life. Indeed, you may feel there has never been a separation. The best laid plans can go astray. Do not spread your net too wide or think you can make a hit overnight. Be sensitive. Gently feel your way forward. Do not be guilty of assuming too much. Your judgment is suspect, so do not push your luck. This could apply particularly in dealing with people who speak a different language.

31. WEDNESDAY. Disconcerting. Share a load with your partner. There is a lot of joy awaiting Sagittarius people who do the right things together. A lonely, frustrating day is foreseen if you are selfish or cannot find the right partner to do what you like. Children may need extra attention, which can be wearing. Get someone to help out and the boredom will disappear instantly. Not a day to take chances with money. If you go to the races, listen to the tips given by your mate; you will undoubtedly back an also-ran. There may be plans for a future marriage or engagement that need to be worked on this year or even this month.

1. THURSDAY. Guarded.   You may be reminded of your own personal limitations. A love affair can go astray if either of you are not playing it straight. You can be deeply in love with someone and feel it is not yet the right time to declare yourself. Financial difficulties can make a personal venture a nonstarter. Someone could be working on your behalf behind the scenes. It may be that an official can be privately persuaded to see things your way. Thus you may not be so badly treated as you think. A kind word will work wonders if you are engaged in looking after the sick. Do not take material things so seriously. You have a lot to give.

2. FRIDAY. Difficult.   Pressure will be on you to produce an answer. You are capable of giving as good as you get. Face up to demands and do what you think is appropriate. An employer may be away, leaving you with a lot of responsibility on your shoulders. Make no attempt to cut corners or compromise. Keep your actions aboveboard. Do not try too hard to please those who are critical and carping. Originality is called for coupled with a feeling for what is necessary rather than what is demanded. Keep your money well concealed if traveling with wages or an excess of cash. You could be approached by someone disguised as an official.

3. SATURDAY. Rewarding.   Make an effort to get something out of your system. The affairs of others out of touch with the world may interest you deeply. Try to come to terms with what you can do and what you are allowed to do. Be constructive. Work may be necessary, and this can cramp your style. But it is not the day to let a chance slip through your fingers. Better to show a small profit than lose a contract or a job. A health problem can clear up. You could be left out on a limb in some way, yet mightily relieved that you have come to a parting of the ways. A dream may put you on the alert. Study what goes on in your unconscious mind.

4. SUNDAY. Exceptional.   A lot is happening around you. Take advantage of an official's generosity. A love affair can be given parental blessing. Some serious talking may be done behind closed doors; you may be aware of this or may be blissfully ignorant. In either case it should be to your benefit. Action is demanded from a partner. Together you can perform wonders. Do not seek to discourage initiative. Go along with someone who wants to be in the front line. Traveling should suit you. Do nothing

in isolation. Let others do their own thing. Be sociable with whom-
ever you meet. A new opportunity could be coming your way.

5. MONDAY. Mixed. Be ready with bag packed. A business
trip could suit your purpose. Teamwork has its ups and downs.
You are aware of your duties toward a partner and also see that
you cannot have all your own way. If the situation is getting a bit
tense, make an effort to get away for the day. Contacts from afar
can bring good news and some hopes of making a deal. It is high
time you thought about expansion. Nothing happens without a
little push. Be positive and get the ball rolling. A close relationship
will benefit from more freedom and more action. Do not allow the
grass to grow under your feet.

6. TUESDAY. Challenging. Your sense of mission can be exploited. Others should benefit from your attention. This is fine so
far as it goes, but do not exhaust your resources. With nothing to
give, you can be wasting your time. An extremist may test your
patience. Misguided people will ask your assistance. It could serve
better ends if you are direct in what you say and do. Genuine
hardship can be recognized and alleviated. Good advice ought to
be heeded. But there is an equal chance that someone will try to
deceive you or will supply false evidence and ill-timed suggestions.
Double-check any information that you uncover. Statistics can be
wrong. Beware financial dealings.

7. WEDNESDAY. Confusing. Take heed of the still small
voice. A confrontation with your banker can clear up doubts. If
there is one mess you must tidy up, be purposeful. You will receive
plenty of support for whatever you intend doing. Look to private
or secret sources if you are engaged in any type of research. There
will be some attempt to keep you from digging up too much; get
around this by keeping your ear to the ground. Do not seek to air
any dirty linen in public. There are those who love you quietly and
with true feeling in private. Seek their company when you have
dealt with your personal problems.

8. THURSDAY. Disconcerting. A relationship may reach a
crisis. It may be difficult to master emotions when you are with
someone special. Be positive. Avoid getting into an intimate situation if you feel you are losing control. A journey could take your
mind off someone or something. Active cooperation with an adventurous person can get you out of a rut. Be generous to those
around you who are eager to help you advance. Studies should be
pursued with more vigor. Now is the time to come out of hiding

and make obvious progress. A secret will be kept. If examinations are ahead, get down to the hard work of preparing.

9. FRIDAY. Tiresome. You will have high hopes early in the day. This is the time to get things done and seek recognition or moral support. Before noon you could be up against some official disfavor. Do not seek support of those with influence, especially in a backdoor or secret way. You will come out the loser and be unable to prove any misdemeanor on the part of authority figures. A loved one may let you down; this can be quite unavoidable. Do not bear a grudge as this will be self-destructive. A journey may have to be canceled, or a trip undertaken by someone you care for can be against your wishes. Be optimistic and keep plugging away.

10. SATURDAY. Disconcerting. Steer well clear of the law or people in authority. The big stick rather than the carrot will be used. Dogmatic people will try to impose their will on you and yours. It will be most difficult to understand what motivates officials. It may be better if you leave well enough alone and play for time. Responsibility can bring you recognition, depending on your ingenuity or independent stand. Provided you avoid close involvement and are open in your dealings you should make progress. Do not rely on inside information. There is a possibility that your name may be mentioned adversely; avoid arguments.

11. SUNDAY. Buoyant. Rejoice in your popularity. Resources should be bolstered and insight sought. You may be in love and eager to proclaim the fact. One of your own sex can be a bit edgy or catty. A business partner may be eager to do extra work today. Insist that on this, your day of rest, you have a lot of other necessary duties to perform. Relationships can improve generally after the doubtful period earlier last week. Treat important people with respect, but at the same time, make your own position clear. You have achieved something and merit respect from anyone. You will be confident and aware that popularity has been hard earned.

12. MONDAY. Positive. Keep your wits about you. Changes, adjustments and modifications will suit you. Restlessness will make you eager to get around and do things for other people. There is a danger that you can say too much or interfere in the affairs of others. This will be all right only up to a point. You are well able to talk yourself out of any problem situation. However, beware of leaving a bad impression in other ways after you have moved on. An after-dinner speech can be a wow. Put a personal point of view across if it will help settle a financial deal. Do not make grand promises that cannot be fulfilled.

13. TUESDAY. Manageable. Financial problems can develop. Do not mix business with pleasure, or personal funds with company income. A superior, possibly a financial manager, may keep aloof from any delicate situation. This should be viewed as a benefit, offering a refuge if you get into really deep water. A joint venture can be launched or promoted if you and your partner are both prepared to give it all you've got. Be an optimist. You should have good publicity or good professional advice to keep you on the right track. A long journey could be to your advantage. Widen your scope. Do something direct and positive about expansion.

14. WEDNESDAY. Wearisome. Cut down on social entertainment. Expenses are apt to mount up. A friend may try to pour cold water on your efforts to get something going. Take note, but do not be inhibited if you feel you are right. Your judgment is usually as good as the next, so you should not be a pessimist. Your help may be called for in a worthy cause. Where you expected to be making progress there may be a reversal. This is not the end of the world, only a transitory setback. Build up resources until you have enough to meet your requirements. It is unwise to overspend in anticipation of things getting better.

15. THURSDAY. Successful. Be quietly independent. Someone who thinks you are dumb may be in for quite a shock. Keep something up your sleeve for an emergency. This applies no matter who the company you keep. It is better to retain some inner strength and sense of your own individuality rather than make a show of your talents. A surprise development can boost your income. Make a private arrangement on a one-to-one basis. Technique is as important as content when you come to the point of wanting to reveal a secret. A professional or scientific touch will work wonders. Someone may think you are quite wonderful.

16. FRIDAY. Mixed. Avoid being adventurous. It is time to build up resources and concentrate on preparations for the future. An overly optimistic view of the immediate future will distract you from what is most important. If you have serious shopping to do, stick to the places where you are known and where reliable traders are to be found. Buy in bulk if necessary. The Christmas period is fast approaching and you should have a knowledge of requirements. In any case this is a year, as you probably have found out, when a full freezer is necessary to withstand unexpected social demands. Avoid arguing with a partner or customer.

17. SATURDAY. Exceptional.   A day to remember for years to come. You could hear of or be involved in a secret liaison. Something of great importance should happen today. You may not be quite conscious of what is going on, but you can be sure the final outcome will be revealed tomorrow or the next day. An important person will have private words with you, and you will feel happy. The health of someone you love should take a positive turn for the better. This will be a cause for quiet rejoicing. Official permission may be given by a parent if you make a sensible, respectful request. Do not underrate the value of diplomacy.

18. SUNDAY. Hectic.   You should feel enthusiastic, but keep your spirits in harness. Someone may take you up on a challenge if you get carried away by your own high spirits. Discussion is one thing, arguing is quite another. Your partner may have ideas that conflict with yours. A long journey could make a pleasant break; seeing too much of the same person can be a bore. Philosophy can be a solid standby when you are backed into a corner. A sermon will appeal to you. In-laws should provide an outlet and are ideal for easing family hostility. Others may not be able to keep up with you once you get going. Be considerate.

19. MONDAY. Positive.   Start the workweek on the right foot. Take immediate action to assert your position. You will have an enthusiastic following if you explain yourself clearly. A journey could answer problems and, at the same time, can take you away from affairs or conditions that would retard you. Studying and independent research will be rewarding. You may be offered a position that suits you admirably. Make an honest declaration of your principles if called upon to speak in public. Your wit and charm will persuade the most stubborn-headed person in any audience. Once more you may be indebted to an older relative for help.

20. TUESDAY. Tricky.   Although fund raising can intrigue you, remember that charity begins at home. Unwelcome handouts from your private purse can leave you in dire straits. A new system of accounting may appeal to you, but let someone else try it first. You are prone to go off the tracks today and thus could end up worse off than you started. Shopping can be a trial. Avoid instant foods and poorly prepared or packaged goods. Use your initiative. You can come out the winner if you are up to date without being too clever. A new gadget can be a success. A monthly bill can shock you; some you win, some you lose.

21. WEDNESDAY. Uncertain. You will be glad you have private means. Reserves of energy, money or supplies may be raided to meet an emergency that is rather a pleasure. Be gentle to those around you. Give aid where it is needed, and do not be too worried about eliciting repayment promises. You will be aware that your own needs are protected should you have any problem. Something could make you slow down or stop to think. So long as you keep your mind on what is ahead and do not fret about things that are never likely to happen again, you will be fine. Lightning is said never to strike in the same place twice.

22. THURSDAY. Sociable. An older person, probably a family member, seems to be on your wavelength. Their support could be a feather in your cap. Do not hang back if asked to explain something important. This could be the beginning of a successful personal venture. Local affairs can take on new meaning if you are asked to serve as a board member or adviser. This is one way in which you can contribute as an active member of your community. Publicity should be undertaken or promoted at this point. Be willing to back up what you intend doing. A sponsor may be found to push you on your way. Tot up all you have to be thankful for.

23. FRIDAY. Uncomfortable. Communications can break down. You will be doubly glad to see a friendly face or hear a gentle word of encouragement. Take the initiative with someone you love. A business partner will stand in efficiently if you have to take time off. Do not expect too much to go right with overseas contacts. It may be impossible to get an interpreter if you cannot make yourself understood to a substantial client. Barriers are likely to be erected by officials or professional people. Legal advice may be necessary in order to make headway. You are better when being assisted than on your own. Share and cooperate.

24. SATURDAY. Outstanding. If you have good news, spread it around. Contact members of the family you have not seen recently. A happy atmosphere will make you more at ease with neighbors. Little things mean a lot, and you will be glad to be part of something that is alive and active. Weekend shopping can be more exciting than usual. It may be that you have a lot of ideas about presents for Christmas and can do some early bargain hunting before the rush starts. Seek variety or novelty. An arrangement that suits you can be made well ahead of the event. Company will make you feel lighthearted; enjoy them.

25. SUNDAY. Caution.   You may feel you have to assert yourself. Someone with seniority can upstage you. Do not take this too much to heart. You are probably a little too conscious of your need for security and can be a bit of a martyr. Such an attitude does not suit you at all. If a partner tries to browbeat you or gives you a hard time in other ways, there is no reason to indulge in a shouting match. Home truths can be hurtful. Do something constructive about any personal failings. The failings of others may have to be tolerated. You may be a bit outspoken on this subject, which could make matters a lot worse.

26. MONDAY. Satisfactory.   The future may depend on past performance. Do not fail to take note of a long-term agreement. Family matters can be strengthened by imaginative, resolute action from all concerned. Finalize a contract or deal concerning property. A private settlement can be made with someone related by blood. You should feel a lot more secure than you did yesterday. Be careful what you say or with whom you associate in the evening. Someone may have to make a journey in a hurry or at an inconvenient time, destroying the family harmony that has prevailed all day. It is impossible to make everyone happy.

27. TUESDAY. Intense.   You will feel entitled to show off. A love affair may now be well beyond the casual stage, giving boost to your morale. A parent will be eager to make you take the right road and reveal your talents. Excellent for show-biz prospects. A legal argument may be slowing down progress, even though you are certain there will be a happy outcome for you. It may be necessary for two parties to make a break or come to a decision before your light can truly shine. Be patient; all will turn out as it should. You may be able to act as a go-between for friends who cannot agree. An expensive item may be of only passing interest.

28. WEDNESDAY. Mixed.   The course of true love never runs smooth. You will feel sure your intuition is not failing. Love grows strongly, and you may feel ready to burst. Outside events may have you in a pickle. You can be uncertain or dazzled by what is going on. There could be a moment of truth when you have to face up to practicalities. Make up your mind about what you are able to do and the time you will need to do it. Do not doubt your feelings. There is no reason you cannot be idealistic and enjoy your opportunities without confusing this with the financial aspect of life. In time you will be able to put things in true perspective, but at the moment you can cope with only one thing at a time.

29. THURSDAY. Rewarding. Get your message across loud and clear. Talents should not be hidden. A declaration of intent will do a lot to make you and someone you love feel happier. This lighthearted day should not be weighted down with too much thought of responsibility or problems of the future. Children may be much in your thoughts and are apt to take up some of your time. There should be an opportunity to make a demand that is allowed. Powers of persuasion should be used to the full. If you have an idea for a book or an article, make an extra effort today. Some will say that nothing said means nothing accomplished.

30. FRIDAY. Variable. Consolidate any gain you have made. Tot up your earnings so far this year. It could be your last chance to organize your affairs according to your means. Be precise. Leave nothing to chance. If you get a year-end bonus, do not go wild. You have a lot to buy and a month yet to go. A health matter could be much less worrisome. This is reason for joy, but keep that within bounds or you will be back where you started. Someone from afar may disappoint you. Thank your stars that other events counteract any letdown. A bird in the hand is worth two in the bush. High expectations can fail. Avoid gambling.

DECEMBER

1. SATURDAY. Intense. Know your own mind. The actions of others can create problems for you. It is essential that you be direct and make your point. A partner will be difficult to handle if allowed too much freedom, for freedom can turn into license. Be positive when you need to solve a love problem. There is no time to tiptoe around an issue. Get to the point or you will be shouted down or tuned out. A legal tussle could reach a significant point. There will be attempts to push you into a corner or up against the wall. You will cope because you have strong convictions. The rights of others are important to you, but you are no pushover.

2. SUNDAY. Mixed. Personal relationships are edgy. Better to get well away from your usual haunts and seek enlightened company. Immediate problems will press in on you and can make you uptight. A distraction is needed. This is a day of rest and one where you should be able to withdraw or seek knowledge. Everyday struggles will get you down, causing you to moan that surely there is more to life than this. Get out and see how others live. Life is far too important to be spent arguing petty personal points. Someone dear to you may have a change of heart. This could be a blow at the time, but later you may understand why.

3. MONDAY. Frustrating. Look after the interests of dependents. Little may appear to go right if you are immersed in figures and facts. Some credibility must be given to feelings and intuition. A logical solution could escape you, leaving you feeling out on a limb. Relax and allow things to fall into place. You cannot push affairs along to suit your own purpose. At some stage there will be a confrontation. Money problems can be ironed out through direct discussion. Be prepared to face the facts, although they may be hard to come by. Do not sign any document, especially if money is involved. Research will be impeded by busybodies.

4. TUESDAY. Worrisome. A monthly review of family finances may be disheartening. But you should be used to this by now and will know what to do. Reserves may be raided just to meet bills. You will have private thoughts but can keep them to yourself. On the surface you are apt to give someone a hard time. Training has made you aware of the shortcomings of those who depend on your sustenance. Do not bother trying to explain why you cannot take on more responsibility. Let matters sort themselves out; responsibility will thus fall on the right shoulders. Be patient if someone is stringing you along.

5. WEDNESDAY. Successful. Official clearance can be given to overcome a lengthy delay. You will be feeling hopeful and looking forward to a trip. Travel abroad could be in your mind if not already arranged. Plans for an overseas trip should not be delayed. An official can probably sweep aside protocol if you want to go somewhere in a hurry. You should be benefiting from previous studies. Or you may be encouraged by a partner to make headway through study. Be sure of your principles. The respect you attract while in a work situation could be associated with the high standards set by your chairman or department head.

6. THURSDAY. Satisfactory. You will know where you are going. A sense of mission should aid in your search for personal development. Be pleased that officials or tutors are aware of your potential. While you may not want to blow your own trumpet, you should appreciate the direct help of influential people who understand what you need to achieve success. Traveling is good for you. This could be your lucky day for taking a trip or an examination. Do not hide your talents. It is important that you grasp any opportunity to publicize or promote yourself. Take heed of those who remind you of the past. A dream may disturb you; have faith.

7. FRIDAY. Demanding. Take over extra duties from a partner. Do not refuse responsibility. You will be judged by the way you handle difficult situations. Enough argument to last a lifetime may come from someone you thought was a friend and companion. Those who have known you intimately can touch on sensitive points if you start an argument. The workweek is ending with a lot of loose ends not yet tied up. Do not let this rattle you. You can patch up or finish up tomorrow or next week. Legal quirks can give you a headache if you permit them to bother you. Better assume authority and let others do the worrying. Make your presence felt.

8. SATURDAY. Mixed. An official may resent your success. Take quiet satisfaction in knowing that you have done a job well. Be enterprising if you want to boost your finances. Do not be afraid to show the sensitive side of your nature. Something you have set out to achieve may yet elude you. It could be a little premature to expect success so early in December. You will be in a better position to succeed in another month or so. Do your best to keep something under cover. The time is not yet right to come fully out into the open. Or it may be that you are prepared to keep someone from the full glare of publicity that will do them no good.

9. SUNDAY. Erratic. Get your priorities right. Someone may flatter you, then lead you astray. Getting a swelled head will be no good at all for your public image. If you can charm or persuade others you will be doing the right thing. But to have the tables turned can be disturbing. Protect your reputation. Build up that which will be reliable. Do not expect too much from others, since you are the only one who can make an impact at the moment. Your love life may be troubling. Someone dear to you may have a false impression of your potential and your needs. An attempt at putting on a false show will only exasperate you.

10. MONDAY. Challenging. Get back into the business picture as quickly as you can. Thoughts of the weekend may linger for a while. Company funds could be rather shaky. Do not betray a confidence regarding finances. Too much information can make a bad situation worse. A close friend may be in difficulties; judge whether or not you can help. It may be a good idea to let this friend learn from mistakes rather than come to the rescue. It is one of those days when you have to be very careful to do the right thing. There must be good reason for today's problems. The sooner they are sorted out, the better it should be for all concerned.

11. TUESDAY. Ordinary. Be prepared to mark time. Too much haste will mean less speed. The good intentions of someone at the top should be recognized for what they are. Try to get a grip on financial essentials in order to make a major deal worthwhile. Be aware of the support at your elbow from top brass. There is no good reason to doubt your ability and the eventual outcome. It may be hard to find the provisions you want to have on hand for Christmas entertaining. Be patient; if you place an order now, you should beat the rush later on. Hang on to what you have at the moment. There could be a few hard days ahead.

12. WEDNESDAY. Positive. Keep everything in balance. There will be people around you with a biased view of life in general. Insist on live and let live as your guiding principle. Private feelings can be disclosed to those who are near and dear. Let others make up their own minds. An old romance can be renewed, possibly with added passion. You are not in a position to say too much or to disclose your hand prematurely. Play your cards close to your chest for a little while longer. There will be a day of reckoning very shortly. A financial deal can be finalized quietly behind closed doors. You will be glad something has been finished.

13. THURSDAY. Uncertain. Take a chance to soak up past history. You may be in a very vulnerable position without knowing exactly what is going on. While you have good insight regarding what is likely to emerge in the near future, you could do a lot worse than study precedent. A family tie will prove difficult to deny. Blood relationships have extra meaning at the moment. Make up your mind to do some good while you have the opportunity. A loud person may upset your peace. Although you may feel resentful, be understanding and tolerant. Your love for someone cannot and should not be measured in material terms.

14. FRIDAY. Changeable. Be sure you know what you want. It may be difficult to get down to cases or to establish a working arrangement. Intentions can be confounded by a breakdown in worker-management negotiations. There may be a lack of understanding of your situation. You could be more tired than you think. If you feel lethargic, take a break. Perhaps you will cope well today, perhaps not. Whatever develops, accept the fact that the world will still go on. It is a time to get things into true perspective. A long-term agreement can be settled, probably in the nick of time. Look for a steady increase in production next year.

15. SATURDAY. Cordial. Get on with your Christmas shopping. A market with a foreign flavor could be attractive. Look far afield for the choicest bargains. There could be good news from abroad; someone special may be your guest during the holiday. Examinations will be successful. If momentum is maintained, you should be qualified for a new position by the New Year. No matter what turns up on your doorstep, be optimistic. The cheerful support or advice of older relatives can make you feel on top of the world. Be prepared to give others the benefit of your experience if they seek advice from you.

16. SUNDAY. Outstanding. This will be a day to remember. An important change in your life can take place. You may take the plunge or set the wheels in motion for a changed life-style. Do not delay if you feel initiative is needed. Essentials are very important. You will not want to be distracted once you know what you are after. Your natural spirit of adventure can make you go off solo or undertake the main responsibility of a new project. Waste no time on the little things. Once you have made your move today, you should be all set for a busy and exciting twelve months ahead. Inner confidence will strengthen your resolution.

17. MONDAY. Easygoing. Keep your mind on earnings or assets. Look over provisions on hand to see if you need supplies. If so, get out and shop before the day is too old. Material affairs are important. You will not be short of work; you may find there are not enough hours in the day. Friends and neighbors will see little of you, but will probably leave you to your own devices. Late in the day something will especially please you. An achievement beyond expectations can make you happy. If strange things seem to be on the verge of coming to light, contain yourself for a little while. Changes will be to your advantage. Love life can perk up.

18. TUESDAY. Misleading. Keep your fingers on the pulse. Let intuition or feeling have room to develop. You may be aware that something is not quite as secure as it seems superficially. An attempt can be made to pull the wool over your eyes. Glamour can turn you on, but it can also impair your judgment. Provided you know what you are doing, it could be a great day for romance. Do not leave money lying around. Also be alert for pickpockets if out shopping. There will be more than one person involved in any attempt to steal, so avoid being distracted. A discussion with someone of the opposite sex can turn into a far closer arrangement.

19. WEDNESDAY. Confusing. Your options are somewhat varied. It is appropriate that you stabilize conditions before attempting to make more progress. A very busy day lies ahead. Performance will be under observation, so make no bones about priorities. Keep what is rightly yours and seek a profit. You are apt to get a bonus or word of a pay raise. No doubt you will feel this is only your due, making you quietly relieved and satisfied. Love life can be unpredictable. Play your hunches if so inclined. This is the other side of the coin that demands either expertise or a touch of the unexpected. Do not mix love with money.

20. THURSDAY. Difficult. Decisions may be made for you. If you are obliged to travel far from home it may be essential to appoint a stand-in. While you may not like the idea, there could be little else to do. An official may have to sort out a personal relationship for you. Do not exaggerate your problems. If others wish to make a mountain out of a molehill, that is their affair. Careless people can delay you. Arguments and points of precedent will infuriate you. Put nothing on paper at this stage. It is possible that influence on your behalf will win the day for you. But there will be little to shout about in the process.

21. FRIDAY. Worrisome. A delayed letter can cause upset. It may suit you to let bygones be bygones, but you could be manipulated. Stick to reliable precedent. Refuse to budge if you are in a corner. Once you try to make progress there could be an outcry or an attempt to put you down. Local people may seem uncertain or unjust. Try to get to the bottom of what is going on. Relatives may call off a visit for which you have done a lot of preparation. Travel as little as possible. Read all mail thoroughly before answering. There could be hidden meanings or complications. It may be necessary to make a hasty visit to see someone who is in hospital.

22. SATURDAY. Manageable. Get out early in the day for Christmas shopping. There will be bargains. A financial settlement can be made and you could be better off. There should be a feeling of love and goodwill at home. Someone respected by the family will have an offer to make. You may be entertaining more than usual over the holiday. A property can be found for a young couple who has just about given up hope. Something you have prayed for can come about. You are free to do a variety of things with your money. Come to a quiet decision, and know you have chosen right. Love will open doors. Settle outstanding bills.

23. SUNDAY. Mixed. Undercurrents can be relaxing or disturbing. You may not be able to put your finger on the exact trouble, but should not be too deeply concerned if you are apparently being kept in the dark. Inner feelings can be more true than outside appearances. You will probably be aware that you are in love and that someone loves you. Financial affairs can be in a muddle, or they may cause you no concern at all. The problems of others should be ignored. Do not be smug, but also do not get too emotional about things you cannot control. A full larder can present a storage problem; look for a reserve storage place.

24. MONDAY. Uncertain. The time has come to patch up a personal feud. A great day for mutual revelry or enjoyment with your partner. There should be a reunion that pleases you. The home and family will be under control before evening. This will give you some time to let your hair down before the children take over tomorrow. A senior member of the family may be unable to join in celebrating. If you are on the verge of proposing or seeking parental permission, tread very carefully. Perhaps it would be better to wait until early next year. Too many people can be talking for your liking. You will want less talk and more action.

25. TUESDAY. MERRY CHRISTMAS! This children's day will be one to remember. Let things go with a swing. Guests from afar will be extra welcome in the family circle. There may be an offer you cannot afford to ignore. The refrigerator may be raided by youngsters; keep an eye on their "innocent" antics. Something you wanted kept under cover or in a dark place can get a premature opening. There could be some tears during the day, probably the sort that go with family reunions. Cares can be washed away. A surprise can throw you for a loop. You have luck on your side, so nothing untoward will make a big impact. Keep the party going.

26. WEDNESDAY. Mixed. Sagittarius people have a way with youngsters. Older folk will bore you or be a hindrance. A personal interest can be cultivated. Make a contact who will prove an asset. There could be some arranging to do. Get someone in a talking mood so that you can pop a question at the right moment. It is a day for getting things organized, for laying down the red carpet and generally avoiding silly mistakes. Be patient with someone you love. Although you may be sure you are doing the right thing, it will be hard to convince even your most trusted allies. But you can smooth everything over by explaining what you are doing.

27. THURSDAY. Productive. Impatient people will depart. This is a day you probably have waited for since before the holiday. The time should be right to request a favor from someone important. Take the initiative and state your true intentions. There is a lot going for you at the moment. Keep your control and be prepared to take on responsibility at any time. A promotion could be offered. You may need higher income, so will welcome a constructive move at the top. Parents may be pleased with news of an addition to the family. Surprises are likely to be very welcome. Avoid traveling, but do not deny others the opportunity.

28. FRIDAY. Pleasant. Rest should have done you good. If you are obliged to work this week, you will find things to your liking. Jobs are comfortable, and no pressure will be placed on unwilling workers. Someone who will mean a great deal to you may come on the scene. There can be an added attraction at work. Look after those things that are of material importance. Share ideas regarding decor and furniture. It is a day to come to an understanding without any fear of getting out of your depth. Someone who has been hospitalized will have good news at last. Choose your company well. Some people will turn you off.

29. SATURDAY. Unforgettable. Something important needs to be publicized. Joint happiness should be proclaimed. Your partner can open up a new world for you. You will be in the right mood to share the party spirit. A journey can be undertaken in high hopes. This will be heartening at the end of a year of some hardship and a lot of determined effort. Plans may be afoot for increasing the family or expanding a family business. It is not time to be conservative or narrow-minded. Generosity will be repaid. There may be good news for a student or teacher about a university placement. Make an effort to go out into the world. Whether single or married, you have the support of loved ones.

30. SUNDAY. Difficult. Your partner's opinion should not be stifled. Be prepared to listen, although perhaps not to act. It may take a bit of patience to get things sorted out to mutual satisfaction. Appreciate that Rome was not built in a day. A business partner may have to leave at the end of the year; you are likely to have mixed feelings about this departure. You can be called upon to do the work of two or may be unsure of the replacement. Little may be told you, so perhaps you are better off letting things take their natural course. Be careful not to upset someone very close to you. Doing a job on behalf of another person may not be easy.

31. MONDAY. Intense. Try to get yourself organized before the year ends. There could be some difference of opinion about money. You may be outnumbered and unable to do as you would like. But this is a day to give rather than receive. The family or a particular dependent must come first. Be prepared to put yourself out to some extent. There may be talk of a withdrawal of confidence in a business deal. Get down to cases and try to dig up more information before taking on opposition. You may feel you have bitten off more than you can chew. If that is the case, just take your time. There is another year commencing tomorrow.